THE
BLESSINGS
OF
BREAD

THE BLESSINGS OF BREAD

BY ADRIAN BAILEY

PADDINGTON
PRESS LTD
TwoConPub

Library of Congress Cataloging in Publication Data
Bailey, Adrian, 1928-
    The blessings of bread.

    Bibliography : p.
    Includes index.
    1. Bread.   I. Title.
TX769.B18   641.3'31   75-11173

ISBN 0-8467-0061-1
Library of Congress Catalog Card Number
75-11173
Copyright 1975 Paddington Press Ltd
Printed in the U.S.A.

Drawings by George Underwood
Picture Research by Nora Stein
Designed by Richard Browner and
Richard Johnson

IN THE UNITED STATES
PADDINGTON PRESS LTD
TWO CONTINENTS PUBLISHING GROUP
30 East 42 Street
New York City, N.Y. 10017

IN THE UNITED KINGDOM
PADDINGTON PRESS LTD
231 The Vale
London W3

IN CANADA
distributed by
RANDOM HOUSE OF CANADA LTD
5390 Ambler Drive, Mississauga
Ontario L4W 1Y7

CONTENTS

The author and editor are grateful for the help received with the research for this book and wish to thank the following persons and organizations: Alan Clapp, Secretary, and Connie French, Librarian, of the Flour Milling and Baking Research Association, Chorleywood, England.
Ruth Emerson, Librarian, and Dennis Southwood, of the American Institute of Baking, Chicago, Illinois.
National Association of Master Bakers, Twickenham, England.
Coleson Bros., Bakers, Leather Lane, London, England.
Arthur Ostrow, Continental Baking Co., Rye, New York.
Paul Frank, American Bakeries Co., Chicago, Illinois.
Ariane Castaigne, James Beard, Barbara Kafka, Donna Lubell, Fiona Macpherson.

Picture Credits
Mary Evans Picture Library: pp 16, 17, 20, 21, 33, 39, 40, 41, 48, 50, 53, 54, 56, 62, 65, 68, 70, 76, 84, 86, 87, 100, 111, 112, 113, 114, 115, 126, 132, 134, 136, 142, 143, 144, 158, 167, 179, 182, 183, 187, 188, 191.
Radio Times Hulton Picture Library: 18, 23, 25, 26, 28, 30, 33, 35, 42, 44, 49, 51, 52, 63, 69, 79, 88, 92, 93, 127, 140, 141, 145, 156, 157, 164, 166, 170, 171,172, 190.
From Colorific: pp 8, 12, 16; Tor Eigeland, © Time-Life Books, 1975. pg 94; Larry Burrows, © Time-Life Books, 1975. pg 102; Eliot Elisofon, © Time-Life Picture Agency, 1975. pg 122; Stan Wayman, © Time-Life Picture Agency, 1975. pg 129; Wallace Kirkland, © Time-Life Picture Agency, 1975. pg 131; Dmitri Kessel, © Time-Life Picture Agency, 1975. pg 135; Kit Luce, © Time Magazine Inc., 1975. pg. 169; Gordon Parks, © Time-Life Picture Agency, 1975.
FMBRA: pp 45, 47, 59, 72, 73, 77, 78, 83, 101, 138, 149, 150, 151, 152, 153, 154, 161, 163, 172, 176, 177, 180.
John Hedgecoe: pp 13, 60.
Dennish Southwood: pp 10, 17.
Jon Alexander: pg 168.
Ross Alexander: pg. 137.
Reproduced by permission from the Stone Collection of Photographs in the Birmingham Reference Library: pg 99.
American Bakeries: pg 117.
Continental Bakeries: pg 116.
Levy's: pg 118.
Pepperidge Farm: pg 117.

6

INTRODUCTION

The enjoyment of baking bread evokes a deeply felt and long buried emotion in many people. Two hundred years ago, when the world was rural, and capital cities were no more than modest towns, nearly everyone knew the recipe for bread: flour, yeast, a little salt and water. The whitest flour was a good deal less than white. Bread baked in an oven was a specialty, as most loaves were baked under a pile of ashes, on a bakestone or a griddle. It was often rather hard, dry and probably gritty. Even then it was a treat to eat it while still hot.

When bread moved from the hearth to the commercial bakery we lost an individual tradition, and some people assert that bread has never recovered, that it has never regained its former simple and earthy qualities. In fact, this is untrue. The scope for bread making was never better at any period in history than it is today. The flour was never finer, the cereals never more carefully developed; we have electric mixers, dry yeast, and cookbooks. But are these modern aids the only reason for the renaissance in the ancient craft of bread-making?

I think not. It seems to have come about for a variety of reasons: emotional needs and a loss of security have caused us to become retrospective, to seek past techniques and skills. A fear of the future, which is intense, has brought about a desire to be self-sufficient, or to drop out altogether. Our preoccupation with technology and the dangers it creates – pollution for one thing – compels us to focus on the simple life, or what we fondly imagine is the simple life – natural fibers, macrobiotic diets, wholefoods, brown eggs, curd cheese, yogurt, fruits and nuts – home-baked bread.

In times of prosperity, bread sales decline. In times of hardship, bread assumes a magnified importance. Bread production in World War II was as essential as the manufacture of armaments. I remember the patriotic "National Loaf" of wartime Britain as a rather gray and insipid product, but it was probably very nourishing and full of protein; whatever it contained, the supply of bread gave us a feeling of security.

This, I am convinced, is the real reason behind the renaissance of home baking. It generates an atmosphere of domestic sanctuary – in other words, security in a time of stress.

There are those, of course, for whom the return to the simple life brings no security, but rather a kind of fear; for they love the processed way of life, and would seek to process us to a terrifying uniformity, until we all resemble pre-sliced and pre-packed loaves – for that is *their* security. This book is not for them.

7

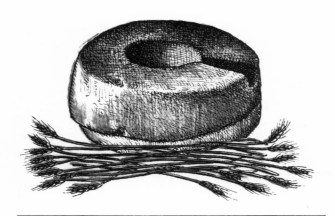

BREAD
FROM THE
STONES

1

Farmers wait for the arrival of a hot desert
wind to carry the chaff away. The primitive method of
winnowing the corn.

The story of bread began when the Ice Age was losing its grip. The frozen, iron-hard earth was softening, just enough to support wild grasses and shrubs where the glaciers had retreated. Sea levels were rising, and rivers changing their courses. Across Europe the green edge of the forest crept northwards in the wake of the ice-sheet. Where Paris now stands, packs of hyenas hunted the woolly mammoth through primitive pine forests and across acres of wild sedge grass. In America, 20,000 years had passed since men first crossed the dark ice bridge that was later to become the Bering Strait, and headed southwards to the great plains. Now, in 10,000 BC, bromegrass flourished in Kentucky and Kansas, and men pursued buffalo over the sage scrub of Montana where future crops of wheat would one day be harvested. One day – but it was to be a long time coming.

The seeds of the wild grasses were harvested, though, as a staple to supplement the buffalo meat grilled on an open fire. The men who had found their way from Europe brought with them the secret of fire, for even Death Valley was bitterly cold in prehistoric times. They also knew the cunning of chipping flintstones to make arrowheads and skinning knives, and how to make grinding stones with which to crush grain. And with the grain they made a kind of crude porridge – mankind's earliest recipe. Stone Age Californians had fish and clams from the sea; they used mortars to pound nuts, roots, and grains, tasty substitutes for the flesh of the caribou, and those animals too dangerous to track across the frozen wastelands. These hunters would eventually drift far south to find, and learn to cultivate, the wild pod-maize which grew alongside the potato and tomato on the slopes of the Andes. One day the fat cobs of corn were to prove a treasure more valuable than Inca gold.

The need to domesticate plants came about slowly, over many thousands of years – the first tentative steps toward what we call "civilization." When men were nomad hunters,

9

Spelt, triticum spelta, *one of the early wheat types, was once very widespread though never a successful rival to emmer. Spelt thrives in poor soils and is still grown in some areas, but the grain in now used mainly as animal feed.*

OPPOSITE:
Early wheat and barley
Triticum boeoticum *(a), the ancient wild wheat, and (b) its successor, Einkorn.* Triticum dicoccoides *(c) is another wild wheat which eventually produced the prolific Emmer (d).* Hordeum Spontaneum *(e) is the primitive two-row barley.*

each required an area of fifteen square miles to search and find food for himself, an area that can provide for five thousand when cultivated.

The place where civilization of mankind first took root was Mesopotamia, because it is here that wild wheat grass and wild barley grew. The dark brown, dusty heads of the primitive grasses bent and swayed under the Shamal, a wind that blows southwards down the Tigris River from Kurdistan. Botanists call the wild wheat *Triticum boeoticum* and the ancient two-row barley *Hordeum spontaneum;* both of them are thought to have been very rich in protein. In neolithic times, the grains were harvested with flint sickles, urgently, before the fragile, hairy seeds were scattered. This way, a man could gather over two pounds of grain in an hour, and a good harvest would yield enough to sustain his family throughout the coming year. The next step was to cultivate a kind of grass that had a higher yield, a hardy plant that shed its seeds not to the wind but to the sickle, and one that could be more easily threshed. Improvements such as these are slow-moving, but prehistoric time is measured in thousands of years.

The idea of harvesting grain and sowing seeds for cereal crops seems to have first occurred to an early race of people called the Natufians, who lived in the Middle East about 8,500 years ago. They hacked at the arid soil with digging sticks, broadcast their seed – and waited. They knew nothing of fertilizers, the rotation of crops, pest control, and selective breeding. They threshed the grain by driving animals over it, by pounding it with their feet, or with sticks. They winnowed it by throwing handfuls in the air, so the chaff would be blown away by the wind. There were disappointments: crops failed because of dust storms and harsh winds, and the harvest was lost in the sand. But the Natufians could always kill a few wild mountain sheep, or return to the fishing boats on the Persian Gulf. Or they could try again.

Perhaps the first real advance they made was the selective breeding of the hardiest

a

b

c

d

e

11

An Egyptian farmer using an ancient ox-drawn plough. Many of the famous cattle breeds with which we are now familiar – Herefords, Aberdeen Angus, and Brahman – were originally draft cattle, used for ploughing and turning millstones.

OPPOSITE: Ploughing a straight furrow. Notice how the soil is cut and turned with such symmetry and purpose – it has taken several thousand years to perfect.

plants. Gradually, the stunted *Triticum boeoticum* that grew on the flanks of the Zagros Mountains gave rise to the first cultivated wheat – einkorn, a poor relation to emmer, a wheat that developed from another wild grass, *Triticum dicoccoides*. While einkorn can thrive in the arid soil of the mountain regions, it would not adapt to the richer alluvial soil of the fertile lands that stretched between the Tigris and the Euphrates; here, emmer came into its own.

Emmer wheat grains, carried in the pockets of neolithic frontiersmen, traveled westward. They were planted by the Danubians and found their way to the lakeside communities of what is now Switzerland, and eventually to the British Isles. The first archaeological examples of prehistoric wheat were found in Egypt by Joseph Passalacqua, at the beginning of the nineteenth century. Later, the botanist Oswald Heer discovered the lakeside dwellings at Wanger in Switzerland, revealed when the lake dried up in the summer

drought of 1854. Heer discovered some carbonized pieces of barley bread made with barley, wheat, vetches and chickweed seeds. Even the opium poppy was cultivated for the seeds which contain not opium, but oil. They may have been used to sprinkle on the loaves, as they are today.

These pioneer farmers of Europe gathered plants that would yield sources of oil and starch: field parsley, vetch, sorrel, wild mustard, rye-grass, and brome. They reaped the wild, two-row barley and crushed the grains between flat-faced stones to make a coarse and heavy bread. The barley was good for beer making, perhaps mixed with millet, which would ferment and make yeast, and the yeast might serve another purpose – to leaven the bread. The women gathered acorns, hazelnuts and beech mast, first soaking them to get rid of the bitterness, then pounding the nuts to make cakes. Some 10,000 years ago, on America's Pacific Coast near Santa Barbara, the Oak Grove settlers were making the same kind of bread.

There is a Hungarian saying stressing the antiquity of bread: "Bread is older than man." Nine thousand years ago, in the fertile valley above the Persian Gulf, the first farmers sowed crops of wheat and barley, onions, peas, cucumber, and cultivated almonds and figs. They domesticated the wild moufflon sheep, kept pigs and oxen and geese. The grains of wheat and barley could be roasted and pounded and made into a flat, tough bread when mixed with water and baked on hot stones. As farming flourished, the population expanded to demand bigger and better crops, and the crops were abundant as were the people who planted them. Out of this pioneer husbandry grew the civilizations of Sumer, Ur and Babylon. The Sumerians developed a system of irrigation in the lands that bordered the rivers, and the goddess of grain, Ashan, and the spirits of the seasons, Emesh and Enten, did the rest:

The gardens he decked out in green, made
their plants luxuriant,

Made grain increase in the furrows,
Like Ashan, the kindly maid, he made it
come forth sturdily.

The next great agricultural advance was the introduction of bread wheat, a cereal grain with a high content of starch and possessing the vital gluten. *Triticum aestivum* is a cultivated wheat that derives from emmer, possibly crossed with certain species of wild grasses known as *Aegilops,* though how this came about is uncertain.

To most Americans and west Europeans, bread is a well-risen, light and spongy, crusty and yeasty necessity of everyday life. But elsewhere bread has very different characteristics. It might be flat and rather tough, like the *chuppatis* of India, black and sour like the pumpernickel bread of East Europe and Russia, hollow and resembling a pocket, like the bread of Greece, or flat and heavy and honeycombed with holes, like the *sang-gak* of Persia, or the *shrak* like a piece of calico, a pancake of wholemeal flour baked on a hot stone – one of the staple breads of Jordan. The last mentioned breads are perhaps direct descendants from the original breads of Babylon and Sumer. Coarsely pounded grains, rubbed on a grinding stone, mixed to a paste with water. Some of these breads might have been partially leavened with wild yeast from barley and millet beer.

Most prehistoric breads were made of simple crushed grains, mixed to a crude dough with water and cooked on a hot stone, or under ashes, or in an oven, so you will see that they were not exactly Wonder Bread or Mother's Pride. The most likely birthplace of ancient bread was Iran. The first leavened bread is usually credited to the Egyptians, and the most popular theory is that fermented bread was the spontaneous discovery of an Egyptian housewife, who left her batch of dough too long in the sun, and wild yeast spores started the bread working. It is certain that fermented bread was discovered long, long before the Egyptians, and came about through a process of

Women baking flatbread in Egypt as they have done for centuries.

OPPOSITE: Ancient Egyptian breads, recently discovered in a tomb near Thebes, sealed in the spring of 1494 BC.

a/ Probably a type of barley bread.

b/ Grain residue from a brewer's mash, containing sycamore leaves used by Egyptian brewers as we now use hops.

c/ A type of fruit bread, rather like our own plum pudding, but here made with grapes and possibly figs, plus a quantity of grain.

d/ Similar to our rye bread in that it is dark and close-textured. It was baked in a cone-shaped clay vessel.

e/ A coarse grain bread, made in a finger-shape in the manner of eclairs.

f/ Egyptian honey cake or gingerbread, usually made in the shape of men or animals.

g/ Grain residue from brewer's mash or from a wine press.

h & i/ Grain from primitive Egyptian wheat, and a full ear of the same type of wheat.

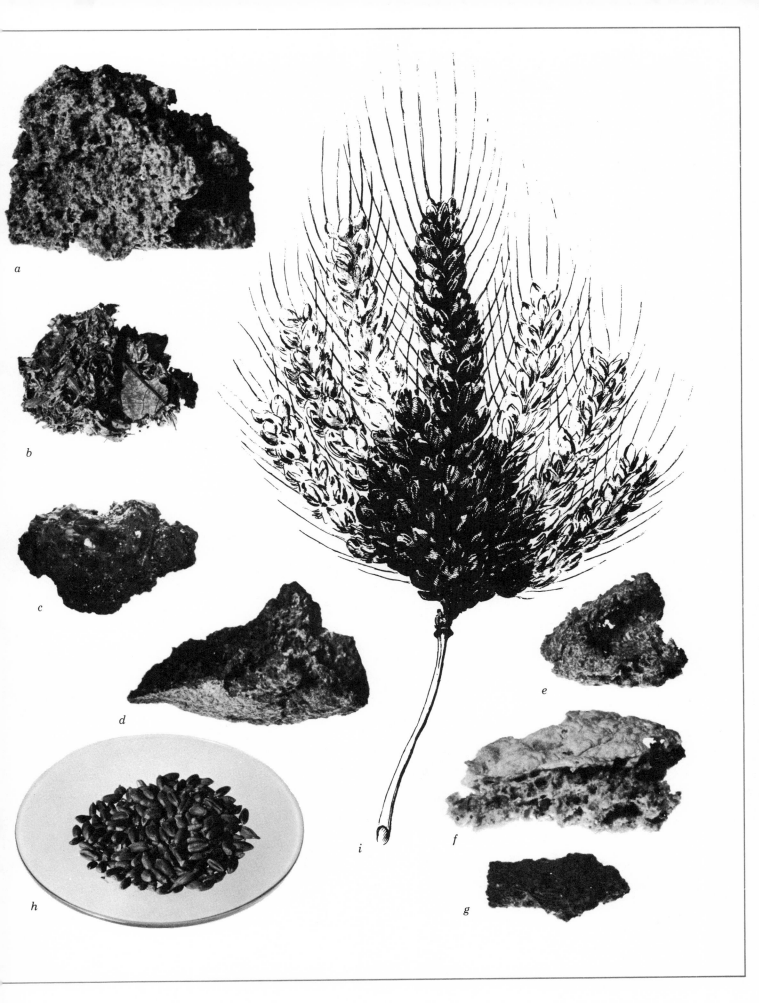

a

b

c

d

e

f

g

h

i

用犁將地土播
起令其宣活次
年在為下種耕
種此地方能滋
潤也

The Chinese grew wheat in the north of China, and were
credited with the invention of the ox and horse harness or
collar. The collar replaced a crude device that pressed on
the animal's windpipe, restricting its power and
movement. The collar is considered one of the most
important inventions in agriculture.

primitive experiment. If you mix wholemeal or barley flour with warm water, or with the wort of beer, or with honey, knead it to a stiff dough and leave it for a day or two in a temperature of around 70 degrees F, it will probably ferment, to become "sourdough" bread. Bread and beer are old partners, and we know that the Stone Age peoples had a rudimentary knowledge of brewing. It follows that they were aware of the leavening properties of yeast, even if they didn't know what was taking place. Had the Stone Age bakers possessed better milling techniques, their bread – and history – might well have been different. But milling would not improve until the time of the Romans, and would not be completely revolutionized until the introduction of the roller mill in the mid-nineteenth century.

By some accounts, the bread of the Egyptians was pretty awful. For one thing it was gritty, because the grain contained particles of sand from the desert, and flecks of mica and limestone from the grinding stones and sickles. Recent examination of ancient Egyptian skulls (and also those of Neolithic peoples) reveals considerable wear on the teeth, not only because of the bread, for their diet included nuts, berries, unmilled cereal grains, and they probably chewed on animal bones; dentistry would have been a thriving profession under the Pharoahs. They greatly enjoyed their bread nevertheless. Not for nothing did the Greeks call them *artophagoi* – the bread eaters, and Egyptian troops when on the march were supplied with four pounds of nourishing wheat and barley bread each day.

As we have seen, the first batches of bread in history came about in Mesopotamia, because of the wheat and barley which grew there, and because of the river valley which irrigated the small plots of land where crops were sown. The Egyptians had a river, too, and a river bigger and better in every way – the Nile. The great thing about the Nile was that the river rose once each year to flood the delta country over an area of 12,000 square miles, and on receding left

19

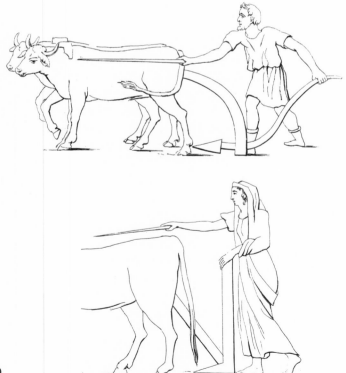

behind a rich deposit of silt, perfect for hoeing, ploughing and planting seeds. Pliny, the Roman chronicler, observed that the Nile played the part of the farmer, "beginning to overflow its banks at the new moon in midsummer, at first gently then more violently, as long as the sun is in the constellation of the Lion. Then when the sun has passed over into the Virgin, it slows down."

Under the brilliant eye of the sun god Re, and with the blessing of Osiris, the god of grain crops (and, incidentally, of the underworld), Egyptian sowers broadcast their seeds over the black alluvial soil. "When the Nile overflows the land, then the servant has no need to plough. Everybody dozes." But when the waters were low, ploughshares had to be sharpened, and ploughmen drove straight furrows across the land. The plough was already ancient; nobody knows who invented it or from where it came. The Assyrians had a plough with a built-in tube which dropped the seeds into the ground, a precursor of Jethro Tull's seed drill of the eighteenth century.

At the beginning of the spring season, *Shemu*, tiny green shoots of corn appeared across the Delta. To the Egyptians the green shoots were the very embodiment of the god Osiris. They called this fertile area "the Black Land," and beyond to the west was the land of the dead, where the great Pyramids at Giza shimmered in the heat haze. The importance of the crop couldn't be overestimated because it was the foundation of the Egyptian economy. The stock of grain represented the country's wealth; money had yet to be invented, and wages were paid in bread and beer. The river Nile stood for life and death – any year that the floods were low might result in famine, an ever-present threat. The farmers must have observed their own version of the European rhyme:

Sow four grains in a row,
One for the pigeon, one for the crow,
One to rot, and one to grow.

The grain warehouses, as carefully guarded as a bank vault, were threatened by insect infestation and vermin, which is perhaps why the Egyptians domesticated and revered the cat, which was worshipped as a deity called Ubasti. And they had better not overlook Nur, the goddess of water, or Geb the earth god, Horus the sun god and, most important of all, Osiris. Then, when the crops were fully ripe, and the whiskered heads of barley and wheat rippled in golden acres, the locusts swept in from the southwest.

We do not have to search among the hieroglyphs for a description of the devastation wrought by locusts in Egyptain times; modern locusts have lost none of the rapacity of their ancestors. At the beginning of this century in western Canada, they smothered an area by several hundred insects to the yard, and the dead ones, gathered up in wagon loads, could be smelled for half a mile. In Germany they spread in armies a mile across and eight inches thick "causing a roaring noise similar to a cataract of water."

But if the crops were spared, then the harvest reapers sliced at them with their sickles, in a steady rhythm to the accompaniment of a reed pipe or flute, cutting, binding and loading on to the backs of donkeys. They threshed the corn with flails, and used a sledge of rollers called a *charatz;* a man with a flail could do eight bushels of wheat a day, with time off for bread and beer. What was the result of this labor of devotion and economy? We know that Egyptian bread was gritty, and could give a man severe toothache, which may be why one of the Pharoahs was reputed to have hanged his baker.

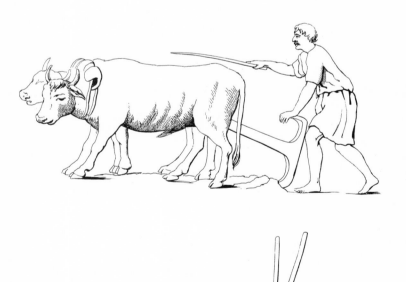

Household bread was known as *ta,* made of wheat with the probable addition of barley, kneaded by the baker's feet and leavened with a piece of the previous day's dough – sourdough bread. It constituted the main diet of the Egyptian laborer, along with onions and beer. Perhaps on occasions the bread would be sprinkled with sesame seeds, or mixed with honey, but it was *ta,* barley beer and onions that built the Pyramids of Giza. Quite recently some examples of ancient bread were found in a tomb near Thebes, sealed in the spring of 1494 BC. The Egyptians evidently believed that the journey to the land of the dead was long, arduous and would provoke considerable hunger, for the tomb contained a large, cone-shaped loaf; a type of honey bread; a loaf containing a mash of grapes and grain, perhaps the residue of a wine-pressing; a heavy loaf of barley bread; a plum pudding of fruit and grain and a loaf containing a sycamore leaf — sycamore was used by the Egyptians in place of hops. Their honey bread was often made in the shapes of men and animals, as gingerbread men are made today.

The improvements of baking techniques are due largely to the passage of time. Greek bread was marginally better than that of the Egyptians; Roman bread considerably better than that of the Greeks. The reasons were the gradual developments of milling, of finer flour and better crops. All the Egyptians had to grind their corn was the saddlestone: a flat, grooved bedstone and a rubbing stone rather like a rolling pin. The operator put a handful of grains in the bedstone and broke up the grain with the rubber, pushing it backwards and forwards. The grinding had to be frequently interrupted in order to add more grain. Moreover, it was hard and tedious work, and the task fell to the women.

Greek mills were an improvement: two rectangular stones, the upper with a slit through which grain could be fed, worked by the to and fro movement of a pivot and lever. The task was lightened by musical accompaniment, and the encouragement of such milling songs as this one, described by Plutarch, which points out that milling was by this time considered a worthy occupation by such great philosophers and poets as Pittacus:

Grind, mill, grind;
for Pittacus too did grind,
though he ruled great Mytilene.

Ancient hand mills could produce about ten pounds of coarse meal in an hour, and only by regrinding or sieving could the flour be graded.

If Greek bread was inferior to that of the Romans, what could it have been like? Roman bread has been described as "so heavy that it would sink in water," and we know that the Greeks were fond of barley, from which they made porridge, bread for their slaves, or barley cakes, without which paradise was incomplete. This is evident from Teleclides' *Amphictyons:* "The streams all ran with rosy wine, and barley cakes fought with wheaten loves to be the first to reach a hungry man's open mouth." They called barley *Alphita* when used as a cereal, but it was also scattered around at sacrifices (in the manner in which we scatter confetti) and went under the name of *Ulai,* but by the fourth century barley was on the way out, and by the time of Alexander the Great, wheat was the staple of Greece.

According to the French master chef Alexis Soyer, in a scholarly work as heavy as the bread he extols, the bread of Athens had a well-deserved reputation. "Its whiteness dazzled the eye, and its taste was exquisite. There were seventy-two different sorts of bread made from the scientific association of milk, oil, honey, cheese and wine with the best flour." But Soyer's facts came from such Greek writers as Herodotus, who were partisan. They described bread made of wine, pepper, oil and milk, called *artolaganos. Ecarites* was a light paste seasoned with milk, new sweet wine and honey. Above all, there was *melitutes* "whose exquisite and perfumed flour was delicately kneaded with the precious honey of Mt. Hymettus." Most of their bread was made of a dough using nine pounds of leaven to twelve bushels of flour. It was baked in ovens, or under ashes, or over charcoal, or in the manner of waffles, using a hinged iron.

It is evident from all we have seen that ancient bread was not intended to be cut into slices and spread with butter. Neither was it something used as an accompaniment to meat. Bread was often a meal in itself. This is why it is

so frequently described as a composite food of cereal grains, mixed with all manner of things such as fruit, grape skins, cheeses, oil, and honey, not forgetting particles of stone and grit – but it was certainly nourishing and rich in protein; einkorn and emmer wheats were almost twice as rich in protein as cultivated bread wheats are today.

The most important single advance in the improvement of bread was the introduction of the rotary mill, which made its appearance in the first century BC. Argument still persists about its origins. The Greeks are credited with "the donkey mill," which implies that a harnessed donkey provided the rotary power, when in fact the name was given to the upper grinding stone, the rubber, because like a donkey, it did most of the work.

It is likely that the rotary mill, or quern, was invented not in a solitary Archimedean flash of inspiration, but by several different groups of ancient peoples at different periods, probably around 1,000 BC. There is a hopper mill on the rotary principle from eastern Turkey of about 800 BC, while the Spanish and the Celts had domestic hand-querns before Roman times. The so-called Pompeiian mill was the largest and most efficient, and the surviving examples from Pompeii indicate that these ground flour on a commercial, or at least civic, scale. The rotary action of milling developed perhaps from the saddlestone's backwards and forwards motion. When you polish a table or wash a floor, the circular movement of the arm seems more efficient than rubbing to and fro.

The improvement of bread depended a great deal of course on the progress of milling, but we know from experience that progress often meets strong resistance. The old ways are always only reluctantly dispensed with, especially in rural communities. It must have taken a long time for millers to accept the revolutionary methods, and the Romans in particular were too fond of their staple *puls* – husked emmer wheat prepared as a thick porridge – to switch suddenly to bread. Roman

24

A primitive, animal-driven mill in the Nile Delta near Cairo. Ancient techniques of harvesting and milling are still employed in countries where traditions are strongly maintained. This mill is still in use.

Roman quern or hand-mill for grinding corn or barley, doubtless to make the dish of puls *or porridge, the staple of the Roman breakfast.*

millers crushed their grain by pounding it with a mortar and pestle and were called *pistores,* "the barley pounders." The pounders gave way in the end to the Pompeiian mill, and the introduction of bread wheat, which promised finer and lighter bread although, in fact, the finest of bread was eaten only by the upper echelons of society.

According to one legend, bread was even used as a weapon when the Capitol in Rome was besieged by the Gauls. Jupiter appeared one night to the Roman general, Manlius and advised him to make bread with all the flour the Romans had in store, "and throw it at the enemy to show them that Rome has no apprehension of being reduced to famine." The bread they threw was probably a vile concoction called *furfuraceus,* "a mass of indigestible bran that the wildest savages among the Scythians could not have swallowed with impunity."

Pliny, the inquisitive recorder of Roman life and times, has plenty to say about bread. He refers to *similago,* the finest flour obtained from bread wheat, *Triticum aestivum.* It was first moistened before milling and produced three grades of flour, the finest requiring two grindings and siftings, with sieves made of linen. "In some places, bread is called after the dishes eaten with it, such as oysterbread, in others from its special delicacy, as cake-bread, in others from the short time spent in making it, as hasty bread, and also from the method of baking, as oven bread, or tin loaf, or baking pan bread."

The importance attached to the whiteness of bread, which has persisted throughout history, stems from the Roman aristocracy who insisted on fine, white bread. Pliny notes that chalk was often added to emmer flour, a habit that persists to this day, as chalk in the form of calcium carbonate is often added to household flour. To a certain extent, the method used to ferment the dough helped to improve the quality of Caesar's bread. The Romans used millet mixed with wine, or sourdough from a previous batch, or wheat bran soaked in wine, then dried in the sun – this last would keep indefinitely, and was the origin of dried yeast. The Gauls and Spaniards, says Pliny, used the scum from their fermenting beer to leaven bread. "Their bread," he says approvingly, "is the lightest of all." At the Roman bread market, the *forum pistrinum,* you went for your daily household bread, following the nationalization of the baking industry.

Eventually, bread became so important to Rome that public bakeries were working overtime to supply the increasing demand. A bakery might produce between 50,000 and 100,000 loaves daily, with slaves working the mills, probably on shifts, throughout the twenty-four hours; in Pompeii there were twenty public bakeries supplying the 20,000 inhabitants. In 123 BC the Roman Government, in a spasm of altruism, sold grain to the population at half-price – it might even have been a step toward political aims on the part of the Senate. A further step was to distribute the grain free in 58 BC – but it was indirectly paid for by taxes, a system not unlike that of Britain's National Health Service. Eventually, the dole was made in bread, and commercial loaves called the *plebs frumentia,* the bread of "corn commoners," were distributed to the unemployed.

In the center of the market stood the statue of Vesta, the goddess of the hearth, and there was also Fornax, the oven deity and the goddess of baking. The market had open stalls of bread, including certain kinds for which one probably paid; household bread might be free, but if you wanted a loaf of *cappadocia,* the finest bread for the tables of the wealthy, made from fine flour, oil, salt, and milk, you sent your slaves to market with a coin or two. You could also buy "a molded bread for refined persons" called *artoplites.* Dogs and slaves (there seems to have been little distinction in some households) were obliged to chew on a solid loaf of *autopyron,* "self-baked" made of coarse bran mixed with a little flour – they didn't sell it, they threw it at you. Lastly, because it was applied at night, was *panis madidus,* a paste of milk and flour,

"with which fashionable ladies and effeminate dandies covered their faces before going to bed"; a Roman face pack.

Most of the houses of ordinary folk in Rome, and in the surrounding countryside, possessed hand-querns to grind their grain and made their own bread. Home-baked bread had the same appeal to the Romans that it has to us. Roman troops, apart from their ration of *buccellatum,* biscuit-bread, carried querns wherever they marched, and the legions that arrived in Britain were probably surprised to find the natives working hand-querns of a similar if cruder type.

As the legions conquered, the countries under Roman rule were obliged to export their products to Rome. From Britain came barley and millet, flax, lentils, and beans, but not oats and rye. All the main varieties of wheat – emmer, einkorn, durum and bread wheat – came from the territories around the Mediterranean, and emmer from as far afield as Britain, which also exported other delicacies like oysters from Colchester. Rye is the only rival to wheat as a

AC exc.   M. de vos inu.

Esuri multa Cereris
me fruge cibastis

bread cereal, and the earliest known use of it was in Bronze Age Czechoslovakia; had the Romans managed to cross the Danube and take northern Europe from the Huns, they might have discovered rye bread. Neither did the Romans have a name for wholemeal bread, because *all* their bread was closer to the wholemeal type than the dazzling white product which we enjoy today. A bread free of specks and bran is difficult to produce on old querns, even if it is bolted through fine cloth. A truly white flour must have taken much time, effort, milk and perhaps a dash of chalk. Furthermore, the wheat had to have been of the best quality. Said Pliny: "The wheat of Cyprus is swarthy and produces a dark bread, for which reason it is generally mixed with the white wheat of Alexandria." It must have changed a great deal since a Greek writer had observed, some three hundred years previously: "It is hard when beholding Cyprian loaves to ride carelessly by, for they do attract hungry passengers." But by all accounts, the bread of the Romans was much nearer to the familiar loaf which we would recognize. Hot from the ovens of the master-baker and one-time slave Marcus Vergilius Eurysaces – whose decorated tomb in Rome faithfully depicts his trade – a crusty loaf with its tempting aroma must have had the same appeal that fresh, home-baked bread has for us today. In the first century AD, such bread caused Juvenal to say dreamily " . . . for him a delicate loaf is reserved, white as snow and kneaded of the finest flour." Bread had come to stay.

Le Labourage

THE TRENCHERMEN

2

Rustic husbandry in eighteenth-century France, sowing the seed, ploughing and harrowing. Farming techniques were always lagging behind other developments. This drawing comes from La Nouvelle Rustique, *published in 1755, during a period of scientific advancement which saw the invention of the steel pen, the introduction of platinum, the production of commercial rubber, and Benjamin Franklin's invention of the lightning conductor.*

Imagine a small, round and flat loaf, so dense that a knife point cannot penetrate and slips off its surface, and you are obliged to break it in half with your hands. A little wheat may have gone into the making, and a quantity of rye. If you were to render it into crumbs you might discover some coarse grains of barley, beans, acorns perhaps, and traces of grit. We have seen how prehistoric bakers made their bread, but this isn't an ancestral loaf from the dawn of time, but the staple of Europe for hundreds of years following the fall of Rome. This was the bread of poverty, the bread of the peasant, baked under an inverted iron pan over which the ashes of the fire were heaped. The English called them ashcakes, and the French *fougasses.*

Far in the north of Scotland, Highland women made barley and oatmeal cakes, and cooked them on a griddle or bakestone. The almost continuous warfare between the Highland clans was sustained on oats. Sneered the English, "The Scots eat the fodder we give to our horses." To which the Scots replied, "England is famous for her horses, Scotland for her men."

Wheat was an expensive crop, the damp climate of Europe was unable to favor a good, hard bread wheat, and even the best barley bread was probably close-textured and heavy. Barley, oats and rye could flourish in poor soil under even poorer husbandry, and rye is the only cereal that can compete with wheat as a bread grain. It had spread from northeastern Europe into France, and into Britain with the Viking invasions, but it possessed certain dramatic qualities that were not even guessed at in the Middle Ages: it was subject to attacks of a fungus called *claviceps purpurea,* or ergot, which turns the grains black and endows bread with a sweetish, musty taste.

The result of eating this tainted bread was a disease known as "St. Anthony's Fire" or ergotism. Contemporary sources described it as a "tingling and burning of the hands and feet, and then a frightful heartburn. Fingers and toes are bent nearly double and clamped; the mouth is full of foam. Often the tongue is lacerated by the strength of the convulsions. There is a severe secretion of spittle. The sick utter that they are being destroyed by a burning fire. They feel great giddiness, and some of them become blind. . . ." It was thought that only by praying to St. Anthony might the effects of the fire be tempered. It was well known that a nobleman and his son, who lived in the town of La Motte-au-Bois where the relics of St. Anthony were said to be preserved, had contracted the disease and been cured. Not a few believed that the relics had brought about a miraculous cure.

As we shall see, ergotism struck again, very recently in 1951, and then the fungus was found to contain LSD, but in the Middle Ages the illness was probably thought to be due to divine retribution. In Limoges, in 943, forty thousand people are said to have died of ergotism. The disaster struck again in 1089, the inhabitants of a French village ran through the streets in the grips of a terrifying madness.

But the peasants of the eleventh century were familiar with disaster, and most of them would know famine in their lifetime. In 1124 "all things became very deere, whereof an extreme famine did arise." In 1205 there was a great frost, and in 1222 "great thunder and lightening and such great floods of water with great winds and Tempests, which continued till Candlemas." Only the self-supporting monasteries were secure in everything save plague and pestilence; the wealthy kept their grain to themselves, the poor were left to face long periods of starvation. So acute did famines become that the populace resorted to acorn bread, or bread made with the roots of ferns.

In France flour was mixed with ox blood, baked on a hot stone until hard, then cut into cakes – a kind of pemmican that might keep for years. The Swedes had a similar recipe: flour and reindeer blood made into biscuits, probably very nourishing and full of protein, in fact. Even then the idea was not new – the peasants in the north of Italy had mixed millet with horse blood

Reaping barley with sickles in the fourteenth century. Judgeing from the figure behind the harvesters, backache was a common problem during the harvest. From the Luttrell Psalter.

OPPOSITE: "God Speed the Plow." The most famous of all English ploughmen, the medieval Piers Plowman appears in one of the earliest works of English literature. Frontispiece from the book.

God spede þe plou₃:⁊ sende us korne) noſh

in Roman times, but it is no substitute for bread. Neither was the final resort of the starving hordes of European medieval famine, cannibalism, which even became exploited as a business when gangs attacked travelers and sold their flesh at local markets.

Shortage of bread was caused by exploitation and greed as much as by blight and bad weather. In England, after the great frost of 1234, men were unable to plough the land, and numbers of people died of hunger while the rich, wrote John Penkethman in *The Assize of Bread,* were "so bewitched by Avarice, that they could yield them no relief." The Archbishop of York, Walter Gray, saw the famine as an opportunity to off-load some old corn, which he had been hoarding for five years in a granary at Ripon in Yorkshire. He offered the grain to the tenants of his manors on the condition they repaid him with fresh corn after the next harvest. According to one story, the peasants entered the granary and were amazed that the corn was infested with serpents, while a voice above cried: "Lay no hands on the corne, for the Archbishop, and all that he hath is the Devills!" The City bailiffs were called in, and they decided to burn down the bewitched granary.

When supplies of bread ran low, it served to accentuate the ever-present hardship of the populations of Europe, in what we can see in retrospect as being a cruel age. The almost constant European wars forced rulers to export essentials, such as grain, in order to support the expense of warfare. In many respects, corn was preferable to money in that it was a form of international currency. In Brittany, rents were paid in grain, and the grain merchants stocked their granaries and sold only when there was a dearth elsewhere, especially abroad, and consequently profits soared.

Many countries passed laws forbidding peasants to grind their own corn, since the millers and lords of the manor could exact taxes and tools in return for grinding their grain and baking their bread. This was the soke system, in which the mills were rented out by the lord to a

OPPOSITE ABOVE: July in fifteenth-century Flanders, a farmer and his wife haymaking with scythe and pitchfork.

OPPOSITE BELOW: Saxon plough. The artist seems to have had as much a problem in drawing the plough as the curious creature pulling it. From the Oxford Caedmon.

35

miller who was obliged to pay a toll for the privilege, usually in the form of grain; the tenants paid the miller, the miller paid the lord. And the lord? He might be obliged to pay rent to the Church, or perhaps the local monastery, since the Church was frequently a jump ahead of the barons where profits were concerned.

According to the household accounts of the Countess of Leicester in the thirteenth century, bread for the dogs was considered more important than bread for the peasants. To feed the hunting dogs of Henry and Guy de Montfort and the Countess's greyhounds over a ten day period, about sixteen hundredweight of bread was required. But to feed the poor for over two months, only three hundredweight of bread was ordered, with the addition of fourteen gallons of beer.

In the massive strongholds of the feudal lords, those thick-walled castles that successive rulers since Charlemagne had built across Europe, bread was the basis of all meals. Supplies were secure because the feudal system of exploitation ensured plentiful stocks of grain at the expense of the peasants. Water mills ground the corn, and William the Conqueror's survey of eleventh-century England, the *Domesday Book,* records some six thousand in existence; the windmill had yet to be invented. Millers, and bakers too, had the reputation of being rogues and thieves; the Miller in Chaucer's *Canterbury Tales* could break down a door with his head, and "Wel coude he stelen corn, and tollen thyres." In Germany, France and England most manorial houses and castles had their own baker to whom the tenants were obliged to bring their dough for baking, like the soke system, and paid for the privilege.

There were other, practical reasons for communal baking. While the tenants might secretly grind their own corn on a hand-quern at home, and risk the penalties, few homes had an oven; cottagers' ovens were not an integral part of a house until the sixteenth century. Special skills were required to build the beehive shape of a bread oven. When Eleanor Countess of

36

Leicester moved her household to Dover she ordered a new oven to be constructed. It took two masons and their assistants nine days to build, at a cost of six shillings, probably working overtime, while the Countess's husband, Simon de Montfort, drummed his fingers impatiently on the sideboard, and the dogs howled for their ration.

With their barley and rye bread, the farm laborers might have boiled onions and greens, beer perhaps, but rarely meat. He would never taste the white *guastel* or *manchet* bread from the lord's table, but he might get to gnaw a *trencher,* now and then.

Trencher bread had been in use since the time of Charlemagne. The word comes from the old Norman-French *tranchoire,* meaning to cut a slice, and referred to a wooden platter, or more frequently a slice of bread, used as a plate. *Trenchers* were slices of coarse, dark bread made of wholewheat flour mixed with a quantity of rye or barley flour. It was made into flat loaves, probably oven-baked and turned over during baking to give an even crust. It was stored four days, then cut square by the baker or servant, who had a special knife for the purpose. Those who dined at the lord's table were served in pairs, and would share one dish between two. You reached into the bowl using your fingers, searched for a piece of meat – referred to as "sops" – and placed it on your *trencher* before putting it in your mouth. The *trencher* was designed to soak up the gravy and the juices from the meat; it was rarely eaten by the person to whom it was served, but by the servants, the dogs or the poor.

For hundreds of years, right up until the nineteenth century, the commonest household loaf was the rye and wheat maslin. In the cities, people made their dough of maslin and took it along to the local baker, who was not infrequently suspected of appropriating portions for himself. In 1266 a strictly controlled Assize of Bread was established. The *Assisa Panis* was by no means a new idea; its purpose

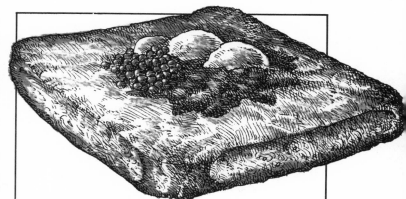

L ay a clean trencher before you, and when your pottage is brought, take your spoon and eat quietly; and do not leave your spoon in the dish, I pray you. Lay salt honestly on your trencher, for that is courtesy.
Do not put the meat off your trencher into the dish, but get a voider and empty it into that.
Do not play with the spoon, or your trencher, or your knife; but lead your life in cleanliness and honest manners.
Heap not thy trencher high with many morsels, And from blackness always keep thy nails."

ADVICE TO A CHILD, 1500

XLVI.

Husbandry.   Agricultura.

The Plow-man 1.	Arator 1.
yoketh Oxen 3.	jungit Boves 3.
to a Plough, 2.	Aratro, 2.
and holdeth	&, tenens
the Plow-ftilt, 4.	lævâ Stivam, 4.
in his left hand	
and the Plow-ftaff 5	dextrâ Rallum 5.
in his right hand,	
(with which he re-	quâ amovet
moveth clods 6.)	Glebas, 6
he cutteth the Land	terram ſcindit
(which was manured	Vomere,
afore with Dung 8.)	& Dentali, 7.
with a Share, 7.	anteâ Fimo 8.
and a Coulter,	Stercoratam,

and

and maketh furrows. 9.	facitque Sulcos. 9.
Then he soweth	Tum ſeminat
the Seed 10.	Semen 10.
and harroweth it in	& innocat Occâ. 11.
with a Harrow. 11.	
The Reaper 12.	Meſſor 12.
sheareth the Ripe	metit fruges maturas
Corn with a Sickle, 13.	Falce meſſoriâ, 13.
gathereth up the	colligit Manipulos, 14.
handfuls, 14. (15.	
& bindeth the sheaves.	& colligat Mergetes. 15.
The Thraſher 16.	Tritor 16.
thraſheth Corn on the	
Barn floor 17.	in areâ Horrei 17.
with a flayl, 18.	triturat Frumentum
toſſeth it in a winnow-	Flagello (tribulâ) 18.
ing-basket, 19.	jactat Ventilabro, 19.
and ſo when the Chaff,	atq; ita, ſeparatâ Paleâ
and the Straw, 20.	& Stramine, 20.
are ſeparated from it,	
he putteth it into Sacks.	congerit in Saccos, 21.
The Mower 22. (21.	Fœniſeca 22.
maketh Hay in a Mea-	in Prato facit Fœnum,
dow, cutting down	defecans Gramen
Graſs with a Sithe, 23.	Falce fœnariâ, 23.
and raketh it together	
with a Rake, 24.	corraditq; Raſtro, 24.
he maketh up cocks, 26	componit Acervos 26.
with a fork, 25. (27.	Furcâ, 25.
& carrieth it on cariages	& convehit Vehibus 27.
into the Hay-Barn. 28.	in Fœnile. 28.

Pecuaria

From Orbis Pictus.

was to establish weights and prices of bread and corn, and to counter the sharp practice of undercutting and racketeering prevalent among the extremely competitive bakers' guilds. The Assize was further intended to keep the price of bread down, following the not infrequent bread riots, and the popular pastime of selling short-weight bread in the markets. It was based upon a complicated (and extremely boring) scale of weights of certain types of loaves when related to the current price of a quarter of wheat.

The bakers were subsidized by an allowance made to them on every quarter of grain or flour which they used for bread making "for the miller fourpence, for the two journeymen and two pages five pence, for salt, yeast, candle and sack bands, two pence, for himself, his wyfe, his tye dogge and his catte seven pence, and the branne to his advantage, which cometh in the whole, in a quarter two shillings for his labour baking." It was the baker's task to sieve and separate the flour from the bran,

L.

Panificium.

Bread-Baking.

The Baker 1.	*Pistor* 1.
sifteth the Meal	cernit *Farinam*
in a Rindge 2.	*Cribro* 2. pollinario ,
and putteth it into	& indit
the Kneading-trough 3.	*Mactra* 3.
Then he powreth	Tum affundit
water to it,	aquam,
and maketh Dough 4.	& facit *Massam* 4.
and kneadeth it	depsitque
with a wooden slice 5.	*spatha* 5. lignea ;
Then he maketh	Dein format
Loaves, 6.	*Panes* 6.
Cakes 7.	*Placentas* 7.
Cimnels 8.	*Similas* 8.
Rolls 9. &c.	*Spiras* 9 &c.
Afterwards he set-	Post imponit
teth them on a Peel 10.	*Pala* 10.
& putteth them thorow	& ingerit
the Oven-mouth 12.	*Furno* 11:
into the Oven 11.	per *Præfurnium* 12.
But first	Sed priùs
he pulleth out the fire,	eruit
and the coals with a	
Coal-Rake 13.	*Rutabulo* 13.
which he layeth on a	ignem & Carbones,
heap underneath 14.	quos infra congerit 14.
And thus	Et sic
is Bread baked,	pinsitur *Panis,*
having the Crust	habens extra
without 15.	*Crustam* 15.
& the Crumb within 16.	intus *Micam* 16.
	H 4 *Pis-*

and the bran he could keep for himself.

Competition between bakers encouraged them to employ the medieval version of the public relations man, who went out into the streets ringing a handbell, shouting that the bread was now fresh and hot. Street-sellers were sent out into the narrow, thronged lanes of the city with a baker's dozen loaves to sell, the baker having added the thirteenth as a form of sales commission; marketplace techniques of selling short-weight and undercutting prices were fierce. Merchants would have had little to learn from the cut and thrust of the modern boardroom.

In Paris, the monks had a monopoly on the public ovens and were said to control the bakery business. Bakers were restricted to sell all their bread at the markets, under the strict supervision of inspectors. Underweight loaves were confiscated and sold to the poor, faulty and burned bread was distributed free, probably with the message that the bread was a

Only the big houses and castles had kitchens in Anglo-Saxon times. The bread was coarse-textured, the soup hearty and the roast meat probably burnt. Compliments were seldom sent to the cook.

gift from God, through the auspices of such and such a religious house.

Bakers had always considered themselves a cut above most other tradesmen because of the demand for their product – the continuous supply of good bread was the infallible guide to a country's prosperity. In medieval London, the bakery business was controlled by guilds, and was practically a closed shop – to become a baker you had to undergo a seven-year apprenticeship. In Germany, the murder of a baker was far more serious than, say, the murder of a shoemaker or even a miller.

In spite of their status, even perhaps because of it, bakers were constantly wrangling with the authorities, who imposed restrictive regulations. French bakers, for example, were allowed to bake small bread rolls, "but not display them for sale." The authorities in London tried this one out on the bakers of the seventeenth century: "No baker, nor any other person, shall make or bake to bee sold any other kinds or sorts of bread (except Simnell, Wastell, and Horse-bread, allowed by the Lawes and ancient Ordinances of this Realm) as Spice-cakes, Bunnes, Bisket or other spiced bread (being out of Assize, and not by laws allowed) unless it be for burials, or on Friday next before Easter, or at Christmas, upon paine of forfeiting all the same Spice-cakes to bee distributed amongst the poore as aforesaid."

Bakers, like the Masons, had their own ceremonies of initiation. An apprentice baker in Paris had first to become skilled at winnowing, sifting and kneading. After some time he became a foreman and could then pay a sum of allegiance money to the King, allowing him to become an aspirant-baker. Four years later he could apply for his master's ticket by going through certain rituals. On a given day he set out from his house, followed by all the town's bakers. The procession headed for the home of the Master of Bakers, and on arrival the aspirant handed the Master an earthenware pot filled with nuts. After a solemn exchange of references, the baker was given back his pot of nuts which he broke against the wall – an act that must have some profound symbolic significance – and was thus accepted as a master baker.

We know something about the medieval types of bread from contemporary household accounts, and the accounts of monasteries, most of which were written in Latin. As always, bread reflected the quality of life, and an important factor in the appearance of bread was that of color. The wealthy demanded that their bread be "white" which was not exactly white as we know it today, but more of a pale, fawn color.

In Norman times the top quality bread was called *guastel,* which the monks called *panis de wastello,* and the English *wastel.* This word might have derived from the Latin *vestellum,* and was originally a bread connected with divine service, perhaps even from Vesta, the Roman goddess of bakers, but this is mere conjecture.

The French, and later the English, had a fine bread called *paindemagne,* literally, "hand bread," later known as *manchet.* There was the *simnel* loaf, from which the modern simnel cake descends, the *cocket* made of whole-wheat flour, the *panis de coketto.* Then there was *cheat, chet* or *treet* bread, made of unbolted meal, *celsus* of coarse wholemeal, and *cibarus* made of roughage and bran.

The bread of the servants in the Baronial castles was known as *maslin,* in France *miscelin* – the name of the flour from which it was made, a mixture of wheat and rye. In the city of York they were very proud of their *mayne* bread, similar to *paindemagne,* which went down very well with York ham and a bottle of the newly imported wine from Bordeaux. *Mayne* and *manchet* were made of finely bolted wheat flour, and were the breads that everyone demanded, the breads that separated the wealthy from the poor, at a period when privilege was never more sharply delineated. Sighed the physician and author Andrew Boorde, "I do love manchet breade, and great

This animal-powered mill was used to grind corn in Venice during the seventeenth century. Mills of this type were once worked by slaves, until slaves became too expensive during Roman times, and animals were substituted. The size of this mill can be gauged by the five foot scale in the bottom right corner.

loaves the whiche be well mowlded and thorowe baken."

It is perhaps difficult to realize the limitations of use to which bread was then put – people didn't make sandwiches from it, or puddings, or stuffings as we do today. They didn't spread it with butter and jam, or serve it as

ANIMALI

P   Piedi cinque

for sauces.

There were special breads, though, for special occasions – French bakers made a dough of flour, eggs and milk for a Christmas loaf, and rye bread kneaded with spice and honey, like the English gingerbread. At Chailly and Gonesse, fine breads were made, especially *pain echaudé* or "pounded bread" (because it was beaten with long sticks) and "sheep bread," kneaded with butter and then sprinkled with wholewheat. There was also an old Norman bread the Anglo Saxons called *surleas,* the word being derived from *sur lit* – dough set to prove under the warm blankets of a recently vacated bed!

But there was one French bread dish destined for immortality – *pain perdu,* introduced into England by the Normans, where it was known as "Poor Knights of Windsor." In America it simply became – French toast. The old recipe takes a slice of *manchet* bread, which is soaked in beaten eggs and cream or milk, mixed with wine and flavored with spice, and sweetened with honey. The slices were fried in butter, a simple idea which the French may originally have borrowed from the Romans. When the English adopted it for their own they replaced the wine with *sack* – the early name for sherry.

Such things were delicacies unknown to the common people; they survive only through the legacy of recipes handed down the ages, in the kitchens of manor houses. Likewise gingerbread, sometimes even adorned with gold leaf, was rarely tasted by the country folk, except at fairs and markets; how could it be when bread itself was, more often than not, a blessing?

The ideal bread has always been a loaf of wheat. While rye and barley, oats and millet and buckwheat might be favored by some, it was wheat that was carried in the pockets of pioneers, and in the packs of conquering armies. When Cortes invaded Mexico, the Spaniards planted wheat. In 1585 the colony under

toast with tea. Middle Ages bread was something you either used as a platter, then discarded, or ate as an accompaniment to meat, for vegetables were practically unknown. In France, where it was not unusual to be served several different kinds of soup at one meal, bread was used as a thickening agent, and also

CLEARING THE WILDERNESS in Pennsylvania

Raleigh planted wheat on Roanoke Island off North Carolina, while Drake was plundering the West Indies. The Plymouth settlers eventually planted wheat and rye among the alien corn which had saved them from starvation. The English navigator Bartholomew Gosnold, the discoverer of Cape Cod, planted wheat on Elizabeth Island, Massachusetts, on his arrival in 1602.

Most of the men who first planted wheat in American soil were immigrant farmers; all were desperately pious settlers who believed that the fruits of their labors were as much rewarded by prayers as by their skill with the hoe. They sowed the golden corn raised in tiny English fields, on a vast, uncharted landscape and took off their hats. Arrivals to the New World who were not farmers would soon learn to be, and when they became a nation, who would question the right of a miller to be the first president?

While the settlers were watching their crops sprout green, a French chemist was planting wheat on land that would one day be the city of Quebec in Canada. Louis Hebert had been granted the land by Louis XIII, a king who liked to bake bread, make jam, and knew over one hundred ways to cook eggs. Hebert had probably sown his grain before he even had time to measure his new acres, for the seventeenth century seems to have established bread as an absolute essential to the French, so that today in France it is inconceivable to dine without bread on the table; even though the bread might not be eaten, they like to know it is there.

Only the aristocracy considered bread vulgar. This is why Marie Antoinette was puzzled when told that the *canaille* were short of bread, and suggested that they try cake. Did she really say it, or was it an apocryphal story designed to convey the contempt held by the aristocracy for the mob? In the towns, the wealthy bourgeoisie for once did not ape the manners of the Court, but ate all the bread they could lay their hands on, and made certain of supplies in times of scarcity. Because the grain

POISON DETECTED:

OR
FRIGHTFUL TRUTHS;

AND

Alarming to the *British* Metropolis.

IN A
TREATISE on BREAD;

AND THE

ABUSES practised in making that FOOD,

As occasioning the decrease and degeneracy of the people; destroying infants; and producing innumerable diseases.

SHEWING ALSO,

The virtues of GOOD BREAD, and the manner of making it.

To which is added,

A CHARGE to the confederacy of bakers, corn-dealers, farmers, and millers; concerning short weight, adulterations, and artificial scarcities; with easy methods to prevent all such abuses.

By MY FRIEND, a Physician.

If thy brother wants bread, wilt thou give him a stone? or if he asks a fish, wilt thou give him a serpent?
JESUS CHRIST.

Dicere vix possis haud multi talia florent. JUVENAL

LONDON:
Printed for Mess. DODSLEY, in *Pall-Mall*; OSBORNE, in *Gray's-Inn*; CORBET, in *Fleet-street*; GRIFFITH, in *Pater-noster-row*; and JAMES, at the *Royal Exchange*.

MDCCLVII.

[Price One Shilling and Six-pence.]

AN ESSAY ON BREAD;

WHEREIN

The BAKERS and MILLERS are vindicated from the Aspersions contained in Two *Pamphlets*;

ONE INTITLED

POISON DETECTED:

And the other,

The NATURE of BREAD honestly and dishonestly made.

PROVING

The Impossibility of mixing *Lime*, *Chalk*, *Whiting* and *burnt Bones* in Bread, without immediate Discovery.

WITH

Plain and Easy Experiments to discover *Alum* and other Admixtures in Bread, instantly.

To which is added,

An APPENDIX; explaining the vile Practices committed in adulterating Wines, Cider, Porter, Punch, Vinegar, and Pickles.

WITH

Easy Methods to detect such ABUSES.

By *H. JACKSON*, CHEMIST.

——*Sed ignotis perierunt mortibus illi.*　　　HOR.

Who dares think one Thing, and another tell,
My Heart detests him as the Gates of Hell.　　Pope's Hom.

LONDON:

Printed for J. WILKIE, behind the *Chapter-House*, in St. Paul's Church-Yard. 1758.
Price One Shilling.

flowed toward the towns, the country people suffered. In Paris there was no organized, single corn market, and bakers were permitted to sell in the markets only after the needs of private indivials had been met.

The provincial towns lived in dread of poor harvests and conditions approaching famine. "The well-to-do have turned *pirattes de bled,*" wrote the Bishop of Chalons, "they scour the countryside for four or five leagues, taking everything on land or on the rivers. One of those who are most active has a band of one hundred and twenty men, with a train of wagons. They break into the châteaux where there is grain, and carry off whatever they find. . . ."

Near Dijon starving peasants attacked the grain boats on the Saone river, and one of the boats was carrying the Provost of the Merchants of Lyon. "It is just as if we were in hostile territory" (they *were*). "Our grain is seized without any formality. The boatmen are attacked by armed men, who threaten to kill them if they offer the least resistance." If crops failed, what might the people eat? Well, there was always the "food for pigs," a root crop that the Belgians and Germans fed to animals – the potato, which had been despised ever since the Conquistadores had introduced it into Europe in 1630. The only champion of the potato was the French chemist Parmentier who, the story goes, presented a bouquet of potato flowers to Louis XVI on the King's birthday, for which Louis rewarded Parmentier with a handshake and permission to "embrace the Queen."

Following the Royal recognition of the potato, it was generally accepted as being "the only substantial blessing which the inhabitants of Europe derived from the discovery of the continent of America." In Scotland the Earl of Dundonald tried to interest people in making bread from potatoes, in order to save wheat flour.

The British Army, in a burst of patriotism, refrained from the practice of dusting their periwigs with fine flour. There were, of course, other ways to supplement the shortage of flour,

and people with long memories suggested acorns and beans. Acorns? The poor could eat acorns and be damned, but the city dwellers of the eighteenth century insisted that their bread be white, even though the term "white" is subject to infinite variation. Whiteness has always been consistent with purity, and perhaps it was this that caused suspicion to fall, as usual, on the bakers.

A London doctor, James Manning, became obsessed with what he suspected was widespread adulteration of bread which, he claimed, "snatched off the healthy after meals, in a Manner new to the Physician, and Terrible to the Survivors." He proceeded to list the ingredients added to flour by the rogue bakers, including such substances as beanmeal, chalk, size, slaked lime, alum and bone ash. "In consequence of this, Bread, which has well been called the Staff of Life, becomes an Arrow in the Hand of Death. . . ."

Manning's accusations were echoed by another pamphlet, this time by an anonymous physician, its title *Poison Detected.* The message was the same, and so most probably was the author. "Good bread, that most substantial and principal part of human food, ought to be composed of flour well-kneaded with the lightest water, seasoned with a little salt, fermented with fine yeast or leaven, and sufficiently baked with a proper fire. But instead of this wholesome bread, the craft of iniquitous bakers has found out a more advantageous method of making this food, by the mischievous admixture of many pernicious ingredients ..." and so on.

It is unlikely that the public were very concerned about these accusations, but the bakers were furious. The public were given *A Final Warning,* by one Peter Markham, MD, whose aim was to save the public from "rapine and havoc" at the hands of the evil bakers, who put into their bread "bones which perhaps ought to be at rest." Manning again?

To the defense of the bakers came a chemist named Henry Jackson, who wrote in

LONDON IMPROVEMENTS.

IMPROVEMENT, hail ! Thy busy hand
  To court or alley gives no quarter;
Against thee nothing now can stand:
  Thou art too strong for bricks and mortar.

Before the parapets and tiles,
  Houses and streets promiscuous fall;
Thou hast so altered old St. Giles,
  Few now would know him, by St. Paul.

The gallant captains, Parry, Ross,
  Each made the trial once or twice,
To take a desperate cut across
  Some awful blocks of thick-ribbed ice.

" No thoroughfare," did nature cry,
  So Ross and Parry homewards flew :
London Improvement doth defy
  Each *cul de sac*, and cuts it through.

At parlour, factory, or shop,
  At public entrance, private door,
Or window e'en, it does not stop,
  But rudely pushes more and more.

Improvement, too, performs a task,
  Worthy a scientific hand ;
Turns sand into the sugar cask,
  Thus into sugar turning sand

Adulteration of food in London in 1845. Sand in the sugar, pump water in the milk, plaster of paris and bone ash in the flour. "Old Tom" was a famous dry gin. Rumor maintained that gin was the most adulterated of all products, containing spirits of salts and lead derivatives. It nevertheless was, like bread, the mainstay of the poor.

his *Essay on Bread,* "I have carefully examined the bread of more than a hundred different bakers, and I have been unable to discover the least Particle of Lime, Whiting etc and I am pretty certain that if any of their bread had been mixed with only a minute portion of such Substances, it could not have escaped my researches. These malevolent suggestions have occasioned more mischief than could possibly arise from contaminated bread." "What," fumed Manning, "is your crazy denial of the facts sufficient?" The chemist responded by enquiring whether Manning's "MD" might not stand for "Mad Doctor." "The petty smatterer of physick enumerates Six ingredients, which, he says, Bakers and Millers add to flour viz. Beanmeal, Chalk, Whiting, Slak'd Lime, Alum, and Ashes or Bone. Let him remember that those who eat such bread are very apt to fart soon after, and the more such Admixture, the more violent the explosion."

The adulteration of bread is an urban practice, and by no means only recent. Roman bakers were suspected of adding a whitening agent to their bread, possibly in the form of magnesium carbonate. The English country people, if they could afford to, made their own bread; those who migrated to the cities, following the Industrial Revolution, became the urban poor, and purchased cheap bread made from inferior grades of flour, called "seconds." An analytical chemst, Frederick Accum, was later to vindicate Manning: "Without alum it is impossible to make bread from the kind of flour usually employed by London bakers, so white as that article which is commonly sold in the metropolis. If alum be omitted the bread has a slight yellowish grey hue. . . ."

White was right, and to achieve it bakers added not only alum but ammonium carbonate, magnesium carbonate, zinc sulphate, plaster of Paris, pipe-clay and lots of boiled potatoes to make up the bulk. French bakers were not far behind their English counterparts in the tricks of adulteration, adding bone ash, pea, bean and rye flour, powdered flint and potato-starch. The

An early nineteenth-century cartoon depicts the monopolizing of corn by rogue farmers and price controls by the authorities during the Napoleonic wars.

commercial, everyday loaf was probably yellowish-grey, heavy and close-textured, qualities that were to persist for several decades.

In 1823 the radical English politician, traveler, farmer and journalist William Cobbett wrote, "... think a little of the materials of which the baker's loaf is composed. The *alum,* the ground potatoes, and other materials, it being a notorious fact, that the bakers, in London at least, have *mills* wherein to grind their potatoes; so large is the scale upon which they use that material." Even as recently as 1941, attempts were made to brighten up the greyish, wartime loaf by the addition of chalk, on the pretext that the population suffered a

The BRITISH-BUTCHER,
Supplying JOHN-BULL with a Substitute for BREAD. Vide Message to Lord Mayor.

Billy the Butcher's advice to John Bull (1794): "Since bread is so dear (and you say you must eat), for to save the expense you must live upon meat; and as twelve pence the quartern you can't pay for bread, get a crown's worth of meat – it will serve in its stead."

Troops charge the anti-Corn Law mobs in 1815, who were protesting against the sharply increased prices of corn, and therefore bread. Bread has always been an accurate gauge of economic and social conditions.

51

GIVE US THIS DAY OUR DAILY BREAD

NATIONAL ANTI-CORN LAW LEAGUE

is a Registered Member

Joseph Hickin Secretary

Nº   Registered by

Anti-Corn Law League members card.

OPPOSITE: Thomas William Coke, the Earl of Leicester, one of the great agriculturalists of the eighteenth century. Coke introduced wheat to the farmers of barley-growing Norfolk, and advocated the use of modern farm machinery, in particular Jethro Tull's seed drill. Coke was the first to show the results of the Norfolk four-course system on his estate at Holkham Hall.

calcium deficiency. A nutritionist accused the British Minister of Food, and warned the public, "Today it is one food crank who becomes dictator; tomorrow there may be another. Today it is calcium, tomorrow heaven knows what may be imposed upon us."

But there were important reasons for the adulteration of bread in the eighteenth and nineteenth centuries; these were to be found in the desperate and intense competition between bakers, following the abolition of price-fixing in 1815, and the new Corn Laws. These forbade the import of foreign wheat and kept the price of home market corn artificially high; scrapping the ancient Assize system – which could no longer be enforced in the crowded cities – meant that bakers could now determine their own price for a loaf of bread. The practice of underselling became rife, and even more frantic

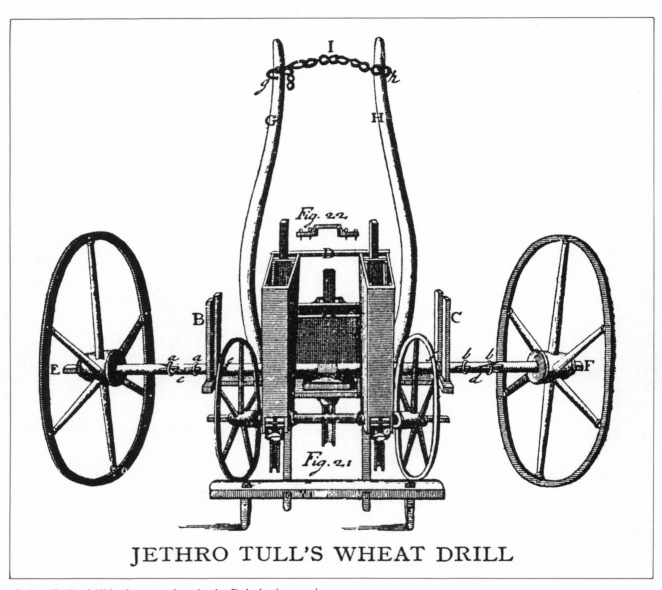

JETHRO TULL'S WHEAT DRILL

Jethro Tull's drill had a precedent in the Babylonian seed drill, where seeds were dropped through a tube set into a plough. Tull's machine used a similar technique, but was far superior, and it brought about a revolution in crop yields.

measures were taken by "cutting bakers" who undersold the undersellers. The result was that a loaf might sell for a price lower than the cost of the flour, and only by adding, say, potatoes, could the baker realize a miserably inadequate profit margin.

Several milling companies then moved in on the act by taking over small baking businesses, and here, large profits were gained with adulterated flour. The Corn Laws were introduced in an attempt to restrict the imports of foreign wheat, the aim being to protect the farmer and to raise revenue, but the Laws merely served to further impoverish an already poverty-stricken laboring class. Such aims were not peculiarly English: similar restrictions applied in Europe, and were later to apply in America.

In England, anti-Corn Law mobs roamed the countryside. One such mob, led by a man bearing a small loaf tied to a pole, attacked Thomas Coke, "Coke of Norfolk," one of the greatest agriculturalists of all time. It didn't matter that Coke supported their cause; today they were starving, and Coke was "one of them," the landed gentry. The crowd pelted Coke with stones when a butcher named Kett let loose a bull, whose tail he had bitten to enrage it. According to an eye-witness, Coke seized the bull's tail and "passed through the midst of the scattered rioters."

It was Thomas Coke who introduced wheat into rye and barley growing Norfolk, and slowly, patiently, brought about reforms by example. No farmer or laborer in England had ever seen such rich harvests of wheat and barley as those of Holkham Hall, Coke's estate. The old method of sowing grain was by "dibbling," making holes with a dibbling iron into which seeds were dropped, while a man followed with a rake and covered the holes. Coke introduced the seed drill developed by Jethro Tull, and the Norfolk four-course system of crop rotation. Wheat was grown in the first year, followed by turnips in the second year. Then Coke sowed barley mixed with clover and rye; the clover and

A Yankee will set hunger at defiance, if you turn him into a wilderness with a flint and steel, and a bag of corn-meal, or flour; and he likes the meal best, because it adheres together less closely than the corn-flour. He comes to a spot, where he means to make his cookery, makes a large wood fire upon the ground, which soon consumes everything combustible beneath, and produces a large heap of coals. While the fire is preparing itself, the Yankee takes a little wooden or tin bowl, (many a one has it in the crown of his hat), in which he mixes up a sufficient quantity of his meal with water, and forms it into a cake of about a couple of inches thick. With a pole he then draws the fire open, and lays the cake down upon where the centre of the fire was. To avoid burning, he rakes some ashes over the cake first; he then rakes on a suitable quantity of the live embers; and his cake is cooked in a short space of time."

WILLIAM COBBETT 1831

William Cobbett, the irascible, radical author, farmer, politician, sailor and traveler. Cobbett, a great reformer of rural life and labor, wrote and published Cobbett's Rural Rides, *and* Cottage Economy. *He was a bitter enemy of the potato, and a champion of bread.*

rye was either cut or grazed in the fourth year, the turnips used as feed for livestock. The fodder crops produced quantities of previously scarce manure which Coke used to fertilize the soil.

The word spread that Coke's crops, sown in the black earth of East Anglia, produced "hat barley" – you could throw your hat to lie floating on the densely packed sea of grain. In spite of the evidence, the new ways were resisted by the yeoman farmers, and Thomas Gray's ploughman, homeward plodding his weary way, feared anything that might threaten his miserable living. There were no such fears in America. Farmers crossed the Atlantic to visit Holkham Hall and see Coke's methods for themselves.

The New World crops of corn and wheat had founded a nation, as the einkorn and emmer of Mesopotamia had done in the ancient world. Tide mills, to grind the corn, had been constructed along the New England coast. The first watermill had been built in 1634. The settlers built a windmill in Newton, discovered that "it would not grind but with a westerly wind," and so brought it down to Boston. The Dutch settlers built a windmill in what is now Battery Park, Manhattan, and decided that the scene reminded them of home; they set to work erecting mills all over Long Island. New York then became the center of the grain trade for the whole of the Hudson Valley, West Vermont, Virginia and Maryland. In 1786 Jefferson said proudly: "There is no neighborhood in any part of the United States without a water grist mill for grinding the corn. . . ." There was bread for everyone: Dutch bread, and English bread of rye and wheat – the old *maslin,* and American bread, the exciting new flavor of cornbread, cornmeal mixed with wheat.

As wheat came to the New World, corn was introduced to the old. William Cobbett had been living in America at about the same time that Coke was turning Norfolk into the "granary of England." Cobbett liked what he saw, and became wildly enthusiastic over maize: "Much of the ease and happiness of the people of the United States of America is ascribable to the absence of grinding taxation; but that absence alone, without the cultivation of Indian corn, would not, in the space of only about one hundred and fifty years, have created a powerful nation, consisting of twelve million souls; a population surpassing that of England and Wales. This plant is the great blessing of the country ... the greatest blessing that God ever gave to man." Cobbett loaded himself with corn cobs and returned to England. "I shall show what a blessing this plant will be to the English laborer," he wrote in *A treatise on Cobbett's Corn* and took the opportunity to attack the potato, which he hated: "It will and must drive the accursed soul-degrading potato out of that land, into which it never ought to have come."

The radical, irascible Cobbett duly planted a field of "Cobbett's Corn," and was subsequently enraged when in England maize lost out in favor of the potato. "I have frequently been asked [and Cobbett hated being questioned] by persons who have come to see my field of corn, especially by the ladies and gentlemen who pass the greater part of their lives under the roofs of houses, 'Will it make bread, Mr Cobbett?'

"Why, Ma'am, suppose it do not make bread, but makes bacon, pork, beef, mutton, turkeys, ducks, geese, and fowls?" snapped Cobbett.

Maize, then, was not to the English taste, and it was difficult enough to get the farmers to raise wheat and barley, so why risk a strange crop that probably wouldn't make bread?

As Cobbett was urging people to try his corn, Coke of Norfolk was experimenting with Meikle's new threshing machine at Holkham Hall. The first threshing machine had been invented by a Scot, Michael Menzies in 1732, but it proved unsuccessful – or perhaps it was before its time. Meikle's was the prototype of the "peg-drum" thresher used throughout America, and in 1800 a winnowing device was incorporated. It was fast, it was efficient, it robbed the farm laborer of his winter work – that of threshing by hand. Worse, it was a new-fangled machine. The laborers grumbled over their cloudy, home-brewed beer, and remembered the distrust with which they had viewed the cast-iron ploughshare, introduced by Robert Ransome in 1785. True, it made easier work, particularly the self-sharpening plough – but where would it all end?

In the last decades of the eighteenth century the Industrial Revolution had drawn men from the villages to the cities, where wages and bread were to be found. The countryside was never prettier and never poorer. In their despair the farm laborers attacked the machines, the farmers, and burned the hay-ricks. Coke was seventy-seven when he was again attacked by a mob who were marching toward Holkham, armed with pitchforks and sticks, their faces hidden by bizarre, crepe veils. Even in old age, Coke was a man not to be tri-fled with; he had been a great fox-hunter in his prime, and was famous for having ridden a fox right into London's Russell Square, where he had killed it with his bare hands. Coke charged the mob in his coach, grabbed the two ringleaders, and bundled them off to

Walsingham Goal.

As Coke was defending Holkham, William Cobbett was riding on his horse into the town of Ipswich, sixty miles to the south. In his *Rural Rides* Cobbett wrote: "Immense quantities of flour are sent from this town. The windmills on the hills in the vicinage are so numerous that I counted, whilst standing in one place, no less than seventeen. They are all painted or washed white, their sails are black; it was a fine morning, the wind was brisk, and their twirling together added greatly to the beauty of the scene ... the most beautiful sight of the kind I had ever beheld." As Cobbett was admiring the scene, an inventor in Switzerland was making some rough sketches of a new machine. It would revolutionize the milling of grain. It would produce the finest flour of a whiteness yet to be seen. The windmill, the miller and his tools would be all but swept away forever. The new machine was the roller mill, and its designer, Helfenburger, would probably never see his sketches become reality, for the realization would take fifty years. Yet the world had waited 3,000 years to taste a fine, white and crusty loaf – what was a mere half century?

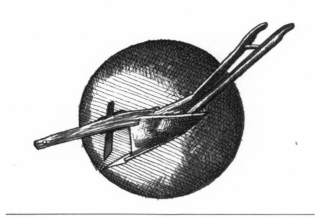

PLOUGHING INTO THE NEW WORLD

3

The men who first broke the plains of Western Canada were Highland Scots. Their leader, the young Earl of Selkirk had, like Moses, led his people to a promised land. The Scots had been crofters (small landholders), exiles from cholera and persecution. All across the Highlands of Scotland the landowners were using mercenaries to evict the crofters by force, burning the tiny cottages and turning the hard-won, stony country into grazing for sheep; the Highland clearances would realize good profits in wool and meat for the English absentee landlords, and renegade chiefs. But Selkirk was loyal to the clansmen, and he was also a pioneer. He purchased shares from the Hudson Bay Company, who granted him 116,000 square miles of wild, unyielding prairie over which the Indians pursued herds of buffalo.

The Scots embarked in the emigrant ships *Prince of Wales* and the *Eddystone* and sailed for Canada, to the new settlement in the Red River valley, where the river runs from Minnesota into Lake Winnipeg. Most spoke only Gaelic, clansmen from beyond the Great Glen – the Gunns from Kildonanan in Sutherland, MacBeths and Mackays, and from the Western Isles were Macleans and Mac-Gillivrays, and the MacEacherns and Livingstones from Mull and Lewis. They had been raised on barley bread, potatoes and oatcakes, kail and herrings, but they arrived unprepared for farming, to raise crops of oats and potatoes and then to plant wheat. Yet, their singular efforts would one day develop and flourish until the province of Manitoba was among the greatest wheatlands in the world.

Now, in 1812, they had only one broken harrow and a few hoes which they swung to bite into the hard soil. Being crofters they were true to the turnip and the potato, but they also planted wheat and barley. The first two crops failed, and the Indians laughed and called them "the gardeners." In the autumn the harvests were all but picked clean by flocks of birds, including the now-extinct passenger pigeon.

Cyrus McCormick invented the reaper, based on the shearing principle, that was the forerunner of the combine harvester.

The following year the locusts got there first and devoured everything but the settlers themselves. The farmers fought the Metis and the Cree Indians, and the fur trappers of Hudson Bay's rival, the North West Company, mainly over a question of territorial rights. Twice the colony was destroyed, their crops were trampled, their houses burned – to the crofters it must have been a familiar story.

The settlement survived, as only a settlement of such people could survive. Their entire past was a history of struggle, against the English, against each other, against the soil and the weather. They may have been encouraged by the example of the French in Quebec, who had produced the first and largest wheat crop in Canada, a yield of some 738,000 bushels.

The story of bread has always been bound with the story of agrarian expansion through crushing hard work; bread was not made by delicate, floury fingers, but by calloused hands wielding scythes and flails. The wheat grown by the colony in the Red River valley was perhaps the first that most of the crofters had ever grown – wheat does not thrive well in the north of Scotland. Here, in Canada, the wheat made good bread, and there was better yet to come.

As we shall see, much would depend on the expansion of the wheatlands, on the development of sturdier and more prolific bread wheats and on mechanization. In Europe, more efficient machines were needed to keep pace with the increasing population. In America, new ideas were swiftly grasped, as might be expected in a young and growing nation; the peasant's deeply rooted suspicion of the new replacing the old had been left behind.

In London, the world's first steam-powered mill was built adjacent to Blackfriar's Bridge in 1780, and was powered by two Boulton and Watt engines. The mill was attacked by millers fearful for their livelihood and burned to the ground. The engines were more or less undamaged, and a new mill was constructed around them. The Albion Mills could produce twenty bushels of flour in an hour, each engine

BELL'S REAPING MACHINE.

M'CORMICK'S AMERICAN REAPING MACHINE.

HUSSEY'S AMERICAN REAPING MACHINE.

driving twenty millstones. The new mill "accidentally" caught fire in 1791, and the owners prudently forbore to replace it, there being little doubt that it would be destroyed again; the nineteenth century was the dawn of the machine-smashing age, the futile attempts by agricultural man (a vanishing species) to arrest progress.

As curious Londoners prodded the still-burning embers of Albion Mill, the American inventor Oliver Evans was demonstrating his steam-driven, completely automated, seven-story mill in Philadelphia. James Watt had a mechanical grain elevator and hopper. Did the machines make better bread? Well, they made *more* bread and produced it faster than ever before. We know that Andrew Meikle invented a threshing machine in 1786, one that improved production on Coke's estate. Now a reaping machine was needed.

Inventions often have an unlikely genesis – the percussion cap on the bullet was invented

The application of McCormick's reaper depended on increased crops. Better yields of wheat came about through the work of Justus von Liebig (left), who pioneered fertilizers, and Gregor Mendel (right), whose singular efforts in the study of plant genetics eventually saw improved types of wheat.

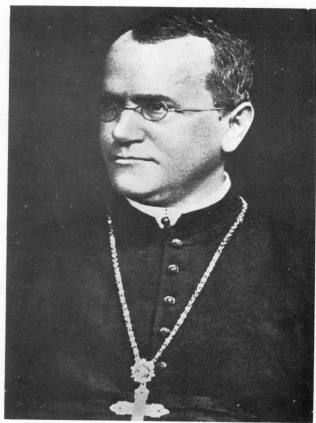

by a Scots preacher, the Morse code by an American sculptor. The first successful reaping machine was invented by another Scots preacher, the Reverend Patrick Bell of Carmylie in Fifeshire, in 1826. Bell's machine was a clipper with scissors and, predictably, it was wrecked by farm laborers and its inventor was threatened. A European harvest scene of 1800 was scarcely different from one of ancient Egypt – minus a few pyramids, of course. Before the invention of reapers, the work was carried out by seven men, six cutting with sickles and the seventh following behind, binding the sheaves. Such a team could harvest two acres a day – an efficient machine could put four of them out of work.

But the nineteenth century was ripe for improvement. The checker-board fields of England might continue to fall to the sickle, and Bell could return to preaching. America, on the other hand, was waiting for John Deere's steel plough, and Cyrus McCormick's reaper. In 1833 an Illinois blacksmith called John Deere

made a lightweight, all-steel plough that sliced through the soil like a sharp knife through sponge cake. Two inventors produced reapers at more or less the same moment – Obed Hussey and Cyrus McCormick, who battled through the courts for the right of first patent. In fact, McCormick's reaper was better adapted to many improvements, though both worked on the shearing principle, in the manner of hair clippers. Australia, short of labor but with potentially vast acres to harvest, came up with a "stripper" that removed and threshed wheat heads in a single operation. Fine, so far, but what about binding the sheaves; could it be done mechanically? America produced a wire-binder that proved too expensive, until J. F. Appelby in England thought of using string.

Increased productivity depended on machines such as these, but the converse was also true – how to obtain greater yields of crops, and improve upon the existing species? In Germany, the chemist Justus von Liebig was studying the effect of artificial fertilizers on the soil. In Germany, too, a priest, Gregor Mendel, was studying the hereditary factors of plants (he concentrated much of his study on the pea) and the probable benefits of cross-fertilization. His conclusions, which remained unappreciated for many years, were that the most desirable qualities in plants could be transmitted. It was a revolutionary concept, and when applied to wheat proved that the characteristics of several varieties might be concentrated into one single variety.

The next great step toward the perfect white loaf came from Canada. A farmer in Peterboro, Ontario, wrote to a friend in Glasgow, Scotland, and asked him to send a sample of seed wheat from Northern Europe, wheat hardy enough to survive the Canadian summer and winter. A cargo ship bringing wheat from Danzig was in port, and a sample was sent to the farmer, David Fife, who planted it in the spring of 1842. Eventually, five heads matured, the rest having failed. While Fife was absent, a cow strolled by and ate two of the stems, but Mrs Fife rushed out of the farmhouse waving her apron and chased the cow away, saving the remaining three heads, an act that was later described as having "changed the destiny of all western Canada."

Red Fife wheat adapted very well to the soil of Canada, producing a good, hard bread wheat for McCormick's reapers. The new wheat traveled west with the young, pioneer farmers, down to the American Midwest, to Minnesota, Wisconsin, Illinois, Iowa and Kansas. America was shortly to become the world's greatest producer of grain, and the grist mills turned ceaselessly to grind the ever growing yield.

The pious rural community with its simple wooden furniture, quilted bedspreads and primitive portraits was not complete without its grist mill. "The old grist mill," wrote the American agriculturist Harry Snyder, "was the local news exchange. The Blacksmith shop, the school, the church, the store and the post office were all near by. The little settlement had either a simple or a pretentious name, according to the fancy of the person who christened the hamlet. The mill was patronized by farmers for miles about. Sometimes, when the farmer brought grist to be ground, his wife or daughter accompanied him. At the store they bartered eggs and butter produced on the farm for dry goods and groceries; the eggs might fetch 10 cents a dozen, and the butter 15 cents a pound. The farmers talked of crops or politics, swapped stories and sampled each other's tobacco. It was slow work grinding the grist, but no one complained."

But even in America the age-old suspicion of thieving millers persisted. An honest miller was credited with the title "Honest Henry" or "Honest Abe." Said Snyder: "It was in a mill that Abraham Lincoln earned the title 'Honest Abe' when, in 1831, he worked for Mr Offult who operated a flour mill at New Salem, in Menaud County, Illinois." George Washington, too, was a miller, who made such good quality flour that it was received entirely on its merits and was rarely inspected in foreign markets, a

George Washington's reputation as a miller, no less than as first President of the United States, was internationally respected. His flour was freely exported to foreign markets.

OPPOSITE:
The working hours of a nineteenth-century baker were long and arduous, the conditions often appalling, his life expectancy less than forty-five years.

considerable achievement in the days when much of the wheat was contaminated.

In the smaller mills, wheat arrived which had been threshed by trampling horses, to which bits of manure were said to contribute to the "nutty flavor" of old-time bread. But on the whole, American wheat and flour was of a high standard, and America's first export trade regulation required that, "all biscuit and flour, made for transportation, shall be well made and honestly and truly packed, for the encouragement of our trade and credit, that those who purchased the same may not be cheated or defrauded."

Even the Army had good bread, like Napoleon's army, which was said to have the best bread in the world. The British navy was less than concerned over the quality of that seaman's staple – the ship's biscuit. These were made at Gosport by gangs of five men, the furner, the mate, driver, brakeman and idleman, all who sound more equipped to handle rolling stock than flour. The dough was kneaded in a trough by the brakeman, who jumped up and down on it, probably with bare feet. Then it was molded, cut and pierced with holes, and finally hard-baked. The problem with ship's biscuits was that the weevils usually got to them before the seamen did, and the men had to tap the insects out on the edge of the table. A contemporary baker wrote: "Where one man dies by the chances of war, two are lost to the nation eating ship's biscuits."

The invariable diet of the English laborer was bread, potatoes and beer, to be later superseded by tea. Although his American equivalent might face hard times where the common enemy was the untamed land and the climate, the bread was sweetened by personal freedom. The pioneer might have little choice between "rye 'n' Injun" bread and a tin of beans, but the rye and corn was grown on his own patch – the New World bread tasted good.

The north of England was marginally better off than the south, where the breakfast of a Devonshire farmer consisted largely of "kettle

Dauglish's aerated bread process, in which the dough was leavened with carbon-dioxide gas. Dauglish founded a bakery at Islington, in London, and opened the first teashop opposite London Bridge Station in 1863. The ABC teashops are now numerous throughout the city.

broth," a mess of bread, hot water, salt and milk or dripping. The poor were as much victims of the feudal system as they had been during the Middle Ages. In early Victorian days, the bread of the Sussex man and his family was likely to be "growy," the name given to bread made of poor quality rye, barley or wheat, and infected by a bacteria which appeared as yellow patches and could be pulled into long ropes.

In Scotland only the wealthy could afford wheat, the mainstay was either oats, barley or the old, medieval *maslin,* a mixture of wheat and rye, or a *bannock* of beans and peas, when poverty struck hardest. Oats may not make bread, but at least it could make hot porridge, and excellent oatcakes. In Yorkshire, oats were mixed with flour, syrup and spices to make *parkin,* or with water to make a thin, fine oatcake which was afterwards hung in the rafters to dry. Making a *havercake* is an art now lost, and likely never to return, for it required a deft flick of the wrist to spread the oatmeal batter across the hot bakestone or griddle.

Elsewhere in Europe rye was the staple – in Poland and in Russia, in Germany and across Scandinavia. Only in Hungary were vast plains given over to crops of wheat later to provide the bakers of Vienna with the opportunity to bake the lightest and most delicate breads in the world. But the sweet, sour and almost spicy flavor of rye – often with the addition of caraway seed – held sway over northern Europe, as it does today.

The middle of the nineteenth century saw the renaissance of a new form of popular literature – the cookbook, designed to appeal to the housewives of the now mighty middle classes, or, if you prefer, the bourgeoisie. One of the first to concentrate on the subject of bread had been William Cobbett in his *Cottage Economy,* published in 1823. While not exactly a cookbook, it attempted to encourage better baking, albeit in a rather extravagant style: "Give me, for a beautiful sight, a neat and smart woman, heating her oven and setting her

bread! And if the bustle does not make the sign of labour glisten on her brow, where is the man that would not kiss that off, rather than lick the plaster from the cheek of a duchess?"

Cobbett's loaf was to be a big, crusty cottage loaf, its ingredients those that only an idealist could have expected – wheat flour, salt, water, with a dash of socialism, a good measure of economy, lightened with yeast and a little humor: "The dough must be well worked. The *fists* must go heartily into it. It must be rolled over; pressed out; folded up and pressed out again, until it be completely mixed, and formed into a *stiff* and *tough* dough. This is *labour,* mind. I have never quite liked baker's bread since I saw a great heavy fellow, in a bake-house in France, kneading the bread with his *naked feet!* His feet looked very white to be sure: whether they were of that colour *before he got into the trough* I could not tell. God forbid, that I should suspect that this is ever done *in England!*"

Between Cobbett's book and Mrs Beeton's mighty work came *The English Bread Book,* by Eliza Acton, published in 1857. She had been shocked by the conditions which she had witnessed in a bakery, and her book urged housewives to bake their own bread. In Victorian London, bakeries were more often than not infested by vermin, particularly since many of them were situated too close to the drains. Potatoes and alum were still being incorporated into the dough, which was kneaded by hand. It was seeing the sweat running in rivulets down the arms of the journeyman baker and into the dough that had so alarmed Eliza Acton. Kneading was gruelling work, usually in a temperature of between 75° and 90° F, after which effort the bakers stretched themselves out on the kneading boards and, with their heads on baking tins in lieu of a pillow, fell asleep; it was said that the average life expectancy of a baker was forty-two years.

While the *English Bread Book* suggested that effort be diverted from the bakeries into

the home, a chemist named John Dauglish had written to the biscuit factory, Carr's of Carlisle, asking for their backing and money to develop his "Invention of an improved method of Making Bread."

Dauglish, however, overlooked one important fact, the intractable stubborness of the average baker, as ever averse to change, even for the better. By the 1900's the profession was still among the most backward in the world. Dauglish's method was aeration, which he had patented in 1856, the idea being to pump the bread dough full of carbonic acid gas, in the form of soda water in a closed chamber. "There are thus," Dauglish claimed, "three economies. One of labor, two of time, three of material. It reduces the time to prepare a batch of dough from eight to ten hours to less than thirty

Advertising from "The Miller" in 1881, a trade publication for the milling industry.
ABOVE: Mills were subject to frequent fires, and fire insurance was a grim necessity.
OPPOSITE: The new Hungarian roller mill.

73

minutes. The results are absolutely certain and uniform. It does away with the need to add alum to poor flour (or *any* flour). It is completely clean, untouched by hand throughout the process. The journeymen are relieved from a circumstance most destructive to health, that of inhaling flour dust in the process of kneading."

Flour could prove destructive on a more dramatic scale – under certain conditions it became highly volatile – and in 1878 a fire in a mill, Washburn's of Minneapolis, caused an explosion that destroyed the mill and killed most of the workers. The mill would be rebuilt, but with an important difference: Washburn, the Governor of the State of Minnesota, ordered that the new, Hungarian roller mill be installed, declaring that the process would give America "the whitest bread the world has ever seen." Hungary, with its important wheatlands, had developed the roller mill which, since Helfenburger's first sketches in 1820, had taken nearly sixty years to realize. The mills promised flour of an unparalleled whiteness because the rollers carried off the bran and the wheat germ that caused bread to remain dark.

The first mills had porcelain rollers, later to be replaced by steel; invention waits upon invention, and the roller mill depended on the application of steam, and also the Bessemer process of manufacturing commercial steel. Soon, electricity would be harnessed to the mills, and the grooved steel rollers could swiftly process the harvest of an entire nation in degrees of varying fineness.

In 1775 Britain had been called "The Granary of Europe." Now, in the next hundred years America, where progress had broken from an amble into a run, was the granary of the world. The combine harvester had been introduced, followed in 1892 by the petrol tractor (steam-powered Britain had tried a steam plough, but it had proved too heavy to operate), while the railway was opening up the wheatlands from Canada to California. Trade routes were established between the wheatlands of Canada and Europe, and remembering the long and bitter struggle of the Selkirk crofters, it was appropriate that the first consignment of wheat direct from Canada was to Glasgow, in 1884.

Once again, Canada made an historic contribution to the story of bread – the introduction of a new strain of wheat, a grain considered to be the most remarkable wheat ever produced in the world. This was Maquis wheat, developed by Canada's cerealist Sir Charles Saunders, from a cross of Red Fife and hard Red Calcutta. Prolific and hardy though Red Fife had proved, it was a late harvesting variety, and botanists were seeking an earlier developer.

Maquis seemed to fit all the requirements of an abundant bread wheat – it was not only a heavy cropper, but it withstood extremes of climate, the cold winters and the hot summers. In the spring of 1903, Sir Charles Saunders planted a single grain of Maquis wheat. The following year there were twelve plants, and within twelve years they multiplied to 250 million bushels. Of Maquis wheat, Professor Boyle of Cornell University said: "The greatest single advance ever made by the United States was the introduction of that class of hard spring wheat known as Maquis wheat. The idea came to us free of charge from the Dominion of Canada's cerealist, Sir Charles Saunders."

The harvests now required an army of workers, in fact, a force half as large as the United States Army was recruited in Kansas in 1903, some 28,000 men. The harvest moon shone on itinerant reapers who rode freight trains or bought excursion tickets to the wheatlands. Each with a blanket and a tin, and a tea pail, the laborers migrated northwards from Oklahoma through Kansas and Nebraska, through the Dakotas and up into the Red River valley. They worked with scythes, sickles, mechanical reapers and combine harvesters, requiring huge teams of horses as traction.

The men who cut the corn had come from cities and states south of the wheatlands –

America becomes the "granary of the world." A grain elevator in Chicago, a California warehouse, advanced techniques in farming.

students, farmers with impoverished small-holdings, ex-convicts, anyone prepared to work through the long, hot summer. Farmers used all the guile and promises they could muster to induce the men to stay and work on the farm, instead of journeying further north — even holding men by force until the train had gone. The harvest migration was world-wide; Irish moving to England, the Italians to the Argentine, Austrians to Germany, and the Spanish to France.

By the turn of the century, bread for everyone was the widely accepted ideal, bread that was fresh, light, wholesome, and above all – white. Isolated attempts by nutritionists to get people to eat wholemeal bread were largely unsuccessful. It should be added that white bread was the ideal of the wheat countries, of Hungary and Austria, of England and America. Elsewhere, rye remained firmly entrenched as the bread of the people; in France, rye bread was demanded by the peasants, the crispy white *baguette* by the bourgeoisie.

Nowhere was fine, white bread more greatly prized than in Vienna where, at the World's Fair of 1873, the roller-milled flour of Hungary was leavened with a "secret" yeast called *Marxner Pressheffe* to produce the famous *Kaiser Semmel* bread, a name which sounds like the title of a waltz by Strauss. The Viennese established a reputation for excellence

unsurpassed to this day, the apogee of the baker's art.

Fierce competition existed between professional bakers, determined to prove the superiority of their loaves, and exhibitions of "Show Bread" were organized. Local competitions in cities throughout America and Britain demonstrated the excellence of the "new bread." Loaves were cut and sniffed and prodded and tasted and photographed, standards were consistently improved. The flour was either American or Canadian wheat, while in England the soft, weaker types of wheat were used for cake making and for cooking the remarkable varieties of English puddings. During the first World War, England decreed that flour should be used mainly for bread, not "cakes and fancy things." Wartime flour included a quantity of bran which resulted

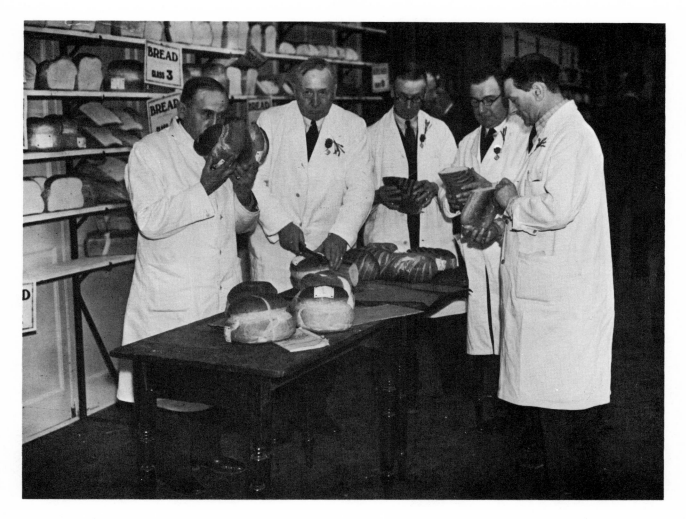

Experts sniff and prod prize cottage and bloomer loaves during the 1937 Baking Trades Exhibition in London.

in flour of quantity but which lacked the accepted quality. "Never mind," commented *The Spectator,* and added the stirring message, "our stomachs must not be too proud!"

It is a social and economic fact that in times of hardship, great is the demand for bread. The converse is also true; peace and plenty show a decline in the consumption of bread, the preference being for meat, vegetables and confectionery. Oscar Wilde remarked: "Give me the luxuries and I can dispense with the necessities." Bread has long been considered a necessity, and this is particularly true in France, which has possibly the greatest respect for bread, and by the 1880's had become the greatest bread-eating country in the world. Notice how the village bakery is a central part of everyday life, and how literally everyone buys fresh bread at least once a day.

79

In other countries a loaf might last several days; not so in France, where bread is inclined to lose its freshness in a matter of hours. It is, however, also the kind of bread that is a perfect accompaniment to French provincial cooking. This bread, the long, crusty French loaf, competes for popularity with that solid, round loaf of rye, the *pain de seigle,* which was usually kept in the table drawer of the farmhouse kitchen. This is the bread that for centuries convinced the peasant he had *really* eaten; it is dark, rich and slightly sour-tasting; as a companion to *chevre* cheese and *vin ordinaire* it has no equal. This is the bread which, on rare occasions, caused the remarkable outbreaks of ergotism previously mentioned.

The last outbreak occurred in Pont-St.-Esprit in the Rhone Valley in 1951, and the tragedy is fully documented in John Fuller's book, *The Day of St. Anthony's Fire.* Rye flour, infected by the fungus *claviceps purpurea* which contains the poison alkaloid ergotoxine, was made into bread and sold to the villagers, with the result that "hundreds of respectable townspeople went totally mad on a single night. Many of the most highly regarded citizens leaped from windows or jumped into the Rhone, screaming that their heads were made of copper, their bodies wrapped in snakes, their limbs swollen to gigantic size or shrunk to tiny appendages. Others ran through the streets, claiming to be chased by 'bandits with donkey ears,' by tigers, lions, and other terrifying apparitions. Animals went berserk. Dogs ripped bark from trees until their teeth fell out. Cats dragged themselves along the floor in grotesque contortions. Ducks strutted like penguins. Villagers and animals died right and left."

Villagers and animals went, in fact, on a massive "trip" induced by the alkaloid drug which bears a close resemblance to LSD, and from which many were never to recover. It was probably the last outbreak ever to occur, for the stringent health checks on all types of flour are such that further infection is extremely unlikely.

We have arrived, finally, in the age of superbread. Bread has undoubtedly never been purer, although there are many people who insist that bread has become insipid, unwholesome and totally lacking in flavor, and because of this belief there has been a recent tendency toward wholemeal flour, from which little has been extracted, and little added. Much of the bread that we buy today can best be described as "technological bread," bread which has been developed from the researches of science. American bread experts decided that the flavor of bread needed scientific description as a rule-of-thumb by which breads can be compared. Thus, fresh bread is "sweet, alcoholic, estery, yeasty, doughy, and wheaty." Stale bread is described as being "sour, starchy and yeasty (old)."

Scientific noses have invaded bakeries and come up with the fact that more than sixty different compounds contribute to the aroma of bread. Health faddists were alarmed to learn that bread, according to scientific analysis, contains the ethyls formate, acetate, pyruvate, tyruvate, levulinate and succinate, plus more than seventeen carbon compounds.

It is hardly the fault of science, nevertheless, since national tastes have dictated preferences for bread, and what goes into the dough. Americans desire a sweet-tasting bread, and because of this, bakers have increased the sugar content – white bread contains from four to seven percent sugar, while the salt added is in the region of only about two percent, based on flour weight. Americans might consider English bread too salty, French bread too sour.

The ideal commercial loaf is no easy to define, as tastes vary considerably from country to country, but as we have seen, the aim has always been toward a loaf that is white as driven snow, never loses its freshness, and has a golden crust. There have been recent trends of convenience bread, that is, bread pre-sliced and wrapped to maintain a longer shelf-life.

Freshness may be prolonged by glycerine saturated fats, such as glyceryl monostearate, while the ideal whiteness is achieved with bleaching agents.

"Superbread," the bread of the future, might be a uniform, processed and bleached and tasteless bread, pre-sliced and wax-wrapped, ever-fresh and without a crust; it may even be brightly colored. Experiments with dyed breads – pink, purple, green and red, have already been seen at exhibitions, and while the flavor is unremarkable, green bread is a bizarre companion to, say, gorgonzola cheese. But perhaps the bread of the future will be "the kind that grandmother used to make," warm, doughy, crusty and full of flavor – farmhouse bread, produced in one of the new high-speed breadmaking plants that can produce 16,000 pounds of bread in one hour. But will we ever agree on the ideal loaf of bread?

Bread of the future? Laboratory experiments with colored dough using the Chorleywood Bread Process, at the research center in Chorleywood, England.

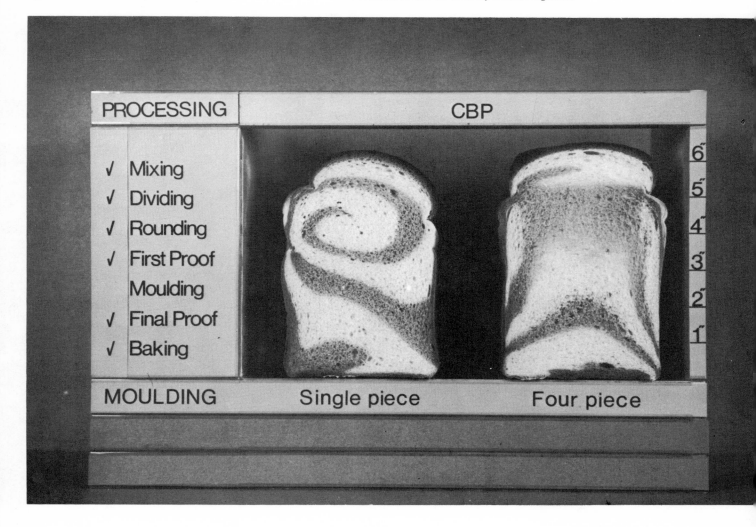

THE GUILT ON THE GINGERBREAD

4

Hades carrying off Persephone.

The beginnings of folklore are interwoven with the beginnings of agriculture, of which bread is the supreme symbol. Although the stories and superstitions surrounding bread, harvests and crops vary from race to race, from society and religion, they are, as we shall see, intimately related.

There are possibly more fables relating to bread and cakes than to any other form of food, except perhaps for salt. Later in the chapter we will explore the reasons that lay behind the rustic rituals and religious festivals, or rather, those which lend themselves to explanation, for there are others that remain defiantly mysterious. Huckleberry Finn knew that a loaf charged with quicksilver, set to float upon the river, would locate the spot where the corpse of a drowned person might be discovered – but he was unable to tell us why.

The myths and mysteries associated with bread and with harvests were certainly well established long before the first plough furrowed the first field. Planting and reaping the crop seems to have troubled the primitive farmers, who hacked at the earth with digging sticks and flint hoes, then planted the seeds and waited for magic to work its spell. Was it wrong to tear the soil, plant the seed and reap the harvest? Why did they find it necessary to make sacrifices – sometimes human – to the goddess of corn, and to act out strictly defined rituals?

That these influences were extremely powerful is evident from the fact that, even today, vestiges of these same rituals are performed in parts of rural England, in the forms of festivals or games on certain days in the year. Early cultures believed the origins of wheat to be supernatural. The Chinese assumed that wheat and rice were direct gifts from heaven. The Egyptians believed that their god Osiris, and the corn-spirit Maneros, were responsible for the sprouting corn. How else could the brilliant, green crop appear so miraculously from the black soil of the Nile delta?

The Greeks, who founded literature on the

Vesta, the Roman name for the Greek Hestia, goddess of the hearth.

rich source of mythology, believed that bread had been bestowed upon them by the great barley-mother Demeter, goddess of the cornfield. According to the Aristophanes, Demeter bore Persephone (who was also known as Core), following an incestuous relationship with her brother Zeus. It was hardly a propitious start to agriculture. Demeter fell in love with Iasion, whom she met at the wedding of Cadmus and Harmonia, which Homer maintains was an occasion at which ambrosia and wine were not exactly in short supply. Demeter and Iasion, bemused by the wine and each other, made love in a thrice-ploughed field. They would have little reason to be surprised, then, when Zeus flew into a jealous rage and struck Iasion dead with a thunderbolt.

Some say that Iasion was the first ploughman, or that it was Erysichthon, whose name means, "earth-tearer," and who cut down the trees in Demeter's sacred grove without her permission. Greek myths require considerable unravelling, for stories are knotted together and plaited with cunning. The gods and goddesses have many and varied faces and each enjoys several names; thus it is easier to disguise the true meaning of the myth. Concealment is one of the first aims of mythology, since the stories are based on human frailty and fears.

The tale of Demeter and Persephone is embellished with humor, savagery and magic. Hades, the dark-browed and sulphurous brother of Zeus, fell in love with Persephone, and kidnapped her while she was picking poppies in a meadow, perhaps to gather the seeds for bread. He bore her off in his chariot, while she screamed "Rape!" to the astonishment of a nearby shepherd, and a swineherd whose pigs were swallowed up in the yawning chasm that led to the Underworld. Persephone's cry was heard by old Hecate, who hobbled off to inform Demeter.

Demeter, overcome by grief and rage, wandered about looking for her lost daughter, blighting the crops, or refusing to allow them to grow, and not permitting herself to eat bread.

Those who got in her way might find themselves metamorphosed into lizards. One, who had enjoyed life as a gardener, found he had difficulty readjusting to the problem of being a short-eared owl. Eventually, through the divine intervention of Zeus, Persephone was returned to her mother for nine months of the year, the remaining months to be spent with Hades.

Robert Graves, in his book *The Greek Myths* suggests that Core-Persephone-Hecate are also Demeter herself in the form of a triad goddess – maiden, nymph and crone. Core also represents the green corn, Persephone the ripe ear, and Hecate the harvested corn.

Persephone, taken underground by Hades, accounts for the ritual in which a corn-dolly was buried in the winter, unearthed in the spring, and found to be sprouting. Similar rituals are associated with Hestia, the great goddess of the hearth and of domesticity, whom the Romans knew as Vesta. She was worshipped in every home as a mound of glowing charcoal covered by a cone of white ash, later as a votive object made of clay or stone in the shape of a female figure, or simply as a mound of clay or stone. The idea, though, is that something dwells inside it, in the same way in which a loaf bakes in an oven, a child grows in the womb.

The Romans had a special deity of the oven, apart from Vesta of the hearth and her Vestal Virgins. This was the goddess Fornax to whom the Latin word *fornus,* an oven, is closely allied. In the sense that words having similar constructions are often associated, *fornus* is not too remote from the Latin *fornix* – a brothel; it serves to point the way in which these myths and superstitions are bound to take us.

It is suggested that symbolism enables us to express hidden wishes and desires, usually of a forbidden nature. Men of the Marquesas Islands who had been baking with banana flour were not permitted to touch their wives on the night of baking day. The oven is a womb symbol, and as for the banana. . . .

In the late nineteenth-century a Swiss anthropologist, J. J. Bachofen, wrote a famous

The Greeks called her Demeter, the Romans Ceres. She was the supreme goddess of agriculture, and mother of Persephone.

The Harvest, painted by Francis William Loring (1838-1906).

work on the theory of prehistoric matriarchy, *Das Mutterrecht,* the supremacy of the Mother-goddess. As H. E. Jacob points out in *Six Thousand Years of Bread*, the name *Bachofen* means "baking oven." "Thus, as happens not infrequently, a symbolic name coincided with the choice of a lifework."

To return briefly to the story of Demeter. She chose, as her protegé, a promising young cowherd by the name of Triptolemus, which means "thrice-daring," and instructed him in the arts of ploughing, planting seed-corn and harvesting. She gave him a plough and a chariot drawn by serpents, and bade him travel throughout the world, teaching men the rudiments of agriculture. Now, it is a well-established, though not necessarily correct fact, that our remote ancestors performed fertility rites in order to promote the growth of crops. When the very last sickle gave way to the McCormick combine harvester, and the old rituals ceased to have any significance, only the harvest supper and the straw corn-dolls remained as curiosities.

The plough and harvest rites had a savage and sinister genesis, and it is a wonder that they vanished without something taking their place, when you consider how durable superstitions are, and that they serve a definite purpose. In ancient Greece, and in the Bible lands, children were burned alive to such gods as Moloch; human sacrifice aims to propitiate terrifying gods and goddesses. In more modern times, these gods had lost little of their savage propensities, the Christian church notwithstanding. The practice of sacrifice was later moderated to burned offerings of bread, or animals that acted as surrogates.

Sacrifices often called for the immolation of rams, which has a closer connection to the subject of bread than at first appears. The word "immolate" comes to us from the Latin *molare* – to sprinkle with meal, which is derived in turn from *mola* – a millstone. The ram recalls the famous ram with the Golden Fleece, sacrificed to Zeus by Phrixus, the son of the corn-goddess Ino (there were many corn gods and goddesses), and it has been suggested that the voyage of the Argonauts, in which Jason returns with the Golden Fleece may represent an episode in the Greek grain trade. Is the Golden Fleece a symbol for ripe wheat or barley?

The many agricultural festivals of Europe are thought to have survived because the Christian church found it impossible to eradicate deeply rooted pagan fun and games. But it is more likely that the church recognized the reasons that lay behind the festivals, albeit unconsciously, and adapted them to suit the Christian faith. Corn-dolls were jolly peasant offerings to Christ, and the bread which is eaten at communion is the body of Christ. At weddings confetti or rice is thrown at the bride and groom; in some countries bread is broken over the bride's head.

The habit of showering barley around at Demeter's temple of Eleusis was something that the Greeks had probably borrowed from the Babylonians or the Egyptians, but the underlying principle is that of fertility. The barley gave way to wheat, the wheat to rice and confetti. In some societies, the rice or a piece of bread was placed in the bride's shoe – or perhaps the shoe would be tied to the back of the honeymoon-bound car.

Even country legends have been given Christian significance. In Shakespeare's *Hamlet,* Ophelia says, "They say the owl was a baker's daughter." This is said to refer to the legend, current in Gloucestershire at the time, and also in Wales, that Christ went into a baker's shop and asked for some bread. The baker's wife put some dough into the oven, but her frugal-minded daughter insisted that the piece was too large, and subtracted half, whereupon the remaining piece in the oven grew into a huge loaf. The baker's daughter, who was given to hooting when surprised, found herself transformed into an owl. We have no doubt that she became a short-eared owl, since the tale is certainly borrowed from the Greek myth in which if we remember, Demeter turned Hades's gardener into such a bird. The story isn't mere rustic fancy, but represents an act or an intended act, nor is the choice of bird arbitrary. Later on in the chapter, we may throw some light on these mysteries which are, so to speak, hidden in that most fundamental of all foods – a loaf of bread.

A great deal of ancient superstition, all carefully worked out, none of it meaningless, is spread throughout the year. Agricultural festivals are common all over Europe, and the more rural the area, the more deeply entrenched are the old beliefs; they persist in spite of any scientific evidence to the contrary.

Many rituals and superstitions are perpetuated by the church, because they are mutually supporting and because they have been long adopted. In Britain, Plough Monday is said to be based on a pre-Christian fertility rite, and is now celebrated on January 6th when ploughs are blessed in front of the altar. They are then dragged through the village by teams of ploughboys, who demand money from each house. If the householder refuses, it is at his peril, and the team exact their dues by ploughing up his front garden.

91

92

The beginning of the harvest was Lammas-tide, when young laborers who had never harvested before were "shod" at the local inn on "Shoeing Night." Each lad wore a halter around his neck and had his foot gently tapped with a small hammer. It was probably an occasion of much ale-quaffing and good-natured pummelling, although initiation ceremonies usually have disguised elements of cruelty underlying the joviality.

Lammas means "offering of loaves" and comes from the Saxon *hlaf-maesse*, a celebration that the Saxons had borrowed from the Celtic *Lugnasad*. The first corn of the harvest is made into flour, baked as loaves of bread and offered in the church to God. In Sweden the loaves were fashioned in the shape of a female figure, and eaten in the home by the family, and this has parallels with the Norse Yule festival in which gingerbread figures with currant eyes were distributed.

As the ripe corn sways and ripples with the soft, warm breezes of high summer, the clapping, reeling, stamping folk dances celebrate the crops. Folklorists maintain that many represent ancient sacrificial or fertility rites, and it is true that most of them have elements of both – sword dances and horn dances in particular. The dances act out a ritual in the form of a mime, but the dancers are usually unaware of the meaning behind the mime – they dance as generations before them had danced. The ritual performed in the fields on the final day of the harvest was both habitual and obligatory, even though the performers had no notion of what they were doing, or why.

It is possible that some of the rituals still take place in primitive societies. Until quite recently they were to be seen in western England where, a century ago, they were commonplace. The end of the harvest was one of the most important days of the year to a village laborer, the culmination of a great deal of effort and patience. The women and children of the village were permitted to search the fields

Haymaking and harvesting with scythes and sickles, time-honored techniques still practiced in some parts of Britain, where superstitions are still upheld.

for ears of corn that the harvesters had overlooked; they were called "gleaners."

From the steeple of the church, the bell tolls a signal that the gleaners may enter the field which has been reduced to stubble, sharp underfoot, and stony. Poppies and cornflowers are now revealed, where before they had blushed unseen. Small animals whose territory was the cornfield have found sanctuary elsewhere – voles and harvest mice have fled at the clash of sickles. The blaze of noon scorches the necks of the distant reapers, goaded by flies, who are harvesting the last acre. Sweat soaks their gloves, and the cotton scarves around their necks. On a day like this a man can drink seventeen pints of harvest ale during the eleven hours of his labor – and champions can put away thirty pints plus a large loaf, cheese, and as many harvest "fourses" as the farmer's wife can bake.

During the period of rest the men talk of new machines that can reap, thresh and winnow all at the same time. What's the good of them, why the hurry? Across the field, the standing stooks of corn shimmer in the heat haze, and because it has been such a fine harvest, the pessimists talk of rain. The skylark's trill rises and falls over the yelw fields, and the entire country scene is soon to be forever folded between the pages of agricultural history. All that will remain are the harvest suppers, the thanksgiving, the corn-dollies and the songs. Perhaps the poet John Clare felt this when he wrote:

Summer's pleasures they are all gone
        like to visions every one,
And the cloudy days of autumn
        and of winter cometh.
I tried to call them back,
        but unbidden they are gone.

As the reapers move toward the last standing ears of corn, an expectant hush falls on the field, there may even be a shiver of anticipation, for it is a solemn moment. This is the culmination of a year's labor, the final act in a scene in which the oldest and most

At the climax of the bun festival in Cheung Chan (an island near Hong Kong), boys race up the 60 foot high bun mountains to seize the highest of the 30,000 sweet buns. Winners are supposed to have good luck. The celebration takes place once a year as an apology to the ghosts of fish and other animals killed for food.

95

Read this page on a Friday and your toast will burn

Bread cures whooping cough. So does sitting a baby on the hopper of a gristmill while the mill grinds a half bushel of corn. Another cure is to give bread baked by a woman whose maiden name is the same as that of her husband, this last is excellent for many complaints.

Set your bread to rise with the sun.
Make a cross on your dough, or on the mixing trough, to make it rise right.
Make a cross on your dough to let the devil out. Bread won't rise if a corpse is nearby. Cut bread at both ends and the devil will fly over the house.

It is bad luck to turn a loaf upside down, or to cut an unbaked loaf. In coastal villages it meant that a ship would sink at sea. It is bad to cut bread on baking day.

"She that pricks bread with fork or knife,
Will never be happy maid or wife."

"This Ile tell ye by the way,
Maidens, when ye leavens lay:
Crosse your dow, and your dispatch
Will be better for your batch."
(Herrick, *Charmes,* 17th Cent.)

If all the bread is eaten at table, the next day is sure to be fair.

To make sure of good bread, mix your dough with rainwater collected on Ascension Day.
Gibbet your bad or ropy bread by running a stick through it, then hang in a cupboard. This will prevent reoccurrence.

Never break cornbread from both ends.

If a boy takes the last piece of bread from the plate, he'll have to kiss the cook.

Wheat should not be cut in the light of the moon, or the bread will be dark.

Harvest all crops in the old of the moon.

"Mist in May, and heat in June,
Makes the harvest come right soon."

To burn bread means a preacher is coming, or your sweetheart is mad at you.

A big hole in a loaf of bread is a sign of an open grave.

If a crumb of bread drops out of your mouth, death will be upon you in a week.

Leave bread and coffee under the house to prevent ghosts from calling.

Epitaph for a miller from Surrey, England:
"O cruel Death, what hast thou done,
To take from us our mother's darling son?
Thou hast taken toll, ground and drest his grist,
The bran lieth here, the flour is gone to Christ."

A loaf falling with the crust down means a quarrel, or a death in the family.

97

experienced reaper plays an important role. The reapers grasp their sickles, and face the last sheaf.

There is something hidden in the sheaf which is neither a field mouse nor a partridge, the reapers cannot see it but, like God, they know it to be there. The "something" has a name. In England the name varies according to the locality. In places they know it as "The Kern," or "The Mell." The people of Hertfordshire call it "The Mare," but in Devonshire it's "The Neck." All are agreed, however, that the names refer to a corn spirit, though in Germany, until quite recently, children were urged to beware of the wolf that hid in the cornfield – the *Kornwolf*. But usually, the corn spirit was identified with a woman, which is odd, since most European languages insist that "wheat" is a masculine word.

In Denmark the corn spirit is a rye-woman, in Poland she is a grandmother called *Baba*. In Prussia she is "The Grandmother," and in Austria she is a black-faced hag of decidedly unpleasant mien, who was thought to lie in wait in the fields. In Scotland the last sheaf hides "The Maiden," which is giving her the benefit of the doubt, for the Irish know her as *cailleach,* "The Hag." The Welsh agree. "Yes," they confirm, "she's the *wrach* – an old hag." The grandmother image appears again in Belfast, and many thousands of miles away to the west, the Cherokee Indians of Oklahoma affirm this by dancing a Green Corn Dance to "The Grandmother."

It is unlucky to cut the last sheaf of corn. The burden of guilt and fear cannot fall upon one man, or one woman alone, but must be shared by all alike. So the reapers turn their backs on the sheaf as if to become dissociated from their actions. Then each turns and throws his sickle by common consent, aiming at the embodiment of the corn-spirit, and cutting it down. Then the oldest reaper takes a few of the remaining straws, and nimbly weaves a "kern-doll" or "kern-baby," with skill born of ancient practice.

Perhaps the stranger of these surviving rituals is this Devonshire one, known as "crying the neck." The veteran harvester grasps the kern-doll and sweeps it in an arc over the corn stubble, close to the ground and between his straddled legs. The others remove their hats and repeat their leader's movements. Then three times they shout, "the neck!" and then, "we haben, we haben!" Or they shout "I have 'im," and the response is, "what have 'ee?" and the reply is, "the neck!"

As the kern-doll is held aloft, a young reaper tries to snatch it away. If he succeeds he runs madly for the farmhouse where a milkmaid is waiting with a pail of water. If he can enter the house unseen, he is allowed to claim a kiss from the maid. If she catches sight of him (that is – if she doesn't want to be kissed) she douses the lad with the water.

The last load of corn is forked on to the cart and the harvesters follow, with a chosen girl – the Queen of the Harvest – wearing a cereal crown, riding back to the farm. Why do the harvesters cry, "the neck?" The word "neck" is thought to come from *neg,* the Danish for "sheaf." An alternative suggestion is that it is derived from the Irish word *anaic,* which means "to wound." But what are all these foreign words doing in rustic, rural, cream-and-cider Devonshire?

The Danish influence following the invasions in the ninth century failed to reach the West Country. And it seems unlikely that the farmers of Devon would borrow a term from the Irish, when they had the Cornish language on their doorstep. If we aim to seek the answer through the study of language, then what about Greek or Latin? What about *necros* – "dead," and the Dutch *nekken,* which means "to kill?" Corn is said to be "necked" when the ears are broken off by wind or rain. Perhaps the reapers are throwing their sickles at the last sheaf in order to *neck* or *kill* it. Maybe this is why they are superstitious. As we have seen, the last sheaf is also known as the "kirn" or "kern," like the plaited kern-doll.

98

The Kern Baby, a photograph by Sir Benjamin Stone, 1901. This is an elaborate version of t Kern or Corn dolly, made of plaited straw from the ste of wheat. Once a widespread practice, the making of c dollies is now done mainly for tourists. It has been suggested that the modern varieties of short-stemmed wheat are responsible for the gradual decline of the art

The bread-and-butter fly, Tenniel's drawing of a Lewis Carroll fantasy, from Through the Looking Glass.

Some suggest that the word "kirn" comes from a Celtic word for a circle or crown – *cerne.* In Scotland, the barley-reapers used to chant: "The corn is shorn, the Kirn's won, Kirnie, Kirnie, Coo-oo-oo!" The last sheaf was covered with a stook, a chosen lass was then taken to the spot and the unreaped barley revealed. These she cut with her sickle, and became "Queen of the Harvest." On the Isle of Lewis they dressed the sheaf as an old woman with an apron, which they filled with bread, cheese and a sickle.

There must have been a rare atmosphere of magic and mystery on the last evening of the harvest, while the reapers threw their sickles at the hag or the wolf in the corn, and the harvest moon climbed over the ridge of the hills, softening the landscape with a pale light.

Gradually, the reapers left, and emptied the fields, and the distant folds rang to the cry of "largess." Why they cried "largess" they would never know. But the ancient Egyptian harvesters had yelled to each other across the silent fields, perhaps the echoes of a long-lost ceremony. There is an account of largess in William Hone's *The Year Book* of 1832, in which "... the husbandmen of the farm assemble upon some near eminence, and call out lustily, 'Holla, holla, holla, – Largess.' The 'holla' they repeat quick, reserving all their strength for the word 'Largess' and on this word they dwell till their voice is exhausted. On a clear night the shout of 'largess' may be heard at a great distance, and the sound is very peculiar and pleasing."

As the wagon laden with corn creaked homeward, the harvesters showered each other and the fields with water. The Harvest Queen, perched on top of the cart with her crown of barley or wheat ears, splashed water on the reapers, who laughed and dodged beneath the cart. And nearer home they all sang:

Harvest home! Harvest home!

We have ploughed and we have sown,

We have reaped and we have mown,

And we have brought home every load,

Harvest home! Harvest home!

Behind the folksy facade of harvest celebrations is a history of sweat, toil and tears. The hours of harvesting were very long, the rules strict. In the nineteenth century absent workers were heavily fined, especially if the absence was due to drink, and a fine might represent more than a week's wages.

Both in Europe and America, harvesters were hired from either the roving bands of itinerants, or in entire families, men, women and children. The men would reap, the women collect the corn, the children bind it into stooks. The rural life, hard though it may have been, evoked powerful associations and memories, and this is the stuff of folklore.

Robert Burns, the exciseman, poet and lover of all things relating to barley, especially whisky, remembered a certain Lammas night and wrote:

Corn rigs, an' barley rigs,

An' corn rigs are bonie:

I'll ne'er forget that happy night,

Amang the rigs wi' Annie.

Neither would Laurie Lee forget "Cider with Rosie," in the book in which he recollected his childhood days, a time when the combine harvesters had arrived to reap the English fields, and old men shook their heads, and the summers were long and hot. "The villagers took summer like a kind of punishment. The women never got used to it. Buckets of water were being sluiced down paths, the dust was being laid with grumbles, blankets and mattresses hung like tongues from the windows, panting dogs crouched under the rain-tubs. . . . Small heated winds blew over our faces, dandelion seeds floated by, burnt sap and roast nettles tingled our nostrils together with the dull rust smell of dry ground."

The crops of wheat and barley and the seasons have given us our songs, and even rye is not forgotten. Among the acres of the rye, Shakespeare's pretty country folk would lie, in the springtime. Across America's great corn belt, the fiddles played the old jig of Weevily

Artistry with dough, a harvest cornucopia, symbol of plenty, also of fertility.

Wheat, from the colonial days of "rye 'n' Injun":

I don't want none of your weevily wheat,

I don't want none of your barley;

I want some of the good old rye,

To bake a cake for Charley.

They sang: "Shine on, shine on harvest moon," and celebrated the fruits of the harvest. The harvest supper was the highpoint of the agricultural year. In England the laborers were rewarded with the Mell Supper. "Mell" is another word of doubtful origin, but may possibly derive from the old English for *meal.* Some called them Churn Suppers, because of the huge churns of cream that were said to feature on the tables.

Harvest suppers still feature prominently in towns and villages throughout Europe; in America the Thanksgiving Dinner is a folk memory of harvest suppers, more than the celebration of an historic occasion. In the villages corn-dolls are still made, but they are now sold to tourists. Loaves baked in the form of a sheaf of corn, and glazed a glossy brown, are available on hire from town bakeries.

The ritual breads have all but disappeared, save for the consecrated bread of Eucharist, Mass or Holy Communion; the hot cross buns of Easter, the pancakes of Shrove Tuesday, the matzos of Passover.

Why does bread play an important role in festivals and observances? Surely it must be a symbol of something – the Christians believe that bread and wine taken at communion are the very embodiments of Christ, His blood and His body. The simnel cake of Easter and Mothering Sunday might well be a descendant of the cake which the Athenians baked in honor of the god Cronus. So might the Scottish Beltane bannock, for they each have in common a decoration of twelve balls or knobs surmounting the cakes. It has been suggested that the twelve knobs on the Athenian cake represented the twelve Titans, of which Cronus was a principal member.

But why should the Scots celebrate

Hot cross buns, eaten in Britain and America during Easter, an example of a pagan ritual bread that has been given Christian significance.

OPPOSITE: The Jewish feast of Passover, in which the matzo represents the unleavened bread made by the Jews after their expulsion from Egypt.

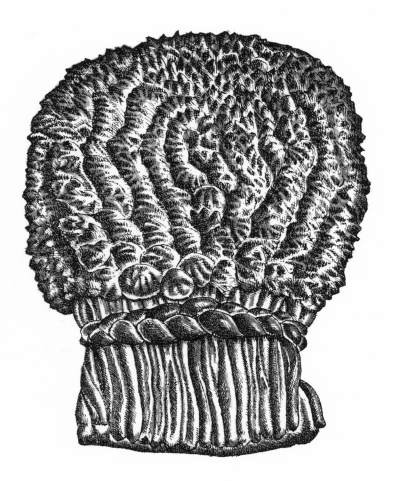

Cronus? At the festival of Beltane, fires were lit and local couples held hands and jumped through the flames. Wheel-shaped cakes and bannocks were rolled down hillsides, and the Beltane bannock daubed with soot. Sir James Frazer, in *The Golden Bough,* suggests that a blackened portion of this cake was used to determine the Beltane *carline* (*carline* means "old woman") who would draw it by lot, and she was the victim doomed to die in the sacrificial fire.

Is the *carline,* then, the same figure as the hag of the harvest? During *Tannel,* or *Tander* – both come from an old Norse word for fire, folk jumped over lighted candles and ate dough cakes flavored with caraway seeds. Similarly, the Greeks had a ritual known as the "Supper of Hecate" in which devotees placed round cakes bearing candles at crossroads, during the full moon.

Some say that our festival breads are relics of fire worship or that they were used in lieu of sacrifices at the festivals of the winter and summer solstice. In his book *Journal of Hellenic Studies,* published in 1886, Sir Arthur Evans wrote: "It is characteristic of a whole class of religious cakes that they are impressed with a wheel or cross, and in other cases divided into segments as if to facilitate distribution. This symbolical division seems to connect itself with the worship of ancestral fire rather than with any solar cult. In a modified form they are still familiar to us as hot cross buns."

The bun bearing a cross fulfils the same functions as the Jewish matzo and the communion wafer, namely, the identification with God. The origin of the word "bun" may give us further clues in the mystery of bread folklore. According to Leopold Wagner in his book *Manners, Customs and Observances,* the Egyptian bun originally had horns instead of a cross, or might have been horn-shaped (like the French croissant) and identified with the bull.

Alternatively, the bun might have been sacred to the bull-cult of Mithra, and Wagner suggests that the word comes from *bous* or *boun,* meaning "oxen." But if we side-step this involved etymology and plump for the old French *bugne* to the old English *bunne,* both meaning "a swelling," we may be nearer the truth, especially if we consider that vulgar aphorism for pregnancy – "a bun in the oven."

The folklore of bread probably began with prehistoric rites of cannibalism, because the idea of cannibalism comes not from a dearth of food, but from the belief that the strength, the power, the sexual potency of these devoured, may thus be inherited. Let us return for a moment to the story of Demeter and Persephone, and Iasion of the thrice-ploughed field.

We remember that Demeter's protegé, Triptolemus, was "thrice-daring" and that Demeter herself was a triple-goddess. When we look into the symbolism of the number "three," we begin to unravel part of the myth. Robert Graves wonders whether Triptolemus's name might be due to his having three times dared to plough the field and to couple with the corn-princess.

Another title of Triptolemus was "King Rarus," because Demeter taught him the art of ploughing in the Rarian Plain. But *rarus* means womb, and ploughing can be likened to sexual intercourse. Furthermore Demeter is not only a bread/corn goddess, but is a variation of the great mother-goddess herself. The significance of the number "three" can be found in Sigmund Freud's explanation of symbols; "three" represents the male sexual organ, and so does the symbol of the cross, also the triangle. Triptolemus – and Iasion – dared to possess the goddess in the face of Zeus the father of all the gods.

The sexual symbolism hidden in the folklore of bread cannot be underestimated; the ancients unconsciously recognized the significance of bread, especially after the discovery of leavening (because the bread would swell) and the introduction of the bread oven, which again leads to parallels with sexual intercourse.

The reason why the buns bear a cross is

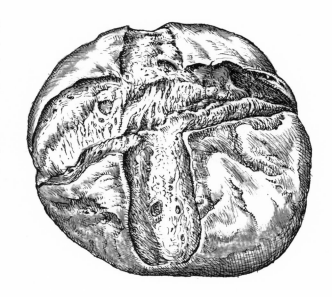

The wheatsheaf design in bread symbolizes the fruit of the harvest. A cross cut in bread had several purposes. Superstition says that it "lets the devil out of the loaf." The practical reason is that a cut helps the loaf to expand without cracking.

generally accepted as being an Easter celebration of the Passion, and that bread which symbolizes a ritual feast, such as the Last Supper or the Passover, has a purely religious significance. The matzo symbolizes the unleavened bread that the Jews ate traveling through the desert after their expulsion from Egypt. At the Jewish feast of Purim, triangular cakes filled with poppy seeds, called Hamantaschen, are eaten. The Egyptians baked dough cakes in the shape of boars, dedicated to Osiris.

The Aztecs ate the body of the god Huitzilopochtli, in the form of bread baked in his image. On All Soul's Day, bread or cakes were eaten in the shape of triangles or ovals; All Souls is partnered by All Saints, Hallowe'en and the ancient Celtic Samhain, each having a connection with death, resurrection, ghosts, witches, and wild fire at midnight. The Scottish and American observance of Hallowe'en – largely ignored by the English, who celebrate Guy Fawkes Night instead – has echoes of sacrifice. An unleavened oatcake called *harcake*, – *Hárr,* one of the Norse names for the god Odin – was eaten in the north of England on November 5th, but it also features as a harvest cake, or "soul-mass cake," left for the ancestral ghosts to enjoy during the night of All Souls.

In some counties in Great Britain, cakes known as *fourses* were given to the men working during harvest time. These are traditionally supposed to be handed around at four in the afternoon, but *fourses* really means a bread divided in four parts. They are identical to old-fashioned cakes called wigs; like *fourses* they are triangular, and said to resemble the gentleman's wig of the eighteenth century. But "wig" really means "wedge" in Old English, deriving from the word *wigge.* Wigs were quite unlike the hair-pieces then fashionable, but simply triangular breads flavored with caraway seeds, and like all of these special breads, were descended from the ritual cakes of fire and fantasy.

The useful but somewhat bizarre custom of

"sin-eating" used to be practiced in Wales, and those English counties on the Welsh borders. The diarist John Aubrey noted in 1686: "In the County of Hereford was an old custom at funeralls to have poor people, who were to take upon them all the sinnes of the party deceased. One of them, I remember, lived in a cottage on Rosse Highway. He was a long, lean, ugly lamentable poor raskal. The manner was that when the Corps was brought out of the house, and layd on the Biere, a Loafe of bread was brought out, and delivered to the Sinne-eater over the corps, as also a Mazar-bowle of Maple full of beer, which he was to drink up, and sixpence in money, in consideration whereof he took upon him all the Sinnes of the Defunct, and freed him (or her) from walking after they were dead."

Salt and bread were invested with magical properties, and by eating both, the sin-eater took on the troubles of the deceased, who was then relieved of having to remain an earthbound spirit, going around haunting people.

In many parts of Wales, salt was eaten in place of the bread, but both have the same symbolism, namely, that of fertility. We remember how bread was placed in one of the bride's shoes at a wedding; the shoe is a womb symbol – like the oven, and in Germany salt was placed in the bride's shoe in place of the bread. At Greek theaters, the actors pelted the audience with barley bread shaped as phalli, and well-kneaded with lots of salt. But what was the purpose of sin-eating?

Sacrificial or ritual bread is really a totem object, something that stands in for, and displaces, the subject of both veneration and fear. The subject is always the stern and wrathful God, and the desire is for our union and identification with him. What we are really doing is devouring his potency, for as we have seen, bread can be invested with powerful, phallic characteristics.

The sin-eater is not only taking on the sins of the dead, but symbolically divesting the

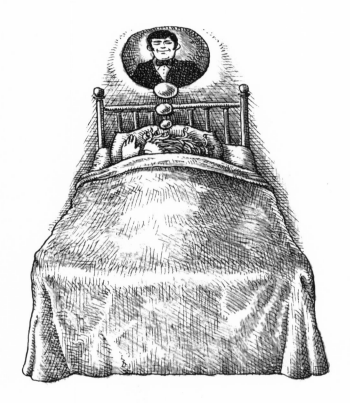

corpse of any malignant tendencies directed against the living relatives. That a delicate, light, spongy, crusty and golden loaf can be associated with sexual potency might at first seem absurd, but many myths and legends support it. A hot ash cake, made of dough and called "Groaning Cake" or "Dum Cake" was given to girls to eat while walking backwards to bed, where they would dream of their future husbands. Bread and cheese together have great power, especially against the "evil eye" (a subject that begs an entire book to itself, but is associated with impotence) and so does bread combined with sweat, which is supposed to have aphrodisiac properties, likewise bread made with urine.

John Bourke, in *Scatalogic Rites of All Nations,* 1891, remarks that urine was used by many countries in the manufacture of bread, and that a Paris baker in 1886 had mixed his flour with urine; the quality of the bread was thought to have deteriorated when the practice stopped. Bourke also mentions that early Christian sects used to incorporate human semen in the bread of the Eucharist – semen and urine as agents of potency are closely identified with each other.

In time, symbols become either modified, or made more obscure. Water has taken the place of the potent, salty fluids, and the water splashed about during the harvest festivities, referred to above, is probably a fertility gesture, the underlying theme being one of impregnating the Earth-Mother; it was important to tip a small quantity of one's harvest ale on to the ground before drinking it, as a libation to the corn spirit.

But what of the hag in the corn, the maiden, the mother and the grandmother? And what would have been the significance of the kern-baby? The hag is obviously Demeter; the triad goddess is a young girl, a mother, and an old woman. It would seem that most people regarded her as a malevolent spirit, and as such she would be Hecate, who amongst other things was the goddess of death.

The spirit's fearsome aspect is shared by that of the German corn wolf, but she had certain sexual characteristics, as had medieval witches. The last sheaf on Scotland's Isle of Lewis was an old woman, dressed in an apron filled with bread and cheese. We have just touched on the properties of bread and cheese and their combined fecundity, and it is worth adding that they were highly recommended for wives in confinement.

There's an old story about a cook who was having problems with his baking: the loaves would either burn, or not rise at all. The trouble was ascribed to a domestic servant who was suspected of being a witch, so the village priest was called in to exorcise the oven, and during the ceremony the suspect's apron burst into flames.

The apron conceals those parts that modesty and morals cause us to hide, but symbols have a habit of asserting themselves nevertheless. The rock of ages upon which the entire fabric of myth and folklore is built is made of infantile wishes and fears. The cornfield is as rich an area of fantasy as the graveyard, the sea, the distant hills, the nursery, the bedroom and the bakery.

We have peopled these places with witches, wolves, ghosts, and fairies. The hag of the corn reappears as a malevolent old witch in Grimm's "Hansel and Gretel," in a house made of bread, with a roof of cake and barley-sugar windows.

The symbolism of bread provided the storytellers with plenty of inspiration, particularly the brothers Grimm, and Hans Christian Andersen. Like most children's fairy stories, they have a strong element of cruelty or sadness. A woman has no shoes to put on the feet of her daughter, who has just died, so fashions a pair from bread dough, and bakes them hard. The child is buried wearing the bread shoes, but returns to haunt her mother, since there is a great proscription both in heaven and hell against treading on bread. The mother is obliged to exhume the body and remove the shoes.

In a story of Andersen's, a wicked little girl named Inge, takes a holiday from her wealthy employer to go and visit her old, peasant mother. She is given a loaf of wheaten bread as a gift for the old woman. On the way, Inge encounters a stretch of marshy ground, and uses the loaf as a stepping-stone. It turns out to be an unwise move. As she steps on the loaf, she sinks through the marsh into hell, her foot imprisoned forever by the bread.

Because agriculture is one of our oldest pursuits, it comes in for a good share of folklore and fable, and because the earth is a provider of food, this is possibly the main reason that we associate earth with the maternal figure, hence the term "Mother Earth." Ploughing the earth and sowing seed from which we made bread to be popped into ovens, aroused the anxiety that, in some way, we were guilty of incestuous desires.

It is likely that the kern-baby is a phallic symbol of these desires, and so are the sickles, those that cut the last sheaf. If this is true, we might then consider that the last sheaf, the hag, is the *object* of the desires. But if that is what we secretly wish, why does she possess the forbidden twin characteristics of sexuality combined with senility? We may just as well ask why we love and fear God, or why it is that the revered Hindu goddess Parprati, a benign mother figure, can change without much encouragement into the demon-goddess Kali with her lips of blood and girdle of human skulls.

At one time, witches and ghosts and fairies were rarely absent from any cottage – they were not always malevolent. The fossils of sea urchins, turned up with the plough, were called fairy loaves, for their resemblance to the round cottage loaf, and their presence in the home ensured a plentiful supply of bread.

Millers were the inheritors of much denigration and innuendo. It is doubtless a giant miller who chants: "Fee, fie, fo, fum, I smell the blood of an Englishman, be he alive, or be he dead, I'll grind his bones to make my bread." This "nursery rhyme," designed to scare children, might cause them to grow up with a prejudice against millers. They were thieves, hence the phrase, "as bold as a miller's collar," because the collar, "takes a thief by the throat every morning."

As for the tolls the miller exacted from his customers for grinding their corn, they were thought to allow the miller every opportunity for thieving. Says the miller's son to his father,

Father, O father, I'm your bonnie boy,
And stealing corn is all my joy,
And if I should a living lack,
I'll take the whole and steal the sack.

That was an American version of an old English song, and possibly represented a sentiment shared the world over.

Our acknowledgement of the importance of bread as a staple and stable factor of life, is reflected in modern folklore by slang words such as "dough" and "bread" for money, and the now archaic *mouler* which also means money, and may have come from the German *müller* a miller, or *mühl,* to mill or grind. But the attitudes to millers plumbed deeper areas of fantasy. It was supposed, in some obscure way, that they were strong, which inferred both physical and sexual potency – even if the evidence was to the contrary.

Chaucer's miller's thumb of gold has always been thought to refer to the miller's ability to appraise the quality of the grain or the surface of the millstone, or as a method of stealing grain. Ernest Jones, the biographer of Freud, points out that "Gold as fertilizing principle, usually in conjunction with a second sexual symbol, is a favorite theme in mythology." The ram with the Golden Fleece is a further example of this, and so we might infer that the miller's thumb is a phallus.

The miller comes in not only for accusation, but for envy as well. The Norse Saga of Amlodhi, from which Shakespeare's *Hamlet* was probably derived, tells of a prince who owned a mill, operated by nine goddesses on the edge of the world. They ground meal for Amlodhi, taking turns to grasp the "twisting or

Chaucer's miller. "Wel coude he stelen corn."

111

The Muffin Man

YOU'VE heard about the muffin man,
    the muffin man, the muffin man,
You've heard about the muffin man
    who lives in Drury Lane?
Well, here you see that muffin man—
    that celebrated muffin man,
And if you try his muffins, you'll be sure to buy again.

MUFFINS

CRUMPETS

A muffin seller on a foggy day in London, 1880.

boring stick" that turned the millstone. Later, it seems, the mill got out of control and began grinding salt at the bottom of the sea.

It is a well-known fact that "grinding" is a vulgar euphemism for the sex act, and that the term is very ancient. Today, millers are no longer associated with these characteristics; milling is a push-button business and highly impersonal.

The old country ways survive only in old country corners where you might discover a hand-quern or a cheese press in action. Yet there are many city dwellers who would revert to the quern, if they had the time, in the belief that stone-ground flour might prolong and enhance life, and that the old ways hold some kind of spiritual communion with the soil, an extra dimension of which we have been cheated by the twentieth century.

In 1975, in York, England, a civil servant and one-time baker borrowed an antique baker's cart from a folk museum and, dressed in antique clothing, pushed the cart piled high with hot cross buns through York's narrow, medieval alleyways distributing free buns to the people.

Well within living memory the muffin men, balancing trays of muffins on their heads and ringing handbells, walked through London's streets. Curiously enough, muffins that are so popular in New York City are now practically unknown in London; they are just starting to be sold once again in London's shops, delicacies imported from America.

When the practice of home-baking began to decline, the superstitions were lost, never to return. People forget to cut a cross in their loaves "to let the devil fly out," or to leave bread and coffee around to prevent ghosts from calling. Perhaps in rural areas of America they are careful not to break cornbread from both ends, perhaps the Mennonites and the Amish of Pennsylvania bless their sugar cakes and buns.

There is a pub standing alone on a derelict site in London's east end, where they still observe the old custom of preserving Easter

Molitura.

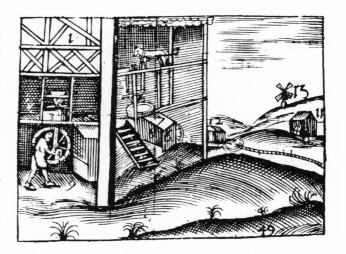

Grinding.

From Orbis Pictus.

113

PEEK, FREAN & CO.'S

CAKE FOR SCHOOL TREATS

PEEK, FREAN & Co's

BISCUITS

PLUM PUDDINGS

Were a Great Success Last Season.

IN WHITE CHINA BASINS,

FOR

1-lb., 1½-lb., 2-lb., 3-lb., 4-lb. & 6-lb.

SIZES.

Basins Included in the Price.

The 1-lb. 2-lb. & 4-lb. can also be Packed in Free Tins, Hermetically Sealed, for Sending Abroad.

❋❋❋❋❋❋❋❋❋❋❋❋❋❋❋❋❋❋❋❋❋❋

NEW THIS SEASON!

MINCE MEAT.

Manufactured by PEEK, FREAN & CO. with the care and nicety acquired by many years of experience in producing Biscuits and Cakes.

Packed in 1-lb. & 2-lb. Glass Jars and 6-lb. Tins.

OBTAINABLE FROM GROCERS.

Advertising – the modern mythology – sells bread for health and beauty. Hovis, with its soft-sell approach in 1893, touched on maternal instincts with this picture of a Victorian child. The fact that Queen Victoria ate Hovis for tea did more than a little to boost sales.

HOVIS

(REGD.)

Supplied to the
QUEEN and
Royal Family

Cure for
Indigestion

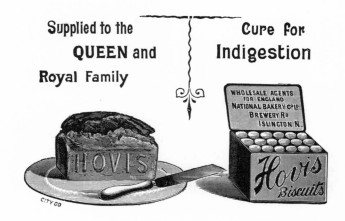

If any difficulty be experienced in obtaining "HOVIS," or if what is supplied as "HOVIS" is not satisfactory, please write sending sample (the cost of which will be defrayed) to

S. FITTON & SON, Millers, MACCLESFIELD.

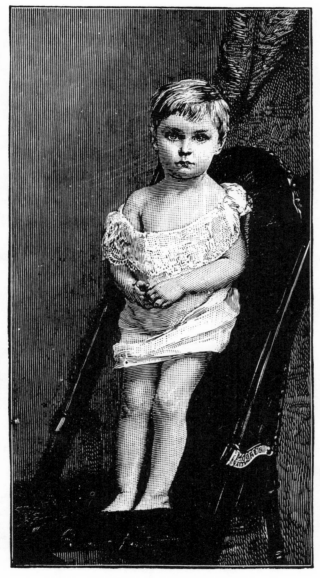

How fresh can you get?

Breads with wholesome good taste.
Pepperidge Farm remembers.

Oatmeal

Cracked Wheat

Whole Wheat

Corn & Molasses

Wheat Germ

For a new booklet of exciting
sandwich recipes, send your name
and address to: Sandwich Leaflet,
P.O. Box 1397, Elm City, N.C. 27822.

*Nutrition is still the big message in bread advertising, with
a glance backward to a wholesome past, and forward to a
healthy future. Freshness is important, too.*

"Big enough to get a drink by myself. That's how big I want to be!"

He'll never need Wonder Bread more than right now.

The time to grow bigger and stronger is during the "Wonder Years"—ages 1 through 12—when a child reaches 90% of adult height. Help your child by serving Wonder Enriched Bread. Each slice supplies vitamins, minerals, carbohydrates and protein. Delicious Wonder Bread!

WONDER.®
ENRICHED BREAD
helps build strong bodies 12 ways.®

Helps build strong bodies 12 ways®

buns. The story goes that a widow's son went to sea one Easter day, many years ago, and never returned. Each year she kept a hot cross bun in the belief that she would see him again. Hanging from the ceiling of the bar is a net full of ancient, dusty buns, and the pub is called "The Widow's Son." The tale is certainly apochryphal.

These buns, and loaves baked on Good Friday, were thought to possess great magical powers. It was said that they never went mouldy, and were suspended from the ceilings of homes and bakeries from year to year as lucky charms. The habit of retaining Good Friday buns was once common all over England. Yet in Russia the practice of baking on Good Friday was dangerous, and no one would have been surprised to find that the baker's hands had turned to wood.

In the late nineteenth century the maintainence of superstition passed from the cottage folk into the bakeries, and from individual bakers into the huge multiple combines and their advertising agencies.

The agencies are employed to create modern folk tales, to excite controversy over the merits of different kinds of bread: wholemeal, stone-ground, brown, white, pre-sliced and packed. To give them names with a heroic ring: Wonder Bread, Mother's Pride, or with individual appeal: Levy's, Hovis, Sunblest. The advertisers assure us – with good reason and sound marketing – that our flour and our bread has never been better, that "Graded Grains make Finer Flour," that "You don't have to be Jewish to eat Levy's," and updating an earnest plea with: "Make Hovis your daily bread."

Over forty years ago, an advertising copywriter came up with, "Bread for Energy," a message as simple as the bread itself. Today we demand much more of our bread: "Wonder helps build strong bodies twelve ways," says an advertisement for Wonder Bread, but this isn't enough, for Wonder Bread must be made to last: "One squeeze tells you we're 'THE FRESH GUYS.'" In Britain our bread is

"Fresh to the last slice."

In Britain and America, the sale of packaged, pre-sliced bread that remains ever fresh, is far greater since the introduction of supermarkets, and a way of life that caters for convenience foods. Only the children remain indifferent to the type of bread that they eat – it doesn't matter what it is so long as it's smothered with peanut butter or honey, or both.

The children have seen to it that the folklore of bread is preserved in their games and rhymes, though many rhymes are echoes of a bygone age:

Why? – Z!
Butter on your bread,
If you don't like it
You'll have to go to bed.

In Missouri, children who had never even tasted gingerbread used to chant:

Red head, gingerbread,
Five cents a loaf.

Similarly, English children sing:

Why? – Wheat is better than rye,
You would know it if you had it to buy.

But rye bread went out of favor over a century and a half ago.

We have willingly traded much of our folklore for the sake of convenience and mass-production – combine harvesters, furthermore, have no fear of the corn-goddess. Yet there is a movement in the cities for a return to the grass roots. Shops specialize in stone-ground wholemeal flour and fresh yeast. The supermarkets are selling plastic-wrapped

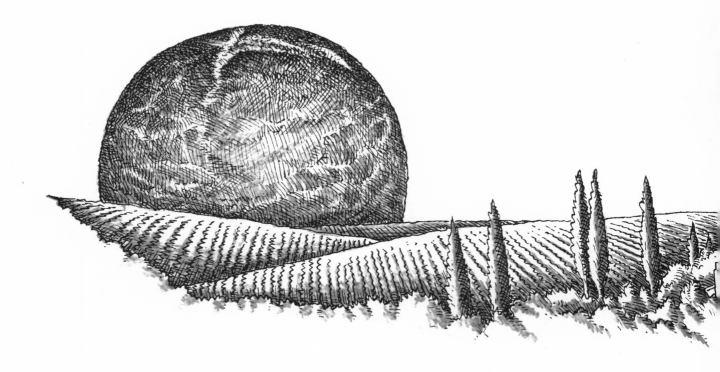

(how else?), unbaked dough so that housewives can bake their own bread just as grandmother did, and feel a sense of achievement that she took for granted.

Some things, though, die hard. Every year at Hallowe'en and in Britain on the 5th of November, pagan fires burn brightly. A large majority of the crowds who come to watch the crackling flames and the burning effigies, do not realize they are supporting a ritual once associated with human sacrifice. They come wearing heavy coats and scarves, and they carry umbrellas as it's sure to be raining. They are twentieth-century people, and they eat hamburgers and hot dogs, they drink Coke and Pepsi and lemonade and beer. In one village an ox is roasted on a spit, and the cooks slice the juicy portions of meat to make beef sandwiches for the crowd, as they probably did a hundred years ago. But the loaves of bread that make the sandwiches are now enriched, bleached, conditioned, pre-sliced and wax-wrapped, and they are spread with butter churned a thousand miles away from the village.

An eighteenth-century ploughman would have regarded this bread, should magic have conveyed him into the 1970's, with awe and wonder. He wouldn't have recognized it as a loaf, but more as a cake perhaps. It might have given him acute indigestion – and where was the cross to thwart the devil? Such is all that remains from several thousand years of mystery and superstition surrounding bread – the staff of life.

If you stand on the edge of a field of corn just after the harvest, you might perhaps feel that sense of mystery passed down through generations of families who at one time in their history have tilled the soil. You might fancy you heard the cry of "largess" over the roar of the machines, a cry that prompted an English country poet to write, nearly 140 years ago:

Twas near upon as light as noon;
A *largess* on the hill,
They shouted to the full round moon.
I think I hear them still.

COUSINS
UNDER THE
CRUST

5

In Georgia, USSR, a woman baker gathers an armful of puri, *a sourdough wholemeal bread baked in a jar-shaped oven called a* toné. *The oven, and the bread, somewhat resemble the Tandoori cooking of North-west India and Pakistan.*

The truly great breads of the world are those which have continued to sustain a nation or community through periods of peace and plenty, famine and war, breads which are part of a heritage: pioneer breads like corn pone, rye 'n' Injun, journey cake; peasant breads like black rye, Mexican *tortillas;* Indian *chupattis,* Scots oatcake, Irish soda bread; good times breads like Vienna bread, Jewish challah, Indian *paratha,* Welsh *bara brith,* brioche and croissant; religious and festive breads like matzos, Ukrainian *kalach,* Russian *kulich,* Italian *panettone,* the ubiquitous gingerbread.

Each of these breads is individual, and each owes its size, shape, flavor and character to a variety of determining factors. Why is French bread nearly always in the shape of a long stick, with diagonal slashes across the top? Why are some breads plaited, others fashioned in cubes or some regular, some eccentric? The shape is important and can reveal the ingredients of the loaf, the country of origin, even the humor of the baker.

What we may describe as "peasant communities," those which are stolidly agricultural, obviously favor a loaf of a kind that is hearty, rough-hewn and infinitely sustaining. The shape doesn't really matter all that much – round will do, or long or fat, but the loaf must be of a fair size to feed a large family whose appetites are keen, sharpened by the wind and weather. A black rye loaf with a shiny crust, scattered throughout with caraway seeds, cut into thick slices and generously buttered – that's what the farmers of northern Europe and Russia mean when they speak of bread.

At the other end of the scale are plaited breads covered with poppy seeds and kneaded with milk – fancy, festive, frivolous and possibly sweet. This is the kind of bread that befits a society proud of its artistic achievements – the sort of bread that the Strauss family might have enjoyed.

If breads are so representative of the societies which bake them, what can we say of French bread which must satisfy the critical faculties of the severest gastronomes in the world? Should it not be the apogee of crustiness, lightness, sweetness and delicacy? Should it not be a *poème* to the art of the *boulanger*?

But the French, of course, are fundamentalist. The bread is long like a stick so that it can be chopped into convenient pieces for the table; it must be cut diagonally to permit the maximum area for the spreading of pâté or butter.

We may search forever for the reason why the French have developed a preference for crusty bread. The crust must not be too thick, but there should be plenty of it. The long shape of the loaf gives more crust than crumb, and the slashes across or along its length help achieve this; the crust, by the way, is more easily digested than the crumb.

The French *baguette* and the *flute*, as the most popular types are called, is really urban bread, the loaf of the café or restaurant table, its companions the breadbasket, the menu and the wine glass.

In the country, rye is still an important cereal, and the *pain de siegle valaisan* from the alpine regions is said to be the most ancient

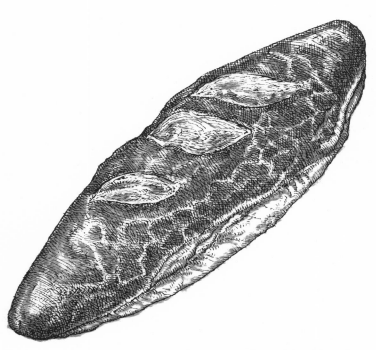

To the French, no meal is ever complete without bread; their choice is usually one of the types shown here – bagette, flute and ficelle.

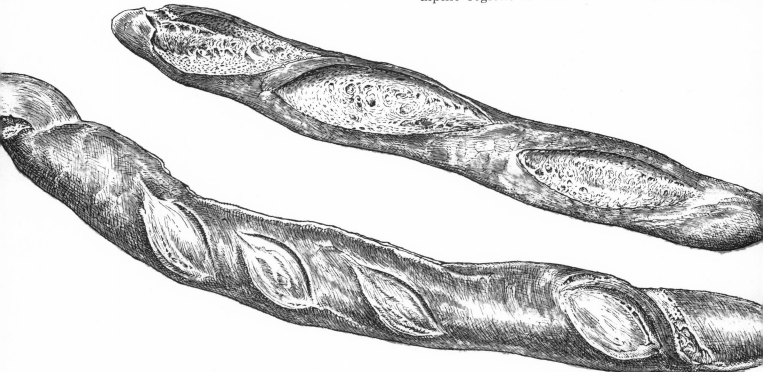

of French breads. This is the bread that accompanies smoked hams and sausages, ancestral cheeses and robust red wines.

An important point when considering the nature of bread is its relation to agricultural communities. As we have seen, bread developed along with civilization; bread, farming and the hearth are inseperable, which is why today's snowy-white, tasteless sandwich bread fails to evoke pastoral longings. We might say that bread, apart from symbolizing many human characteristics, is a powerful link between mankind and the soil – bread is truly the staff of life.

This, perhaps, is the reason why rye bread is so important to those communities that till the land. Rye has properties which might be seen to be shared with the earth itself. Rye bread is dark, earthy, solid, salty, sour, spicy, filling and nourishing.

Its counterpart in the wheat growing areas is wholemeal bread, with which it shares many qualities. Another, and more mundane, reason for the popularity of rye is because it is a cheaper cereal crop than wheat and flourishes on poor soil, as do oats and millet. Even so, when wheat arrived in quantity and became available to all, rye bread stood its ground.

In Germany, land of two hundred breads, *sauerteig* rye makes the two favorites, *Vollkornbrot* and *Graubrot,* without which beer and *wurst* would be robbed of a dimension. The Russian taste for black bread shows rye at its most earthy. Pumpernickel rye is enjoyed all over northern Europe, and has been carried close to the hearts of immigrants on their way to the New World, similarly the taste for pastrami-on-rye, which the Jews brought from Bohemia.

In Britain, rye is practically unknown. The Scots are great bakers with wheat flour and oats and prefer bread fermented by a brewery-style yeast. The Welsh still bake barley bread, on a *planc* or griddle, and like the Scots are fond of sweet breads filled with currants. The Irish also share this liking for fruit bread, but the national

Parisians have always demanded a constant supply of fresh bread, particularly since French bread quickly stales. A bread vendor of 1880.

loaf is, of course, the wholemeal soda bread, cut into wedges or *farls,* baked on a peat fire, and eaten with salty butter.

As for the English, they are wheat-eaters to a man. They said goodbye to rye sometime around 1850, and the reasons were due to the Industrial Revolution which had lured the laborer away from the land into the towns, and the importance of the class system, the like of which is paralleled only by the caste system of India.

The ramifications of the class system are as complex as a game of three-dimensional chess. The aristocracy frequently ignored the existence of bread and refused to serve it at table. The lower echelons of the upper class served bread rolls, or very thinly sliced toast. Their sons at school might have muffins, crumpets or buns, which were also eaten by the upper echelons of the middle class, who also had toast. Everyone else – the lower middle class, and the working class for whom no sub-divisions were permissible, demanded bread and buns of all kinds.

England's most important crop, barley, went to make beer, whisky and gin – and to what better use should it be put? Rye was for peasants and foreigners, and anyway, it tasted rather bitter. Wheat was the bread of gentlemen, and was not everyone now a gentleman?

The loaf of the city-dweller was white, and while there was little variation in the flavor, there was plenty in the shape. British bakers made, and still make, bloomers, bricks, busters, cobs and coburgs, cottage and farmhouse, lemons, leopards, muskets, splits, tigers and trilbys, to name a few.

Bread shapes betray their origins, and many of these English loaves were born in the nineteenth century when the dough left the cottage hearth and came to town; some loaves are square because they have been baked in tins, while others, like the cob and cottage loaves, serve to remind the town-dweller that the countryside is not far away.

The individuality of some types of bread depends on factors that limit them to within certain areas. The sourdough bread of San Francisco, for instance, cannot successfully be imitated, the authenticity and unique flavor is said to be due to the climate. Perhaps the yeast spores of the foggy Pacific bay are subtly different from those anywhere else in the world.

French bread is a challenge to bakers outside France, but it is not impossible to accurately reproduce. One famous American cook is renowned for her real French bread using American wheat flour. She had baked, it is rumored, over two hundred and fifty loaves before being satisfied with the results. The singular qualities of French bread are said to be due to the flour, the water, the yeast, the ovens, the atmosphere, the language, the Eiffel Tower, the aroma of coffee and Gitane cigarettes, the temper of the *femme de boulanger* and, of course, politics. Like the previously mentioned class systems, the world can be divided into several styles of eating. There are those who sit on the ground and eat, and those who sit on chairs at a table. Now we may subdivide: there are those who eat with chopsticks while sitting on the floor; those who eat with their fingers, sitting on the floor; those who sit at table wielding knives and forks.

Not to confuse matters too much, there are those who sit on chairs and eat with chopsticks, or eat with their fingers; sit on the floor and eat with knives and forks, balancing a plate on their knees. There are even those who eat standing up, or even walking in the street. *Sometimes running.* For these victims of a galloping, jet-age society, the hot dog and the hamburger between bread rolls has been invented.

The point of this discourse is to show how the breads match the style. The chopstick people eat rice, so do not use much bread. The floor sitters and cnair sitters who eat with their fingers require types of flatbread that can be used either as a plate (like the medieval *trencher*) or as envelopes for food, or so that they can tear pieces off and dip them into

John Montague, the fourth Earl of Sandwich, Secretary of State and First Lord of the Admiralty, didn't exactly invent the snack which bears his name, he merely popularized it. Yet he is far more famous for the sandwich than for his connection with the Sandwich Islands, named after him by Captain Cook. Montague was, they say, an inveterate gambler, and reluctant to leave the gaming table at any time, called for a constant supply of ham sandwiches – the choice being limited to ham, beef or cheese. Today, almost anything that can be placed between two or more slices of bread makes a sandwich. Some sandwiches are several feet in length, and demand heroic digestions. Others are small, crustless and feminine. There are sandwiches totally and unashamedly dedicated to starch, such as the formidable "chip butty" of Liverpool, England, which contains french fries between two slices of white bread. The Japanese make sandwiches of seaweed, the Danes make sandwiches that require a steady hand when eating them – smørrebrød piled high with shrimp are not for the nervous – the Greeks solve their sandwich problem (how to get a complete meal of grilled meat plus a salad into a sandwich) by putting the filling inside a pocket of bread. The Italians deep-fry cheese sandwiches – the *mozzarella in carrozza;* the Americans invented the hot dog, the hamburger, the steak sandwich, and a delicacy which the French regard with considerable perplexity and caution – the peanut butter and jelly sandwich. The French, on the other hand, have been known to give their children sandwiches made of chocolate and olives. *Chacun à son gout....*

sauces or scoop up pieces of meat.

These flatbreads are sometimes leavened, like the *naan* from the Punjab, or unleavened like the Armenian *lavash* and sesame-seed *churek*. The table and chair, knife and fork brigade demands the kind of bread that accompany food served upon plates, or used as integral parts of the dish: Danish open sandwiches, salt-beef sandwiches, bread and cheese, French toast.

Many of these breads have been elevated from the ground to the table. American cornbread falls into this category, especially the rye 'n' Injun bread of early colonial days, the corn pone ashcakes and hoecakes, the spoonbread of the south. They are staples, like the Mexican *tortilla* and the Indian *chupatti*, sympathetic to the diet of the people and the techniques of baking.

Almost every country in the world has its version of flatbread, even pancakes, waffles, matzos and oatcakes are reminders of a time when baking was done over an open fire, on a griddle or bakestone. The Indian *chupatti* is made of wheat flour called *atta,* mixed to a stiff dough with water, pressed or rolled into a flat, unleavened disc and baked on an iron griddle. It is a natural partner to the lentil stew known as *dal,* and curry and rice.

Chupattis played a curious role in the Indian Mutiny when Britain, who had been fighting the Russians in the Crimea, and was engaged in a war with China, was now obliged to defend her colonial policies at the Sepoy Mutiny of 1857.

In his book, *The Nightrunners of Bengal,* John Masters describes how the *chuppatis* were carried from village to village as coded messages of the uprising. A *chupatti* divided into five parts meant the fifth month, and into ten parts meant the tenth day – May 10th, 1857. A runner bearing two *chupattis* runs slap into a night patrol, lead by a British officer. "... I don't know what it means, sahib, but it must be done." The man went on with more assurance.

"When I get to each village I am to call the

Several countries of the world have a staple flat bread, usually unleavened, like the chuppati *of India. Even pizzas, pancakes, waffles and matzos are types of ancient flatbread. Here, a Mexican baker shovels* tortillas *into an oven.*

watchman and, when he comes, say, 'Out of the east – to the north, to the west, to the south!' Then I give him two *chupattis,* first breaking one into five equal parts and the other into ten equal parts. And I am to promise Fire, Justice, and Punishment on him and his village, unless that night or the following night he, too, makes and delivers six more *chupattis* – two each to the north, west and south."

In the north-west of India, in the Punjab, and in West Pakistan, the *chupatti* gives way to the delicious *naan* bread, made of flour leavened by fermenting curds and baked in a jar-shaped oven called a *tandoor. Naan* goes well with pieces of chicken, fish or lamb, also broiled in the *tandoor.*

In the south of Russia, the Georgians bake bread in a similar fashion. Their oven is called a *toné,* in which a sourdough wholemeal bread known as *puri* shares much with the bread of the Punjabis. These breads are slapped against the hot walls of the upright oven and baked, and so is the Armenian *lavash* which is baked in large sheets and resembles chamois cloth.

All breads are cousins, some more distant than others, yet with a remarkable similarity. In Yorkshire, England, a bread called *haver* used to be made until a few years ago. *Haver* is an old Scandinavian word for "oats" and the bread was a thin, oatmeal batter, cast by a dexterous flick of the wrist onto a hot bakestone. It, too, resembled chamois cloth and is no longer made on account of a shortage of dexterous wrists in that part of the world. But what has it to do with Scandinavia?

When the Danes raided Britain in the ninth and tenth centuries, they introduced a type of bread that was cooked on a bakestone or griddle, and then hung up to dry, and the method persisted in the dales of England until about 1960; *haverbread* was hung up to dry in the rafters of the farms. The soldiers of the Lancashire Regiment were known as "The Havercake Boys," because they carried oatcakes on the march, in small sacks, hence the term "haversack." A tenuous but recognizable thread has carried us from Armenia, through Denmark, to the north of England, which is a good thing because that's where we are going.

In the north, and particularly in Scotland, the climates and seasons have engendered a remarkable variety of breads, and the native habit of "high tea." Now, high tea is a kind of clarion call to the assembly of some fifty different kinds of bread, although the choice has latterly dwindled. Certainly in the eighteenth century, Edinburgh bakers, who had been influenced by their Parisian counterparts, baked more than fifty kinds of tea bread, and Marian McNeill, in her lovely book *The Scots Kitchen* said: "If every Frenchwoman is born with a wooden spoon in her hand, every Scotswoman is born with a rolling pin under her arm." Some Scotswomen conclude, however, that this is because every Scotsman is born with a bottle of whisky in his hand.

The reasons for the popularity of breads are partly due to the short daylight hours – in the winter eight a.m. until four p.m. – the national delight in starchy foods, and the inclement weather. A Scottish farmer needed a hearty breakfast that would carry him through till tea time, just after dusk.

Breakfast included porridge, haddock or kippers, bacon and eggs, the bread rolls called *baps,* and others known as "butteries," *buttery rowies,* the nearest thing to a Scottish croissant; all this, and that great Scottish invention marmalade, set the farmer going until high tea.

High tea and breakfast are practically interchangeable. Both feature a hot dish, often kippers or haddock, and though porridge and marmalade are omitted, bread and tea are the cornerstones. The great tea bread is the scone, which the English rhyme with "bone" but the Scots pronounce "skonn" to rhyme with "gone" and, further to our discourse on etymology, comes from the Gaelic *sgonn,* meaning "a shapeless mass" (which it in no way resembles), or it may derive from the Dutch *schoonbrot* meaning "fine bread." Why? Who knows?

130

A modern Dutch baker who still delivers his bread in a horse-drawn van.

VIRGO — Unmatched enjoyment.

*Says the butler, "Bless the young ladies! How happy they
all do seem to be! Bless their little hearts."
Tea at home in the 1840's by George Cruikshank.*

Such Scottish tea breads as the Selkirk bannock are fruity, filled with currants and raisins, as are the Welsh currant loaf *bara brith,* and the Irish *barm brack.* The famous "black bun" of Edinburgh – not a bread, but a cake – is so heavy with fruit that it is as difficult to pick up as a Glasgow drunk on a Saturday night.

It is by no means always a simple matter to trace the origin of breads by their names. Selkirk bannock is easy – a bannock that comes from Selkirk the word "bannock" has been distorted from the Latin *panicum* – bread – but

"scone" is questionable. The Bulgarian Bird of Paradise bread is so called because it is gaily decorated, and the croissant because it is crescent-shaped, but pumpernickel is difficult to trace, and so is the American bread called Anadama.

The story that this cornbread got its name through someone named Anna is a favorite kitchen fairy tale of New England. The origins of Anadama bread are not known, but it probably started life as a simple hoecake or ashcake of cornmeal. "Anadama" doesn't sound much like an Indian word, but it might be Latin through English. *Anadema* means "wreath of flowers" or "garland" so the bread might have been a pilgrim's harvest thanksgiving bread. Alternatively, it might be a confusion of *adamantum,* which is the Latin for "untameable," a word synonymous in the seventeenth century with "diamond." Perhaps hard-baked corn pone was like a rock!

In the days before roller-milling, when all breads were wholemeal to varying degrees of fineness, and the finest flour was probably off-white or a pale fawn, the baker's delicacies for the English gentry were the buns that bore the name of a town or district. London had the Chelsea bun and the London bun, while the city of Bath produced the mighty Bath bun, full of dried fruit and sprinkled with crushed sugar.

Eighteenth-century Bath was exquisitely fashionable, perhaps the most fashionable spa in Europe. Was Bath not the resort of Beau Brummell and the Prince Regent? Were not the Nash terraces the most beautiful in England?

It is pleasant to imagine the Beau munching Sally Lunn's famous teacakes in her little bakery, except that historians are now fairly certain that she never existed. There was a sweet dough cake in France called the *solimeme* which may have found its way to Bath, for the *solimeme* and the Sally Lunn cake are very similar – the teashop is still there, and the Sally Lunns sell like the hot cakes they are.

The story of the croissant may be equally fanciful. This crescent-shaped, light and flaky delicacy is reputed to have first been made in either Budapest or Vienna, after the city had been besieged by the Turks in 1683. Some bakers, working late at night, felt an unusual vibration beneath their feet, and concluded that the Turks were tunneling beneath the city. The bakers gave the alarm and the Turks were repulsed. As a reward, and instead of the usual weighty medal, the bakers were permitted to bake and sell rolls in the shape of the Turkish national emblem – the crescent moon.

There may be a grain of truth in the legend, but the crescent bread roll called the *kipfel* had

The pride of old Chelsea, the famous Chelsea bun.

The temple of the cream cake, a Konditorei *in Vienna, possibly Demel's, in 1873.*

French bread became world famous in the nineteenth century. A French bakery in New York City, 1882.

been around long before the Turkish wars of the late seventeenth century. Perhaps the introduction of the croissant was an example of public relations to promote sales.

It is possible that the croissant is one of the most ancient of all bread shapes, and its connection with the Turkish emblem is intriguing. Could it have been originally fashioned in the shape, not of a crescent moon, but a bull's horns? A temple containing rows of bull horn symbols, found at Catal Huyuk in Turkey, dates the emblem to neolithic times.

This is mere conjecture, however, but what is certain is that the Turks, retreating from Austria, left behind them two of the most civilizing influences ever to benefit the west – coffee and croissants.

Vienna's fame as the city of bread and cakes, of baroque confectionery, came about through a number of contributing factors: the white flour from Hungary, milled by the new roller-mill process; the beautifully soft mountain water; the singular character of the yeast; a highly concentrated atmosphere of art and music and the elegance of the Hapsburg court; plus the extraordinary collection of influences – Bohemian, Hungarian, Turkish, German, French, Italian and Jewish.

Vienna bread was, and still is, world-renowned for its richness and delicacy, and during the nineteenth century the various types of Vienna breads were as celebrated as opera stars: *lanker* and *linzer,* crescent and *Kaiser* (the *Kaisersemmel* was stamped with a picture of the reigning Hapsburg), the French, Turkish, Russian and Italian, the serpent, coil, scroll, twist, curl, *succoff, bugo, tyke, blitz* and *runt, roseate, spenick,* finger, pinchback and Jew's roll.

A large majority of Jewish breads came from Eastern Europe, from Hungary, Austria and particularly from Russia. Those that have found a natural home in the delicatessens of New York City are foreign no longer – strudel, cheesecake, black breads, poppyseed rolls, challah, bagels.

Bloomingdale's bread counter in New York City, 1970's.

The matzo and the bagel are singularly Jewish, especially the matzo which is said to owe its origins to the Exodus, and is a reminder of the time when the Jews were unable to leaven their bread, hence the strict proscription on leaven during Passover.

The bagel, "the roll with the hole," is one of the few breads first boiled then baked; this it shares with the old version of the English simnel cake – heaven knows why. The close cousin and possible origin of the bagel is the Russian *bubiyky* roll.

The bagel is practically a breadstick, like pretzels, the *solomka* of the Ukraine, the *kaaki* of Tunisia, and not forgetting the Italian *grissini*. *Grissini* are indigenous to the city of Turin, crispy, good to eat while impatiently

135

136

awaiting the pasta or minestrone, and excellent for driving home a point in argument.

Is it not strange, though, that the Italians are all but innocent of bread? But of course they have pasta, and they also have rice, they have a few festive breads, and the world can thank Milan for the *panettone*. There is bread in Sicily and bread in Sardinia, but bread as a theme with variations – bread *con brio* or *molto esspressivo* – is rather scarce.

Can pizza be described as a bread? The base of a pizza is dough, and in one sense all flour that is mixed with water to a dough and leavened with yeast is bread. As we know, all cakes were at one time made of bread dough, before the introduction of raising soda and fine white flour, and we can tell those cakes of ancient origins by the manner in which they are leavened.

Such cakes are really festive breads, like the delicately perfumed *panettone*, Germany's *Dresdner Stollen*, Russia's frosted *kulich*. It would be interesting to see how different these breads might have been a hundred or more years ago.

Danish pastries are sweet breads, and they must have improved considerably with the improvement of wheat flours and milling. The Danes themselves call their pastries "Vienna bread" because the technique of making them was brought to Denmark by Viennese bakers, hired to replace the bakers of Copenhagen who had been dismissed over wage claims.

It would be interesting to discover what the Viennese call the Danish pastry. In a similar fashion, the English have decided to call the jelly roll "the Swiss roll" perhaps because it reminds them of the Swiss *birnbrot,* a favorite Swiss fruit and bread affair. Visiting Swiss coming to London, on being served "Swiss roll" are therefore somewhat bemused, and suspecting that they might be victims of the curious English sense of humor, have taken to calling the Swiss roll the "English roll." Upon such trifles are international relations sustained.

Bagels are first boiled, then baked. "The roll with the hole" being made at a bakery in New York City.

OPPOSITE: Sandwiches for the football fans, hoarse and hungry. The kitchen at Wembley Stadium, England, before the Cup Final of 1925. (Sheffield United won.)

You have, no doubt, been wondering how we could get this far without mentioning the mighty doughnut. While it is an extreme oversight, for the doughnut does comply with our original definition of great breads, we have also omitted the *Baba,* the *Savarin* and the dumpling.

A great bread may also be the one you happen most to enjoy. For some it is the sticky malt loaf which they cannot let alone. For the Spanish it is unquestionably the deep-fried *churros.* For the English, muffins and crumpets. For the Americans, cornbread, rye bread or Boston brown bread.

There are hundreds and hundreds of different breads in the world, and if you were to single out one – just one – it would surely be, in the end, the one you bake yourself. 137

SECTION OF A GRAIN OF WHEAT MAGNIFIED.

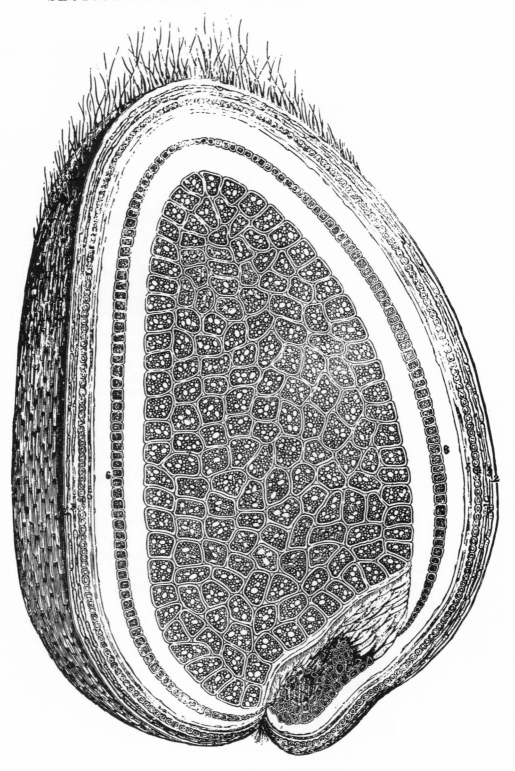

EXPLANATION OF DIAGRAM.

1.—SUPERFICIAL COATING OF THE EPIDERMIS, SEVERED AT THE CREASE OF THE KERNEL.
2.—SECTION OF EPIDERMIS, AVERAGES OF THE WEIGHT OF THE WHOLE GRAIN, $\frac{1}{2}$%
3.—EPICARP,   Do.   Do.   Do.   1 %
4.—ENDOCARP,   Do.   Do.   Do. $1\frac{1}{2}$ %
5.—TESTA OR EPISPERM.   Do.   Do.   Do.   2 %
6.—EMBRYO MEMBRANE (WITH IMAGINARY SPACES IN WHITE ON BOTH SIDES TO MAKE IT DISTINCT).

7.
8. } ENDOSPERM { GLUTENOUS CELLS CONTAINING FARI- Do. Do. 90 %
9. NACEOUS MATTER }

THE NAME OF THE GRAIN

6

A grain of wheat is really a dry fruit, a seed or berry if you prefer, or a kernel. This kernel is made up of three main parts: the endosperm, which is the white starchy substance that makes white flour; the germ, rich in vitamin E, and containing a quantity of fat, plus some enzymes; and the bran, which is the shell or husk of the grain, and a source of vitamin B-1.

There is an important protein contained within the endosperm, this is the gluten that gives bread its characteristic, porous structure. Without gluten, bread would not be a well-risen, well shaped product.

A piece of dough is an intensely active chemical laboratory. When we add warm water to flour the proteins in the gluten form a strong complex of molecules. Gluten contains the proteins glutenin and gliadin, and also a catalyst – chemists call it a "diastase" – which has the power to convert some of the wheat starch into sugar. The sugar encourages the yeast introduced into the dough by the baker. The yeast returns the compliment by producing an enzyme called "zymase" which splits the sugar into ethyl alcohol and carbon dioxide gas, which gives the scientifically minded the following formula: $C_6H_{12}O_6 + 2CO_2 + 2C_2H_5OH$.

Because it is a tough, durable and elastic substance like, say, bubble gum, the gluten is blown into thousands of tiny bubbles by the gas. When the dough has been given time to rise – or "prove" as bakers say – it is put into a hot oven which has the action of drying and hardening the cells of gluten into the spongy product we call bread.

Another important factor governing the quality of the dough is found in the quality of the water, which can have a considerable effect on the fermentation process. A hard water slows the fermentation, while a soft water quickens it. Usually, a hard water is alkaline, and contains a quantity of calcium carbonate, and traces of other minerals. Soft water is slightly acid and will produce a better dough. So if you live in a hard water area, you can correct the dough by adding a little white vinegar to the water.

Wartime harvest in Sussex, England, 1941. Women volunteers who worked on the land rather than in factories quickly adapted to the rugged, open air life of the farm laborer. They were called "Land Girls."

Having briefly examined the chemistry of dough, let's look at the character of the wheat. Some wheats are richer and stronger than others. "Hard" wheats possess gluten to a greater degree than do "weak" wheats. Although many varieties of wheat have been introduced, including dwarf plants from Japan which eventually superseded the mighty Maquis wheat developed by Sir Charles Saunders in 1900, the main types are *Triticum vulgare,* from which bread is made, *Triticum compactum,* used for cakes, and *Triticum durum,* the flour used in the manufacture of pasta and also some French and Italian breads.

The hard or strong wheats include those from Canada, long called "Manitoba's" and the hard red spring (HRS) wheats of the United States. Spring wheats are those planted in early spring, swift growers that are harvested in August-September. The hard red winter wheats (HRW) of the American Midwest and Argentina are planted in the autumn and harvested late spring or early summer. The

140

dwarf wheats from Japan, mentioned above, were introduced in 1940, and were later crossed with a semi-dwarf wheat to produce the successful "Gaines" in 1962, and the "Nugaines" in 1966.

These are hard wheats, as grown in America, but the wheats of western Europe, and in particular British wheat, are both soft and weak. The weakness is due to the action of an unhelpful enzyme called alpha-amylase, with the result that all the bread wheat used in Britain comes from Canada and the United States. Although the climate of Europe is too wet for hard wheats, experiments are being carried out with improved strains, and the general opinion is that in ten years, Britain will be producing hard wheats in some quantity.

Broadly speaking, the character of wheat is determined by factors governing the proteins and enzymes. Gluten, for example, is subject to degrees of quality, depending on the presence of phosphates in the soil. While chlorides and sulphates make gluten hard and brittle, phosphates produce an elastic and flexible gluten.

At the beginning of this century, Profes-

142

two-row barley   *winter wheat*   *oats*

sor T. B. Wood of Cambridge University in England, set out to determine the agents and conditions responsible for the quality and shape of bread. He discovered that the amount of phosphate regulated the shape of the loaf, and the texture was subject to the vitality of the gluten diastase. The difference between wheat and other cereal grains is simply one of gluten as far as breadmaking is concerned.

The only grain that can compare with wheat is rye. The American agriculturalist Harry Snyder said: "It is better that a taste for corn, oats and barley be cultivated in food preparations adapted to them, rather than to force their use on breads." Those who have made studies of cereal grains agree that all major crops had been cultivated by about 3000 BC, and that no new crop has been introduced since. The exception is maize *(zea mays),* which Christopher Columbus named from the American Indian *mahiz* or *marisi;* little is known of its cultivation before the arrival in South America of the *conquistadores,* though it is certainly several thousand years old.

The coarsely ground kernel of the yellow corn is called corn meal and can be separated

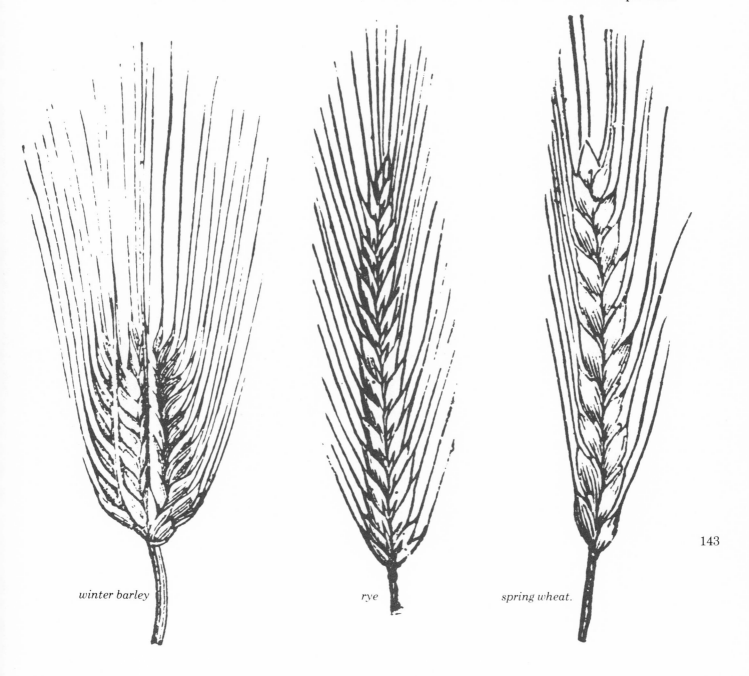

winter barley   *rye*   *spring wheat.*

143

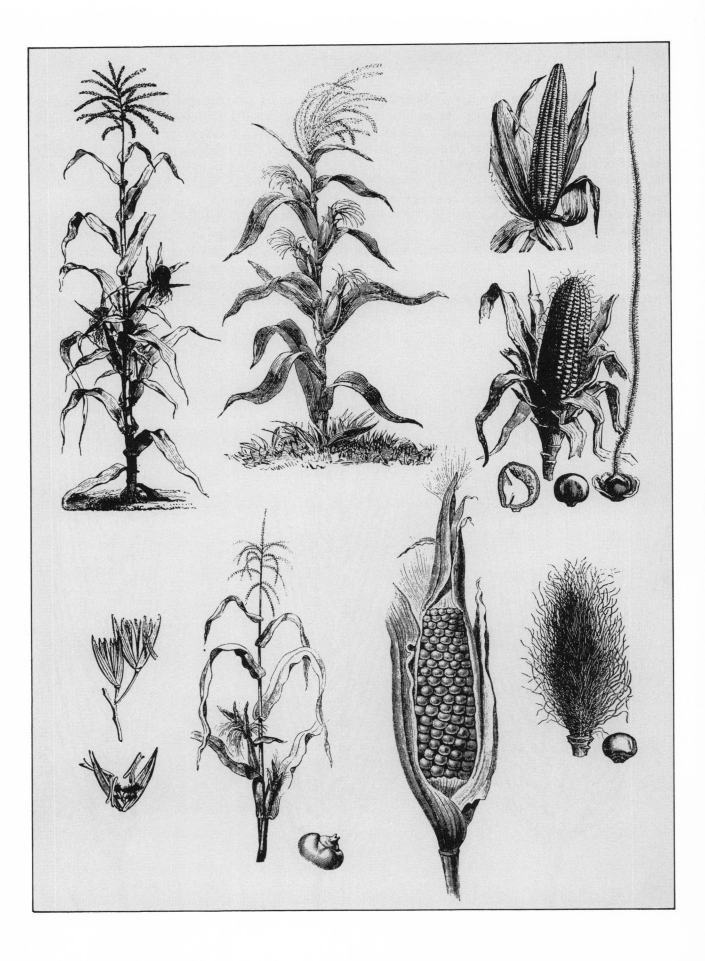

into yellow and white meal, the yellow being a source of vitamin A, while the whole kernel is a source of corn oil. White meal, finely milled, produces cornstarch.

Cornbread varies considerably, and everyone seems to have their own recipe. The old cornbreads were not mixed with ordinary flour nor were they leavened, but today we mix the meal with white flour or rye, and leaven with baking soda or yeast.

The early ancestor of rye was a grass called *secale montanum* which probably crossed with another wild grass *secale silvestre* and eventually produced a grass identified by the Russian biologist Vavilov, which he named after himself, as biologists are wont to do. This *secale vavilovii* finally produced the successful *secale cereale* which we call rye.

Rye is milled to make a flour which,

Winter oats in an English summer landscape in 1949. The oats, sown in winter, are here harvested by a reaper and binder.

OPPOSITE:
Various types of maize, zea mays. In America it was called Indian corn; in Europe it had various names, including Indian corn and Turkish corn because it reached Western Europe from America via Turkey.

145

although it contains gluten, cannot be activated in the same manner as wheat flour. A quantity of wheat must always be added to rye flour in order to get a well-risen loaf of bread. Rye flour is obtainable in a variety of grades, which range from a pale, delicate color and slight flavor to that which produces a dark, heavy, sour type of bread.

The very dark, coarsely ground rye meal is known as pumpernickel flour, as it is mainly used in the production of pumpernickel bread. Rye owes much of its characteristic flavor to fermentation, because rye flour ferments more swiftly than wheat flour, and the fermentation needs careful controlling to achieve the right degree of "sourness."

Although rye is a close rival to wheat as a popular flour for breadmaking, in terms of history rye is a mere newcomer. The most important crop of early civilization was barley. Barley *(Hordeum vulgare)* originated from the wild *Hordeum spontaneum,* which probably first grew in Abyssinia. Barley bread is still popular in Wales, and until the last century, barley bread was baked in Scotland, but it was never a serious rival to oats *(avena sativa)* developed from the wild *avena fatua,* which has sustained poets and Highland regiments for generations.

Two of the most famous varieties of oat plants were discovered by accident. In 1788 a laborer living in Eskdale, Scotland, noticed a patch of oats growing beside his potato patch. He was struck by the distinctive appearance of the plant, so he harvested the grains, and sowed them in the spring. The new plant proved to be extremely hardy and prolific and was named the "potato oat."

The other incidence of accidental discovery was made by a Scottish farm boy, Alexander Thompson, whose nickname "Sandy," was given to a variety of oats found growing on the farm where he worked. The use of oatmeal in baking is limited to oatcakes, gingerbread and a number of local specialties, such as the Yorkshire *parkin.*

There is no place within the scope of this book for a really comprehensive examination of the different grains, our main interest being the milling of certain cereals into flour and the flours used for baking. Not to confuse matters too much, hard and soft wheats are milled to produce "strong" and "weak" flours respectively.

It is rather difficult to tell a strong from a weak flour in the kitchen, but you will probably find that a weak flour is somewhat silky when rubbed between the fingers, while hard or strong flour is faintly granular. A strong flour will absorb more liquid than a weak one, stands up to thorough kneading or mixing to produce a well-risen, nicely shaped loaf.

The flour known as "all-purpose" flour is intended to be suitable for a range of breads and cakes likely to be baked in the home. Its title is rather misleading, for it is not suitable for every kind of loaf or cake, and it is also unspecific, since all-purpose can mean a blend of weak flours, of hard and weak, or even a blend of hard flours. It is possible to convert hard and weak flours by adding starch or gluten respectively.

Wholemeal flour is roller-milled flour which retains most of the grain, and 100 percent wholewheat flour is the whole grain milled by stone-grinding. Graham flour is the name given in America, and in France, to flour which contains the finely ground bran, and is another term for wholemeal flour. It was so-called after the American from Northampton, Massachusetts, Dr. Sylvester Graham, a Protestant clergyman of the early nineteenth century, who urged its use. In fact people took little notice of Graham, who was considered something of a crank, for what everyone wanted was white bread.

The French, who are notoriously resistant to anything that might threaten their dietary habits, especially if it comes from Britain or America, call wholemeal bread *pain biologique* as though one ordered it from a pharmacy. *Pain biologique* is presently the subject of a fashionable volte-face since it has become the

choice of the wealthy, while the poor continue to demand *baguettes,* and the rye bread, *pain de seigle.*

"Bleached" flour is a term applied to some white flours; most are chemically treated to preserve the desired whiteness by removing the yellow carotenoids present in the flour. "Enriched" flour describes a product containing added nutrients such as vitamin B-1, nicotinic acid, iron, riboflavin, calcium and phosphorus. The aim of enriching flour is to replace those minerals and vitamins lost in the milling process, when a proportion of the wheat grain, such as the bran, is sacrificed to obtain fine, white flour.

Additives are put into flour for the purpose of improving its scope: enzymes increase fermentation; oxygen produced by chemicals such as potassium bromate or chlorine dioxide will strengthen the gluten. Other additives help resistance to bacteria molds.

The general public is still suspicious of additives; perhaps it is a lingering memory from the nineteenth century, when bakers adulterated flour with chalk, size and alum. People concerned about maintaining healthy diets suggest that chemicals are injurious, but additives are included in our flour only in the minutest traces.

"Self-raising" flour is simply one that contains a leavening agent, and is identical to plain flour with salt and baking powder added. The advantage of self-raising flour is that the agents are thoroughly homogenized with the flour to obtain baking uniformity.

At the end of the nineteenth century, self-raising flour was becoming widely available. You can trace the development of bread, cakes and confectionery by the history of yeast and raising agents. Although the Hungarian Max Fleischmann is credited as the inventor of dried yeast, New England settlers had made a wild yeast preparation of hops, rye, Indian corn and water, mixed to a dough and left to ferment, which was then sun-dried and cut into cakes for future use. But wild yeast is

The modern, clinical, high-speed "Do-Maker" bread plant, a system of increased productivity developed in England.

both unstable and uncertain.

Fleischmann's yeast was a reliable product made of brewer's yeast and skilfully marketed, replacing many of those raising agents generally known as "starters" of which sourdough (because it is highly acid and "sour") is the most ancient type. Cowboys and forty-niners carried yeast cakes and sourdough starters with them to ferment their daily bread.

Rye bread is usually associated with a sour starter, as is the famous sourdough bread of San Francisco, which may have begun life as a specialty of the chuckwagon cooks or in the prospecting pans of the goldminers.

The word "yeast" derives from the Sanskrit *yas,* which means "to seethe." The yeast used in baking is *saccharomyces cerevisiae,* a

149

Doughboy and dough mixer. Superbread. Ever fresh, ever tasteless, bland, spongy, pure white, untouched by hand, wrapped in plastic and thinly sliced. All you have to do is eat it.

unicellular, swiftly multiplying fungus, becoming active at around 78°F, and the action is destroyed at 140°F.

Compressed yeast, sometimes called "German yeast," is a yeast culture which has been hydraulically pressed, cut into cakes, and wrapped or bottled. Dried yeast is the same product from which the water has been removed – dried yeast is usually in the form of granules, sold in packets or tins.

The introduction of baking powder in 1856 brought about a renaissance in cake and bread making. Layer cakes, sponges, Swiss rolls, soda bread and scones were now possible, and new types of cakes and puddings were constantly developed. Baking powder contains sodium bicarbonate and cream of tartar, which together with moisture and heat liberate carbon dioxide gas to raise the dough or batter.

The traditional use of yeast to leaven bread has given us that product we know and love, but for modern mass-production, yeast isn't quick enough, so it is now used in conjunction with a mechanical mixer. There is continuous experimenting today in laboratories dedicated to research into flour milling and baking.

One of the world's most comprehensive is at Chorleywood, England, where a special process for high-quality, standardized and mass-produced bread was developed. It was called, understandably, the Chorleywood Process, and is used to make 80 percent of Britain's bread.

The principle of the Chorleywood process is to combine a prefermented brew with the flour and mix it at high speed. A brew of water, yeast, sugar and salt, some skim milk powder, soya flour, calcium carbonate, some oxidizing agents and yeast nutrients is allowed to ferment. It is then incorporated with bulk flour and fat and mixed in a high-speed blade mixer.

In both England and the United States, the

152

Bulk fermented bread with an old-fashioned appeal. A selection of breads from the Chorleywood bakery, England.

best known processing machine is the Wallace & Tiernan "Do-Maker," where the brew, the flour and the fat are pumped at constant speed, under pressure, and passed through an enclosed chamber containing two large impellers. The dough is worked intensively for about sixty seconds and is fed to a mechanical cutter which scales the bread for the oven. One of the main advantages of the process is that of speed, for it avoids the traditional slow fermentation.

Other methods of "setting the sponge" as bakers say, is with chemical doughs, such as the whey/cysteine product in use in America, called "Reddi-Sponge," or by the use of ascorbic acid. The natural development of high-speed fermentation is obviously high-speed baking, and to this end micro-wave ovens point the way for the future. Micro-wave baking will produce a crustless, perfectly baked loaf before you can say, "quern," and if you desire a crust, then the loaf is simply popped into an infra-red oven.

This is, admittedly, a long, long way from the peat-fire flame and the hearth breads of the country peasant, and there are many who would have us believe that our bread has suffered accordingly; hence the continuous controversy over white and brown breads. What *is* certain is that some large, white "family" loaves, wrapped in jazzy wrappers, possess a spongy, "spring-back" texture and resilience more in keeping with foam-rubber upholstery than with bread. This is bread without guts, character or taste, made to a bland uniformity, untouched by hand, the product of a technological age.

It is no good blaming the bakers, nor the millers, for the public demand the kind of loaf that is convenient, a loaf that has been sliced for them, with a crust that makes no threats to dentures, and keeps fresh for over a week. It is undoubtedly convenient. But is it bread?

153

FOR
AND AGAINST
THE GRAIN

7

The great bread controversy – should our bread be white or brown – is both curious and intriguing. The argument has persisted for a long time, and has involved social distinction, snobbery, superstition, symbolism, nutrition, plus a host of unsupported and, in some cases, unprovable facts.

First of all, let's see what is meant by "white" flour. Until the introduction of the roller mill in the late nineteenth century, all flours were grades of wholemeal, because even the best French-dressed millstones were not capable of isolating the white endosperm from the bran. As described in chapter 6, the wheat grain is made up of the endosperm, which constitutes the bulk of the grain and makes white flour; the outer covering, or bran; the germ, containing a proportion of fat; and the scutellum, which separates the germ from the endosperm.

Stone milling merely pulverized the wheat kernels, but roller mills have a better technique. The grain, instead of being crushed, is torn apart, freeing the endosperm from the bran and the wheat germ. The endosperm, now called semolina, passes through five sets of rollers, the bran either being lifted off by air, or graded through screens. The semolina is further reduced through rollers until the desired fineness or extraction is achieved. The end product is fine white flour. Should the entire kernel be milled and all parts retained, the flour is said to be of 100 percent extraction, because the whole of the meal has been saved. A flour of 85 and 75 extraction indicates the amount of the kernel retained as flour.

For thousands of years, the fineness of flour depended on the manner in which it was sieved or "bolted." The finer the bolting cloth, the finer the flour. In the early nineteenth century the best flour was obtained by "high milling" in which the stones were set wide apart and the grain was milled twice, then bolted through silk gauze. Because of the labor and time involved, fine flour was an expensive product, enjoyed mainly by the privileged classes who declared it

155

to be more palatable and thus suitable to their refined digestive systems.

The less than privileged were not far behind in declaring that they too preferred white bread, for it was more palatable without butter (often a luxury) than brown, and brown bread was held to be a purgative. White bread, then, separated the rich from the poor, the banker from the student, the captain from the deck hand. It used to be said of a person living in temporary ease and comfort: "He is eating his white bread now," implying that all good things must come to an end.

During the Middle Ages, England had its White Bakers and Brown Bakers; the latter made bread from wholewheat flour. Among other duties, the Brown Bakers were expected to make loaves for the poor of London. The bread probably consisted mainly of bran which cannot be digested, but even so, the poor were not exactly deprived. Bran has laxative properties, and it also strengthens teeth. Wholemeal bread is rich in proteins, vitamins and fats which help to maintain a healthy diet. On the other hand, medieval bread was coarse and heavy, but the European peasant probably had strong teeth, powerful jaw muscles, and a digestive tract like the town drain.

Hundreds of years later, when our systems were daily reamed out with roughage, America witnessed a reversal of the pattern. This was when Governor Washburn of Minnesota declared white bread for all, with the result that everyone suffered from constipation. It was left to the food faddist Harvey Kellogg to encourage the bowels of a nation by introducing roughage as a breakfast cereal in the form of All-Bran. When white bread took its place on the tables of rich and poor alike, attitudes shifted from the area of privilege and snobbery to the fairly unexplored and promising area of nutrition. White bread had held the center of the stage for too long; it was now the turn of wholemeal.

What Sylvester Graham had attempted to do in America, so Dr T. R. Allinson advocated in Britain. "The rich should eat it so that it may

Waiting hungrily in front of an English village bakery.

OPPOSITE:
Brown or white? Two subjects of an ancient, and still popular, controversy. At one time the controversy was a question of class – now it's a question of nutrition.

157

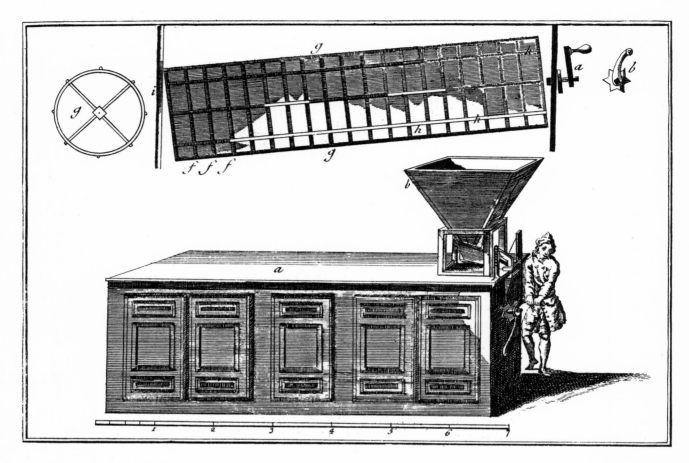

Graded grains make finer flour. A bolting machine, 1730. The finer the cloth, the finer – and more expensive – the flour. The whiter the bread, the more elegant the table on which it was served. This bolting machine consisted of a drum covered by cloth. The meal was fed into the hopper, and by turning the handle the operator separated much of the endosperm from the bran.

carry off some of their superfluous foods and drinks," charged Allinson in 1890, a time when the rich indulged themselves mightily, "and the poor must eat it, then they will not need to buy so much flesh foods ... readers are requested to take warning in time, and eat only wholemeal bread; to banish the white loaf from his home is the duty of every good citizen."

The clash of opinions over the merits of white versus brown are as hotly debated today as they were eighty years ago. The argument has since become extremely complicated and highly scientific, possibly to obscure the real reasons for objections which are largely emotional; considering the long religious associations and taboos connected with bread, this is hardly surprising. Because of this, a number of authoritative comments are inclined to be misleading, of which a few are preposterous.

A book titled, *About Bread, the Controversial Cereal,* describes the wheat germ as being a very rich source of vitamin E, which the author tells us is called "the fertility vitamin," the lack of which causes "sterility, abortion, impotency, loss of vitality and sundry sexual disorders...." The implication behind this dubious claim is that those of us who enjoy white bread, from which the wheat germ is removed in processing, may find ourselves sexually deprived. The nutritionist Magnus Pyke has stated that it is by no means certain that vitamin E is at all necessary to the human function, and that, " ... ill-health due to shortage of vitamin E has never been proved to occur, nor have any symptoms of malnutrition ever been cured by administering vitamin E." And since vitamin E is present in nearly all foods, why should we be concerned about the lack of it in white bread?

The subject of vitamin deficiency has become a powerful weapon in the hands of irresponsible dieticians and nutritionists, who choose to overlook the fact that a society that eats bread enjoys a certain economic affluence, and therefore a mixed diet. In poor and in some cases backward societies, malnutrition and vitamin deficiency is all too common; a solitary diet of rice or maize can cause beriberi and pellagra respectively.

Again, the controversy has emotional roots. Vitamins are associated with potency, strength and virility, the lack of them with impotence and defenselessness. Doris Grant, author of *Your Daily Bread,* and who also introduced the Grant Loaf, has indicted white bread on the grounds that it has contributed to juvenile delinquency, asocial behavior and urban violence because of the fact that white bread lacks vitamin B-1!

Persons deprived of this vitamin show symptoms of fatigue, apathy, loss of appetite, arrested growth and, eventually beriberi. Is it any wonder that emotional disturbance is a by-product? Urban violence, juvenile delinquency and sexual disorders are all the result of extremely complex and deep-rooted psychological factors, none of which have *anything whatsoever to do with a diet of white bread.*

It is strange that bread – any bread – should need to be defended, and even stranger that bread is greatly underrated. Even though people demand it daily, few realize that it is an important source of energy, an excellent food, second only to meat as a storehouse of protein.

Whether the bread be white or brown, both are a valuable part of a mixed diet, although it should be added that too much bread may contribute to overweight, on account of the carbohydrate.

There are a number of special breads on the market claiming to be starch reduced, by which it is often supposed that they assist slimmers. It all depends on what you mean by "reduced," for most of these loaves have only marginally less starch than ordinary bread. John Yudkin, the British nutritionist and expert on slimming techniques, says that these bakeries are allowed to suggest that their loaves are suitable for slimmers. "I admit that most of them don't actually *say* they are suitable," writes Yudkin in *This Slimming Business,* "they simply use names like 'Slimcea' or phrases like 'Slim girls eat Ryvita.' In my experience, even this last remark is misleading. I find it is the fat girls who eat Ryvita." These facts do not apply to those diet breads designed for those who are allergic to certain substances, gluten for example.

The question of nutrition – what is good for us and what should be avoided – is irrevocably bound to the governing factor of commercialized foods. The macrobiotic, Zen, wholefood way of life is no doubt a protest against TV dinners and tea bags and chemical pollution, and at the present time it represents a tiny percentage of the social attitude toward food, but the protests are steadily increasing.

Bread made from stone-ground flour, milled from organically grown, pollution-free wheat, is expensive and scarce. Such products

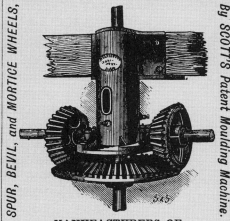
Advertising from "The Miller," in 1881

may be ideal (they are, in fact, Utopian) and commercial, processed foods appear to be the only way in which we can satisfy the present laws of supply and demand.

The average diet of all but the poor countries is better than it has ever been in history. Our awareness of vitamins, of balanced diets and of ways to prepare foods has greatly contributed to the health of each rising generation. To achieve this, we have made several sacrifices. The demand for bread has resulted in the dazzling white, sliced, rather tasteless, spongy loaf replacing the farmhouse type, because it is quick and convenient.

It is improbable that this kind of mass-produced loaf could do us any harm. Although scientists have warned us that sugar is harmful, that an excess of bread will cause us to put on weight, that saturated fats can bring about heart attacks, that strong tea in quantity can cause gout, it should not be taken as a warning to avoid bread, butter, honey and tea.

Bread constitutes a fair proportion of our daily intake of protein, much more so than eggs or cheese, and is rich in iron, calcium and vitamins. "Ah," say the brown bread supporters, "but white flour is robbed of its vitamins and important trace elements during the milling process." This is undeniably true. Low extraction flour loses several vitamins, also calcium, niacin, riboflavin, iron, nicotinic acid, phosphorous and fluorine. However, nobody lives by white bread alone. Other items in the daily diet can supply the lost vitamins, and anyway, millers fortify white flour by replacing the lost mineral salts and vitamins. The brown supporters then counter that by replacing the lost elements, the rogue chemist-millers have *distorted* the true balance of nature.

Although this is hard to prove, it is probably nonsense and takes the controversy into an area of triviality. Much better to stick to a fact such as, "brown bread has the necessary bran which acts as a mild laxative, a quality lacking in white." A good point, and the answer seems to be, "Okay, so why not eat both?"

162

It is difficult to divorce the argument from the rarefied atmosphere of the chemistry laboratory where, if you will forgive the pun, everyone has a retort. A well-tried argument is over a substance called phytic acid which, the white supporters claim, is present in brown bread where it interferes with the absorption of calcium and iron, but calcium and iron are readily available in milk, eggs, meat and cheese.

Few are impartial, but a referee such as Allan Cameron, the Head of the Department of Applied Science and Food Technology in Birmingham, England, writes " ... it is unlikely that the differences in the composition of the bread we eat are at all relevant or significant in the content of our diet as a whole. Unless new evidence is found it seems that the color problem for bread is a myth, not of course that this means there are no differences between different types of bread; only that the differences are not significant."

Perhaps the best qualities of brown bread can be found in its rough-hewn, honest, country texture, and its pleasant, distinctive flavor. As an accompaniment to certain foods, and for sandwiches, brown bread is incomparable – a smoked salmon sandwich is a great delicacy, which could not be achieved with white bread.

White bread is essentially a *crusty,* extremely varied type of bread and its advantage lies in its adaptability and its lightness. Brown bread simply doesn't match cheddar cheese and wine in the way that white does. It cannot be used for certain desserts, as can white bread – apple charlotte, summer pudding, bread and butter pudding, French toast; all require good, white bread.

It is not simply a matter of gastronomy, or of the rigidity of textbook cookery, but a matter of taste and common sense. In the final analysis, what matters most is that bread should be recognized for its tremendous value. Bread should be enjoyed, be it white, black or brown. William Cobbett knew this when he said: "Without bread, all is misery."

A variety of breads baked at the research center in Chorleywood, England.

163

THE BUSINESS OF BAKING

8

Etienne Arrault is a vast, rollicking figure with baggy trousers that always seem about to fall down, and like many French workers of his generation he wears a white, sleeveless vest. After forty-two years as a baker in the village of Monthodon, Arrault has decided to retire. He is sixty-five, and that's quite long enough to be baking *baguettes*. It isn't easy to find Monthodon on the map, a tiny place in the department of Indre-et-Loire, not far from Tours where, they say, the very best French is spoken. What will Arrault do now? He will tend his vines, and make some of the soft, light wine of the Loire. He will dig his vegetable plot and produce some nice, young carrots, and a good crop of spring *navets*. But he will no longer bake bread, even in retirement, though he says he might be tempted to bake the occasional brioche from time to time. Etienne Arrault is well-known for his delicious brioches; they are somewhat flattish in appearance, and not the classical, puffed-up sort.

Arrault will probably tell you that he is retiring, not because he is too old, but because of the decline in the sale of bread. His village is getting smaller, and now there are only 800 inhabitants left. "They are all leaving the farms to work in the cities." And that isn't the only reason for the decline in bread sales. "It is due to the doctors, you see, they are the enemies of the loaf – people must get thinner." Arrault thumps his belly and laughs, "We French eat too much bread."

When Etienne Arrault's father started the bakery in 1901, the French were the world's greatest eaters of bread. Those were the days when you had to bake some really fancy breads to terminate your apprenticeship – now all you have to do is prove you can push the right buttons, and pull switches. Arrault shrugs and returns to the oven. There are ovens and ovens, and they don't make them like this any more. It is fed on logs of wood, as ovens have been for a thousand years, and there are two great iron doors that open like the jaws of a dragon, to reveal the loaves crisping within. Arrault and

his oven produce fifty kilos of white bread every day, and every week two hundred kilos of wholemeal bread that the French – who have only recently discovered a liking for it – call *pain biologique.*

The bakery has a marvelous brick floor, and on it are arranged the bread baskets. Some hold long, crusty loaves, the famous *baguettes,* without which no homegoing housewife would feel complete. In one of the bread baskets there is usually a cat, since cats know on which side their bread is buttered. On slatted shelves by the door you can see the *boules* of wholemeal bread, plump hearth loaves with three short cuts across the top. Now that *pain biologique* is all the rage, you won't find the old rye bread that built peasant muscle and fiber, the *pain de seigle* – like Arrault, *pain de seigle* is due to retire. The bakery is ill-lit, and it smells wonderful. It stand on the corner where the road from Les Hermites divides for St. Martin and Château-Renault, and down which Arrault drives, every morning, in his rattle-trap old Peugeot van to take bread to the farms around the village. But don't the farmers' wives bake their own farmhouse bread? No, and few of them ever did. What's the point of baking your own bread when there are bakers like Etienne Arrault? And what will they do for bread when Arrault retires? Arrault knows the answer to that one. They'll get their bread from Jacques Houry's bakery in Château-Renault, it's smart and modern and that's what people seem to want these days.

The Arraults have never owned their bakery, they merely rented it like the old tenant farmers rented their land, and now some wealthy Parisian will probably turn it into a *pied à terre.*

When you buy a loaf from Etienne Arrault, it is first dusted with a little brush, a kind of deft flick of pride and professionalism, as if he were selling you something antique and very precious, which is perhaps the way he sees it. Like so many local bakers, Arrault belongs to the *Syndicat* in Tours – a kind of bakers' union,

*Elegant ovens for French bread. A mechanized bakery in
the Avenue de l'Opera, Paris, 1885. This was the epoch of
Grande Cuisine, and operettas about artists in garrets
who, no doubt, existed mainly on a diet of bread and love.*

A Jewish Bakery in Brooklyn, New York.

OPPOSITE:
"Man doth not live by bread only, but by every word that proceedeth out of the mouth of the Lord doth man live!"

and he knows they will present him with a gold medal on his retirement, just as they did his father, and probably a small bronze plaque showing a baker at work, which he will keep in a red, velvet-lined case. Well, you need *something* to show for a lifetime devoted to bread, other than a few crumbs in your moustache. Etienne Arrault's wife thinks that baking is a pretty thankless *métier,* and Etienne agrees with her, remembering the long hours and the hot days, but he is secretly sorry that none of his three children have followed him into the baking business – there will be no more bread from the hands of the Arraults.

Arrault will tell you that there's no secret to making French bread – anybody could do it. All you need is French flour, French water and an oven, preferably a French one and, ideally, the oven needs to be situated somewhere in France – it is all very simple. He obtains his yeast in little packets, it is *levure de bière,* brewer's yeast. The special stoneground wholemeal flour with which he makes the *pain bio* comes from Lemaire in Angers. But perhaps it is not all that simple, otherwise why would Houry have asked for the recipe of his *pain biologique*? Over a glass of *eau de vie de poire,* and perhaps in exchange for a small sum, Arrault passed the recipe on to Jacques Houry, the best baker in Château-Renault (8,000 inhabitants, 7 bakers).

Houry started his apprenticeship at the age of fourteen, in *Loire et Cher,* and now he's nearing fifty. His is a success story, though he looks a bit sickly, mainly because he's always covered by a fine film of white flour. Houry wears a sort of uniform with an apron and cap, in keeping with the new, almost clinical appearance of the modern bakery, all glass and tiles and stainless steel, and plastic flowers and a window full of *pâtisserie*. The shop is run by Houry's pretty little dumpling wife, and it opens at 7 a.m. sharp and stays open – even through lunch (of all French *commerçants,* bakers give the best service) until 8 p.m. Houry's oven is his pride and joy and a far cry

from Etienne's old wood-eating monster. It is glass-fronted so that you can see the bread baking inside which is glazed and crisped with steam jets, and the whole affair is controlled by knobs and switches and valves. Houry starts his dough at 2 a.m., and the first loaves are ready when the shop opens. Like Arrault, he uses French flour, and he leavens his bread with Springer's yeast. He bakes about 3000 loaves a week – *baguettes, batards, ficelles, flutes, parisiennes* and huge loaves weighing several kilos for the large families of the country folk. He makes the soft and delicious *Viennoise* milk bread, and the increasingly popular *pain biologique*. And his most popular seller? The *baguette, mais naturellement* . . . . What a question!

After lunch Houry usually has a siesta, as he has been baking all night – do bakers ever sleep? Anyway, it is better than working in a big city, like Paris, for instance. Nobody in their right mind would want to be a baker in Paris. For one thing the people are so damned fussy – *plus exigeant* – that you not only have to bake twice a day to meet the huge demand, but you

have to display a much larger variety of breads, the fancy sort that city folk like – *Parisette, toast rond, pain de mie, cornetti, pain au yoghourt, Tessinois.* What's more, the cities waste so much, they actually throw bread away. One of his assistants was telling him about some neighbors who had recently moved from Paris. He was scandalized by the great hunks of stale bread that the family threw out daily – "never in all my forty-five years have I seen such a thing."

Some bakers are "nearer the dough" than others, bakers like Houry and Arrault, who actually handle the stuff, shaping it into loaves and baking them through the night. In big cities, there are bakers obliged to run their business from behind a desk of files and telephones, having graduated from the oven to the swivel chair, often reluctantly. Such are the Coleson brothers of London. Colesons have been baking bread in Leather Lane since grandfather Coleson started the business in 1866. Leather Lane stretches between the Clerkenwell Road and High Holborn, running parallel to Hatton Garden, which is not a garden but a street of

In twenty years, considerable advances had been made in a profession then notoriously resistant to progress. From 1900 to the 1920's new machinery was being developed and installed. Above: Journalists watching a dough mixer in 1927. Right: A mixer of the 1890's.

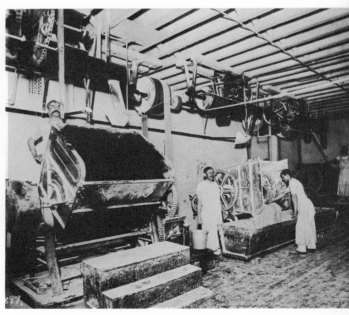

diamond merchants.

It is a strange thing, but many of London's bakers are of German ancestry, with names like Weiss, Moll, Ort, Hahn, Heinzel, Urbach, and Wittekind. These German bakers evidently tried to introduce their own types of bread to the London public, and only one now remains, and that in name only – the Coburg. The once favorite Brunswick is now extinct, perhaps because it was like many German breads, dark and heavy, a mixture of rye and wholemeal. The English prefer light, spongy breads with a crisp, golden crust; there was no place for *sturm und drang* bread on the neat, parochial tea table of nineteenth-century England. It would be like offering a pastrami-on-rye sandwich to Alice in Wonderland. Gradually, the bakers and their bread became anglicized. "We used to be Colehausen," says Tony Coleson who, unlike Houry, is not covered in flour but wears the clothes of a businessman. You might be forgiven for thinking the Colesons were a firm of accountants, and when you hear them talking about dough-making equipment, you are *certain* they are accountants.

The shop is unremarkable. There's a window full of buns, cakes and breads, and inside, the shelves are stacked with bread. There's also a notice that tells you the most popular type of loaf sold in the shop. Not surprisingly it is the bloomer, the loaf which Londoners most appreciate. A bloomer is a large, white loaf shaped somewhat in the fashion of a dirigible, and slashed across the top with diagonal cuts. Most people say the name comes from the fact that the loaf "blooms" or expands in the oven, but so do all loaves. Tony Coleson explains with a chuckle: "No, it is really named after Amelia Bloomer, because everyone said that the loaves looked like pairs of bloomers side by side. Originally it was called 'the Victory Loaf,' and was introduced just after the first World War." The bloomer is only just holding first place because of the recent demand for French-style loaves, the *baguettes* and *flutes,* although there's no evidence that the French have reciprocated by taking to the bloomer.

Surprisingly the Colesons actually *buy* certain kinds of bread. They use quantities of

Above: An electric oven bakes bread in 1922.
Right: Mass-production of hot cross buns for Easter, 1927.
Brushing the buns with sugar glaze.

Peeling tin bread into an electric oven.

Loading sandwich loaves and bloomers into delivery trucks. The bloomer was the recently introduced "Victory Loaf" following the First World War.

mass-produced, sliced white bread for making sandwiches, and do a brisk lunchtime trade. "We buy it because it is tasteless, so in one of Colesons' ham sandwiches you can actually taste the ham," Coleson grins. "Our own bread has such a good flavor that you wouldn't be able to taste the ham."

Colesons' bread is made from English milled flour, and the flour itself is a blend of Canadian wheat and English or Continental wheats. They use compressed yeast and make their dough according to a recipe based on a sack of flour weighing 280 pounds, which is a standard flour unit. "There was a time," remembers Coleson, "when bakers had to carry those sacks of flour up ladders. I have carried a half-sack of 140 pounds, and even then I felt as if my bones were breaking."

Not so long ago there were nearly as many individual bakeries in London as there were pubs. Well, perhaps that's an exaggeration, since there are more pubs in London than could be visited in a lifetime of drinking, and many have tried. Today, the bakers are fighting a defensive action against mass production, higher rates and overheads; the modern problems that confront the small enterprise. Yet the Colesons sell their bread as fast as they can bake it. Just behind the shop an apprentice weighs out the dough – "scaling" the bakers call it – and drops it into a machine that shapes the dough into a loaf. Another apprentice slashes the loaves across the top and places them in order for the foreman, who pushes them into the oven. The loaves are crisped with steam jets and emerge, crackling and golden, giving off that tempting, singular aroma of freshly baked bread that beckons like the wave of a hand to all who pass along Leather Lane. The Coleson brothers are happy that their wives and children have all joined the business. "The older I get," says Tony Coleson, "the more I recommend it. Unlike most other trades, a baker deals with raw materials right through to the sale of a finished product, while a butcher only retails. At the beginning of a day you start

173

with an empty shop, and you eventually end with an empty shop. You meet the public, the job is secure though often mundane, and best of all, bread is a fine product." And what about the hours? Ah, the hours, it seems, are impossible. "Seven in the evening till five in the morning, five nights a week, and you have to keep going because customers are demanding a constant supply of good, fresh bread." The telephone on Coleson's desk jangles, and he spends a few minutes chatting with a satisfied customer, and afterwards says reflectively, "Yes, the hours are impossible, but you get used to it, you know, after twenty or thirty years ...."

Quite recently, Britain's bakers went on strike as a protest against working on Sundays, and there was no bread to be had – not a slice – for over a week. Lines formed outside bakers' shops, and in several supermarkets undignified scuffles broke out between customers fighting over crumbs. But it was only a matter of hours before some realized that the answer was to bake your own bread, and it started a vogue. Now Colesons sell bags of flour, yeast, and instructions on how to bake bread in domestic kitchens. Amateur bakers are inclined to stress the "creativity" in bread-making and talk of "the joy of kneading." In America, the movement toward home-baking began as a by-product of the vigorous protest on the part of young people against commercialized living. Baking seems a way of expression, as much as anything else, and eventually produced such books as the *Tassajara Bread Book* from a Zen community in San Francisco, where bread is part of a philosophy.

Elsewhere, bread comes out of less transcendental ovens, into kitchens where children scramble for anything that faintly resembles dough, the more so if it is sweet.

Betsy Trace lives with her husband and two young children on East 90th Street in New York City. She bakes her family's bread and sees baking as good fun, an accomplishment, but she doesn't bake for "the joy of kneading." She bakes because "commercial bread is lousy, good bread is expensive to buy, and it is much quicker to bake a loaf than to search and find good bread in New York City." It was the New York *Times* that started her on home baking, four years ago, with a recipe for Christmas *Stollen,* and she got quite a surprise on discovering that dough had actually risen. The first attempts are not without hazards, as a home baker recently learned when he left some dough to rise in a warm cupboard where he kept his clothes, and returned to find that the dough had reacted so violently as to devour a pair of his socks.

A lot of people complain that they don't have time to bake, or that when they bake bread they cannot resist eating it when warm, and one slice leads to another ... and if you are young, pretty, like to be chic, teach English at a high school, have a husband who is an electronics engineer, and two children who will eat all you can bake and then some, it is sometimes hard to keep it up. Betsy Trace doesn't have much time to make bread, "but it is enjoyable after a day's teaching, and it is like eating out – the food is better and cheaper if you have it at home."

Craig Claiborne's *New York Times Cookbook* is a source of inspiration. "Most often I bake the Cuban bread recipe; I also like to use Paula Peck's *Art of Fine Baking,* and James Beard's book on bread."

James Beard, larger than life, the acknowledged dean of American cooking with many years experience of baking, is still as active as yeast. He wrote his book *Beard on Bread* to encourage others in the craft and delights of baking, and dedicated it to the English cookery writer Elizabeth David because she shares his "love of bread."

In his beautiful Greenwich Village brownstone, a relaxed and shirt-sleeved Beard expressed his contempt for commercial bread. "It's *terrible,* and expensive, too, although some English bread is better than the American types. In America the French and Italian bakeries can be okay, and breads like rye and

175

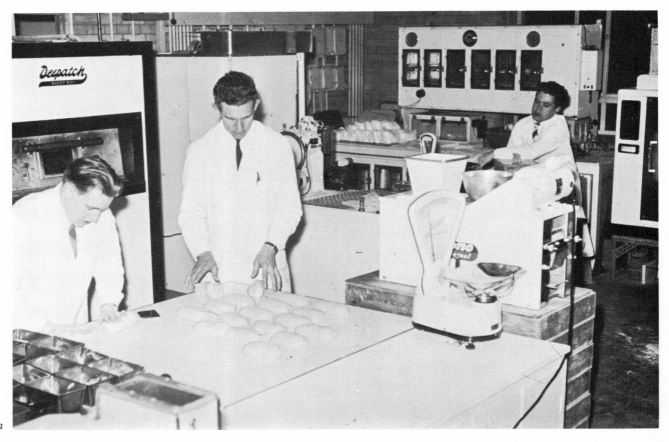

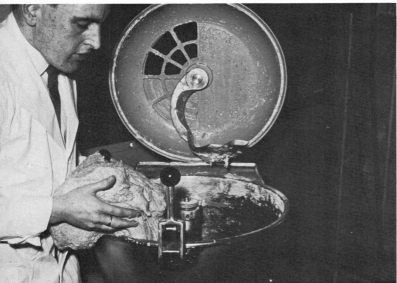

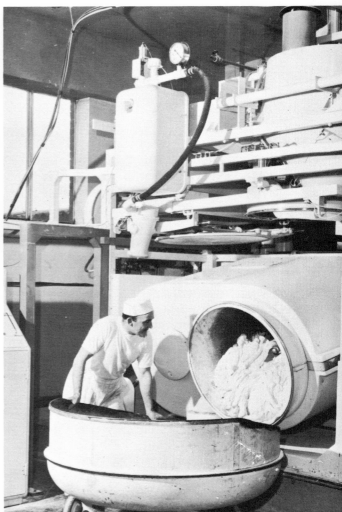

Superbread about to go into orbit. Many people consider that the technological development of mass-produced bread is a giant step for mankind – backwards.

a

b

c

d

a) scaling pan loaves
b) a Stephan dough mixer
c) dough mixer and kneader
d) R. V. K. dough mixer
e) umbrella molder and prover
f) bank of ovens
g) loaves going into the slicer

e

f

g

pumpernickel. There might be a good bakery here and there, but generally speaking, bread is pretty sad."

His book has had a tremendous response from the public, and readers now send him variations of recipes and new ideas, and he realizes that he has touched on a rich source of crusty nostalgia. "Everybody – men, women and children – can and should bake; it's a satisfying emotional experience." Baking a loaf is much easier than people realize, easier in some respects than baking a cake. For Betsy Trace, "cake baking is fun, but too fattening. Sourdough bread is a lot of trouble, keeping the starter going for regular use. Croissants take ages and they're fattening also. I prefer wholewheat bread mostly, and the Cuban bread because I can bake it from beginning to end in an hour and a half, by doubling the yeast and warming the flour." Her methods are in keeping with James Beard's dictum; "You should experiment the more skilled you become. There are so many breads and so many ways to make them."

It is because bread has been so long the province of professional bakers that yeast has acquired some kind of mystique. People will go to any lengths to produce a complicated dish and yet consider yeast baking an unknown territory. It is true that a home-baked loaf takes time, trouble and energy, even with labor-saving helps like a dough hook, which Beard maintains is more efficient than hand kneading and probably better, "but a hand finish gives a nicer texture." And the loaf, once cooked, has such flavor and freshness that it is swiftly eaten, hence the fact that busy people with large families are prone to taking the easy way out by buying commercial bread. "People take bread as it comes along. They are influenced by TV commercials telling you that squishy bread is desirable, the way bread really ought to be."

Until quite recently the flour and yeast companies did nothing to encourage home baking, but now this is changing, and James Beard remarks that one of the few good effects the natural food movement has had is that it encourages people to bake and eat better bread.

Like Beard, but on a more modest scale, Betsy Trace has taught others how to bake. "I said that cake baking is fun, and so it is, but the process is more exacting than bread-making. With bread you can be fairly loose in measuring, it's more variable, and you get to have an instinct which tells you how the bread will turn out. I use mainly unbleached flour, pumpernickel flour and hard wheat flour. Mostly I bake small loaves, they keep better fresh or frozen, and anyway, the big ones aren't eaten fast enough. The family all like my yeast coffee cakes, and they insist on my usual five: Cuban bread, Hungarian potato bread, pumpernickel, onion rolls and basic white – it's what we all like. I'll tell you something though, the kids really prefer Wonder Bread for toasted cheese sandwiches – isn't that typical! I have to buy Thomas's English muffins because they say mine aren't as good, and I buy bagels and Asian breads, like *Pita,* because they take time. I have a secret about home baking which I am happy to share – get a housekeeper to help clean up afterwards."

Cruikshank's drawing of an early nineteenth-century baker with bread basket. In those days the baker often had to bake bread and deliver it, too. Some even found time to smile....

LOAFING AT HOME

9

From "The Miller" 1881.

They say that the oldest craft of mankind is that of flint-knapping, chipping flints to make utensils and weapons, which is why the Stone Age was so called. Hard on the heels of the flint-knappers came the potters, the brewers and the bread makers. Making bread is an ancient craft, it must have afforded the neolithic bakers as much creative pleasure as their pastimes of cave painting and figure carving.

Today, breadmaking has never been easier, never more rewarding. All you require is a work surface, flour, water, yeast and salt. Of course, you also need time – perhaps the most expensive ingredient – plus a means of baking the dough and, equally important to the satisfaction of a good end result, you need a little practice.

In chapter 7 we saw how the flour, yeast and water affect the finished product, because much depends on the quality of each. To make bread you need a strong flour, flour with plenty of gluten. You also need fresh or dried baker's yeast, or a sourdough "starter," or baking soda. Ideally you should use soft water, since hard water has an inhibiting effect on fermentation. If you live in a hard water district, add a little vinegar to the water, this helps to neutralize the alkalinity.

The methods and the quantities quoted in the recipes in most cookery books vary only slightly, because the recipes are standard – white bread is white bread.

The ingredients, though, are inclined to vary from country to country. The flour is different, the water is different, and so is the yeast, even between adjacent states or counties. This is why several trial runs may be needed before you produce bread to your satisfaction. Some recipe books neglect to point out certain basic, important facts, such as explaining that some doughs can be very sticky indeed, those which are too warm, or contain eggs and sugar.

It is a good idea, therefore, to unplug the telephone and disconnect the doorbell when making rich dough breads. Unsuspecting cooks

The Three Minute Bread Maker. About 1900.

have been known to become inextricably wedded to telephones, electric blenders, door handles, small animals and children by a liason of adhesive bun dough, studded with currants.

For the same reason it is wise to have a large, greased bowl ready to receive the dough after being kneaded. This is a point often overlooked, because the bowl you require is always the one in which you have just mixed the dough; it needs cleaning out, and then greasing. But how do you do this if your hands are covered with dough . . .? Kneading thoroughly incorporates all the ingredients, strengthening the gluten in the dough, which will be weakened by the process of fermentation. You can feel the change as you knead; from a characterless mass, the dough becomes silky, resilient and firm. Some special doughs, such as Danish pastry, doughnuts and festive sweet breads, may require a softer, low-protein flour, or an all-purpose flour. If bread flour were used, the gluten would cause the pastry to become too heavy.

People are deterred from bread making because they believe that long and arduous kneading is demanded, but this only true of soft or weak flours; a strong flour requires only a few minutes – it can, in fact, be overworked, thus breaking down the important structure. If you possess an electric mixer with a dough hook attachment, then the problems of sticky dough and long kneading are largely academic.

A question over which there is some controversy is, "should wholemeal dough be kneaded?" Many backers defend the theory that kneading spoils wholemeal bread. The coarse texture of the bran in wholemeal flour fractures the strands of gluten, formed when water is added, thus damaging the structure. We know that gluten in flour is strengthened by kneading and long rising, so does it not follow that kneading might increase the durability of the gluten, and thus able to resist the bran?

Breadmaking, albeit a simple procedure, still depends on such factors as the temperature, time of year, temperament of the baker, even the altitude of the kitchen or bakery. A warm kitchen will encourage dough to rise faster, so will warming the bowl and the flour. Hot doughs, over 80°F, excite fermentation and are likely to become sticky and unstable. If you require a fast-rising dough, use extra yeast and warm the flour, setting it all to rise in a warm place.

A dough will rise in about thirty minutes where the temperature is around 70°F; in a cool spot the dough will take three hours, or overnight on the bottom shelf of a refrigerator. Cool doughs that rise slowly produce better quality bread with a good texture, and will remain fresh longer.

In the recipe section you will find one for "Quick" French bread, where the dough is made with warmed ingredients, extra yeast and no salt, the salt being added only as a wash over the crust.

Salt, like hard water, inhibits the action of the yeast. This "Quick" bread is baked immediately after first rising – purists are indignant – producing a close-textured bread that quickly stales. The idea of "Quick" bread is that you eat it fresh from the oven; it doesn't have time to get stale.

The quality of your bread is regulated by the correct balance of the ingredients. Salt, we know, inhibits the action of the yeast, but it also helps to strengthen the gluten and to give the bread its flavor. Salt also prevents the dough from becoming too sticky, and encourages a crisp crust. Sugar helps to brown the crust.

Sugar and fat, although required in most bread recipes, hinder the complete development of the gluten. Fat, in the form of lard, butter or vegetable oils, produces a richer dough and makes the gluten more supple, as does egg yolk. Most bun recipes and festive breads call for both butter and eggs, but these may produce very sticky doughs, as previously described. Malt extract, used for malted breads, has a similar effect on the dough – the flavor, though, is delicious.

The Home Cake Maker. About 1900.

183

If gluten can be described as the scaffolding that builds the loaf, then yeast is the construction company that puts it up. All the recipes in this book use dried yeast, simply because it is more widely available than fresh yeast. Fresh yeast, being a unicellular plant and therefore a living product, is extremely perishable, and less easy to store than dried yeast. On the other hand, there are bakers who claim that fresh yeast is incomparable, easier and quicker to use then the dried version and imparts a better flavor to the bread.

A point worth remembering about yeast is that it can be kept for long periods at low temperatures, but yeast is killed by temperatures above 140°F. Unbaked doughs, therefore, can be retarded by placing them in the refrigerator, or in the deep freeze.

Fresh yeast can be kept in the refrigerator, in a covered jar, for well over a week; in the deep freeze for about ten months to a year. Because yeast is comprised of 70 per cent water, when frozen it is surprisingly hard, and should be thawed well in advance, or grated into the flour or liquid.

Fresh yeast can be rubbed into the flour, or dissolved in water, warmed to "blood heat." Dried yeast should be set working in water at 110°F. In warm water, fresh yeast fizzes slightly, while dried yeast produces a quantity of froth; both dissolve fairly quickly, say in about fifteen minutes. Since the yeast is an organism, it requires "feeding" with a small amount of sugar to start it "working" but do not add too much as this would retard its growth. Manufacturers usually give quantities on the packet or tin, otherwise calculate a level teaspoon for every ounce of yeast. Recipes usually call for less dried yeast than fresh yeast.

There are several methods for adding the yeast ferment to the flour, and most bakers find the sponge technique gives the best results. Here the yeast, sugar and water are mixed to a batter with one third of the flour. The batter is set to rise and the rest of the flour plus other ingredients, such as salt and fat, are added; the dough is then kneaded in the normal way.

The more usual method is simply to add the fermented yeast to all the flour in a bowl or to the flour heaped on the work table, plus the salt and any other ingredients. The mass is worked into a stiff dough and then kneaded. The quantity of liquid added to the flour depends on the quality of the flour, and is quite variable, which is why you will have to experiment, so do not add all the liquid at once. Bread flour, because of its protein, absorbs more water than cake flour.

The "sourdough" technique of using a "starter" to ferment the dough produces a characteristic flavor, but starters are notoriously difficult to satisfactorily produce and maintain. A starter made in a city, for example, may not be as successful as one produced in the country. James Beard in his book *Beard on Bread,* says, "In New York City I never had the success with it that I had in Connecticut or Long Island or Massachusetts; I have even found variations in its performance from one neighborhood of New York to another."

To obtain a fermented bread, you do not even need a starter. If you add a good spoonful of honey to a straightforward white bread recipe, and leave it to prove in a warm room overnight, the chances are that it will ferment slightly – this was the most ancient method of leavening bread, relying on the wild yeasts in the air.

Practically anything will make a starter, anything, that is, having the qualities to ferment. You can make a starter out of flour and milk, or flour and water; rye flour plus water and a slice of onion; flour, water, sugar and hops; corn meal, beer and tea leaves; old shoes; hot water and sugar mixed with the pulp of old books about bread and magazines devoted to food and wine; water, hops, a slice of onion, a large slice of cheesecake and a finely shredded copy of the Sunday edition of the New York *Times.*

Cooks who develop a passion for using

starters find they have several pots bubbling away on window ledges, which stand them in danger of accusations of witchcraft. The general principle with starters is that they need at least a week to really get going, after which time they will bubble away cheerily to themselves, and can be kept going indefinitely, but need replenishing each time they are used – you remove a cupful from the bowl, and replenish with a cupful of flour, plus a little warm water. If the mixture separates, don't be alarmed, simply stir until it is well blended. If the starter turns orange, don't worry, but if it turns bile green or black, then is the time to throw it away (if it will let you). Starters that have more in common with laboratory technicians than cooks are best left to science.

To put it simply, a starter is a means of fermenting the dough, giving the bread a flavor denied to ordinary bread, and most of them always require an extra boost of baker's yeast in the preliminary stages of breadmaking.

When you have fermented your dough, kneaded it, and set it to rise, you may then have to "punch it down" or "knock it back," as the professionals say. Not all dough needs to be punched down, but the main purpose of it is to get rid of large bubbles of gas, and to make the dough resilient once more, it having been slightly weakened in the first rising.

This second kneading takes only a minute, after which the dough is shaped according to the recipe, and left to "prove," or rise once more. In the bakery profession, this second period of fermentation is called "floor time."

The term "prove" means what it says, it "proves" that the dough is still active, and that it has recovered from being punched down. Professional bakers use a special proving chamber that has moist air or steam circulating, which prevents a leathery crust from forming on the dough.

After the dough has been knocked back, or punched down, it is kneaded and shaped, left about twenty minutes to a half hour to prove, then placed in the oven. The standard method

The rise of home baking. Not many housewives bothered to bake their own bread, but the introduction of kitchen aids, fine flour and baking powder encouraged them to bake cakes. It was also the era of big families with hearty appetites.

SPICE BOXES, BREAD BINS, BREAD AND BEAN CUTTERS.

No. 199. Round Spice Boxes.
Japanned and Filleted.

No.	0	1	2	3	
	6	6¾	7½	8¼	inches
	4/6	5/-	5/6	6/8	each
Plain Tin	—	4/4	4/8	5/8	,,

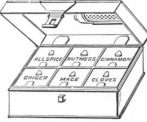

No. 270. Square Spice Boxes.
Japanned and Filleted.

No.	1	2	
	8	10	inches
	11/-	13/-	each

No. 273. Oval Botanical Box.
Japanned Clear.

10×7×3	11×8×3½	12×9×3¾ inches
5/-	6/6	8/- each

No. 271. Oval Seasoning Box.
Strong Plain Tin.

No.	0	1	2
	8 × 5	9 × 6	10 × 7 inches
	4/2	4/6	6/6 each

No. 272. Oval Sandwich Box.
Japanned Clear.

5	6	7	8	9 inches
1/10	2/1	2/6	3/-	3/9 each

No. 276. Round Basket Spice Box.
Japanned Red, Blue or Green. Written and tipped in Gold. 7 inches diam., 3/9 each.

No. 274. Folding Sandwich Boxes.
Japanned Clear.

5	6	7	8 inches
2/-	2/4	2/8	3/3 each

No. 275. Bread Bin.
Japanned Red. Mallett's Patent.
SHOWING INTERIOR.

No. 275. Revolving Bread Bin.
Japanned Red.
Mallett's Patent.

1	2	3	4	6	8 loaf
9/-	11/-	13/6	17/-	22/6	27/- each

No. 277. For Slicing Bread, Meat, Fruit or Vegetables.
Easily adjusted. Fitted with Feedboard.
32/- each.

No. 278. Bean Cutting Machine,
with Best Cast Steel Cutters. Japanned.
11/- each.

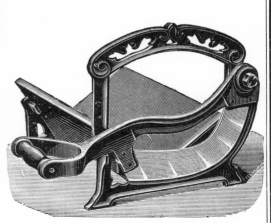

No. 279. Bread Cutting Machine.
To take loaves up to 8¼ × 7¾ inches.
Bronze Finish.
13/6 each.

is to put the dough in a preheated oven, but new
methods have shown that better results may be
gained by putting the dough into a cold oven,
set to the required temperature and left to heat
up. This is a question of experiment, and for the
sake of space and expediency, the recipes that
follow are for preheated ovens.

A crisp crust can be achieved by
introducing steam into the oven. Ovens in a
bakery have steam jets which pump steam
across the loaves, and the nonprofessional is
supposed to get the same effect by placing a pan
of water in the bottom of the kitchen oven.
Actually this is rather ineffectual, although it
does keep the air somewhat moist, which helps.

One method of achieving a crisp crust is to
quickly brush the loaves with water every few
minutes after they begin to color. French bread

needs a top shelf, a very hot oven, and the occasional wash with water in which a little salt has been dissolved. If you have a mind to, you can steam the oven by holding a kettle by the slightly open door. The trick is to use an electric kettle with a long flex, open the oven door just enough to let the steam in, but not enough to let the heat out, but the operation is not without difficulties.

In the previous chapter we saw how those long, French sticks of bread, *flutes* and *baguettes,* were scored across the top before being baked in order to give more crust. But French bread isn't alone in this respect, for nearly all "high-rise" breads are first cut – or "docked" as bakers say – before being placed in the oven. The purpose is to allow for vigorous expansion, and some doughs expand more than others – so that the gases or steam can freely escape without distorting the shape of the loaf.

With the advent of finer and better flours, more successful means of leavening and better baking techniques, bakers have developed bread in all manner of shapes and sizes previously denied to the trade. It is true that the Egyptians and Romans baked breads of attractive shapes, but these were either made in molds, or maintained their shapes because of their densities.

Most of the ancient hearth breads, the barley and wheat breads, were rather flat because the gluten couldn't hold up the loaf, this was due to coarse flour and weak leavening; such doughs needed the help of molds, and if they were marked with a cross or some other pattern, it was for decoration or superstition only.

The technique of shaping certain types of bread and rolls, twists, plaits, croissants and Danish pastries, requires practice. Baking is, after all, a skill acquired after some years of apprenticeship, and the making of *patisserie* can be an art.

For the home baker, the utensils needed are few – scales to weigh ingredients, a thermometer to judge the temperature of

Baking cottage loaves in a Warwickshire cottage in the early nineteenth century.

liquids and doughs, baking pans, muffin and bread tins, pastry cutters, perhaps a few English muffin and crumpet rings, a griddle, a rolling pin, a trustworthy oven and an appreciative family and friends.

It is wise to read the recipe carefully before starting to bake, making sure that all the ingredients are at hand. Plan well in advance and be prepared, should you not be satisfied, to try it over again. You won't even notice the time pass.

Some causes of faults in bread.

The crust is too thick
This may have been caused by insufficient baking, with too low an oven temperature, or perhaps insufficient sugar. A tough crust means that water has been trapped beneath the crust and turns it hard when the loaf is cooling.

Bread stales too quickly
Perhaps the bread has been made too quickly, the first period of rising terminated too soon. Otherwise due to too warm a dough, not enough salt or sugar, oven temperature too low, not enough moisture in dough, soft flour.

Texture of the crumb too open, or contains large holes
Uusally due to excess leavening, failure to punch down, or insufficient salt. Also due to insufficient mixing.

Crumb is too dense and close textured
Not enough leavening, or use of weak sourdough starter, oven too hot, too much salt, insufficient proving. Also caused by hurried fermentation, or over-kneading producing a tough dough.

Too much volume, loaf rises over the tin
There may have been too much dough for the size of the tin, or insufficient salt.

Crust blisters, cracks or breaks
Dough was too weak or too much liquid used, or oven too hot.

Crust too pale
Oven temperature too low, too little sugar used, or loaf placed too low in oven.

Crust too dark
Oven too hot, too much sugar, too much glazing or egg wash. Also occurs with bread that requires a long period of baking and needs to be covered by foil or paper.

Crumb too tacky or ''chewy''
A moist, dense crumb may mean that the loaf has had insufficient baking, that the oven temperature was too low, or the fermentation too rapid. This also occurs with poor leavening, especially in sourdough breads.

Loaf is too crumbly
Due to a slack dough, too much liquid having been used, or insufficient kneading. Also due to oven temperature too low, or dough left too long at proving stage.

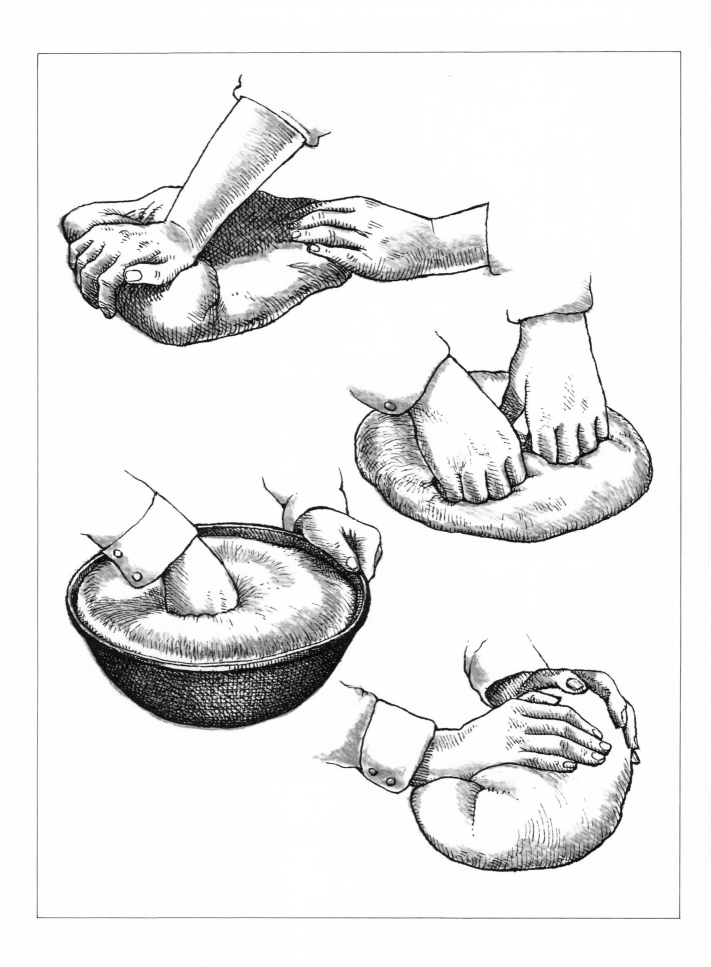

RECIPES
10

Note on the recipes

The flour indicated in the recipes is strong, white bread flour, unless stated otherwise, such as all-purpose flour. The quantities make one or two loaves, except in some cases, where the yield is given. The water or liquid used to set the yeast working should be tepid, and with just enough sugar to get the fermentation underway – too much sugar will kill the yeast, so will hot water. Keep a greased bowl handy to receive the dough after kneading, and cover with a clean cloth. The work surface can be a floured board, or the plastic top of a table. Unfloured plastic tables make a good kneading surface for some of the plain doughs. The stickier the dough, the more flour you may require. The dough has risen sufficiently when doubled in bulk, or when you can make a dent with your finger in the surface of the risen dough, and the dent doesn't spring back. Punching down and re-kneading is usually the work of a moment or two. The longer you leave the dough to prove (to rise for a second time) the better will be the result. The pan sizes vary, of course, but the quantities given here are for either a 9 × 5 inch, or 7 × 4 inch loaf pan, unless otherwise stated. A loaf is cooked when it sounds hollow if the underside is tapped. If it is still soft, return to the oven for further baking. This doesn't harm the loaf, as it might a cake. The temperatures are in Fahrenheit.

Conversion Tables

Oven temperatures

°F	°C		GAS MARK
250–275	121–135		$\frac{1}{4}$–$\frac{1}{2}$
300	149	Cool	1–2
325	163	Warm	3
350–375	177–191	Moderate	4
375–400	191–204	Fairly hot	5–6
425	218	Hot	7
450–475–500	232–246	Very hot	8–9

Weights and measures

PAN SIZES

9 × 5 inches	3 cups	2 pounds
$8\frac{1}{2}$ × $4\frac{1}{2}$ inches	$2\frac{1}{2}$ cups	$1\frac{1}{2}$ pounds
$7\frac{1}{2}$ × $3\frac{1}{2}$ inches	$1\frac{1}{2}$ cups	1 pound
$5\frac{1}{2}$ × 3 inches	$\frac{3}{4}$ cup	$\frac{1}{2}$ pound

AMERICAN CUPS & SPOONS	BRITISH	METRIC
1 teaspoon	1 coffee spoon	7 grams
1 tablespoon	1 soup spoon	14 grams
2 tablespoons	1 tablespoon	28 grams
$\frac{1}{4}$ cup	2 ounces	57 grams
$\frac{1}{2}$ cup	4 ounces	113 grams
$\frac{3}{4}$ cup	6 ounces	170 grams
1 cup	8 ounces	227 grams
2 cups	16 ounces or 1 lb	454 grams
$\frac{1}{2}$ cup liquid	4 fluid ounces	150 ml
1 cup	8 fluid ounces or $\frac{1}{2}$ pint	300 ml

To convert ounces into grams, multiply by 30. As a rough guide for dough-making, 4 cups or 1 pound of flour will absorb 1 cup or $\frac{1}{2}$ pint of liquid.

Basic Breads

How to make a white loaf

4 cups of white bread flour
1 teaspoon salt.
½ teaspoon sugar
1 package dry yeast
butter or lard for greasing
1 cup water

Place your yeast in a small bowl or cup, add the sugar and two or three tablespoons of warm water. Standard recipes usually state that the water should be at "blood heat," but tepid water up to 80°F is about right. Leave the yeast to work, which will take about 10 to 15 minutes to become frothy. Meanwhile, sieve the flour and the salt into a mixing bowl. You can warm the bowl and the flour, but this encourages rapid fermentation, which is not always desirable – patience rewards with a better loaf. Add the frothy yeast mixture to the flour, and also add the water – this can be tepid. Mix to a dough, place on a work surface and knead with your hands until the dough feels firm and springy. If you think that the dough is too soft and flaccid, add a little extra flour. If the dough feels too stiff, incorporate a drop more water. Getting the right consistency is really a matter of experience, particularly since flours vary in the amount of water they will absorb.

Have ready a greased mixing bowl, place the dough inside, sprinkle with flour and cover with a clean cloth. Leave until doubled in bulk. The time this takes depends, of course, on the temperature of the dough and the room, but on the average, it ought to be between an hour and an hour and a half. The next step is to punch down the dough and knead it thoroughly until it is once again smooth and pliable. If you want to make a pan loaf you will require a 9 × 5 inch pan or one with a capacity of about 2 pints. Grease and flour the pan, press in the dough, and leave to prove until the dough has risen to the edge of the tin or above. The proving, or second rising,

195

will take about 30 to 45 minutes, according to temperatures, and during this time, set your oven to 450°. Place the loaf on a middle shelf in the oven, and bake for 20 minutes, then turn down the heat to 400° and bake a further 20 to 25 minutes, until well risen and brown. To test whether the loaf is done, remove from the tin and tap the underside. If it sounds hollow, the loaf is cooked. If it is soft to the touch, return to the oven for 10 minutes.

How to make a wholemeal loaf

4 cups wholewheat or Graham flour
1 teaspoon salt
1 level tablespoon brown sugar
1 package dry yeast
½ oz butter
½ pint water
kibbled or cracked wheat (optional)

Place the yeast in a small bowl or cup, add a ½ teaspoon of the sugar and 2 or 3 tablespoons of tepid water. Leave the yeast to become frothy, meanwhile rub the butter into the flour. Dissolve the salt and the rest of the sugar in the remaining water, add the yeast to the flour, then add the water, and mix to a dough. Knead on a floured work surface until the dough is no longer sticky. Cover and leave to rise until doubled in size. Punch down, knead until smooth, shape either into a round hearth loaf, or place in a 9 × 5 inch loaf pan. Leave to prove until dough has risen, about 40 minutes. Meanwhile set the oven at 450°. Bake the loaf for 35 – 40 minutes, until well risen and brown. The loaf is cooked when the underside sounds hollow if tapped. Before placing in the oven you can sprinkle kibbled or cracked wheat over the top of the loaf.

NB, The flour used in this recipe can be varied. For example, you can mix 3 cups of white bread flour with 1 cup of wholemeal, or 2 cups white plus 2 cups wholemeal.

American White Bread

6 cups flour
2 teaspoons salt
2 or 3 tablespoons sugar
1 package dry yeast
3 tablespoons soft butter
2 tablespoons water
2 cups milk

Heat but do not boil the milk, add butter and all but a teaspoonful of sugar. Dissolve the yeast in the tepid water with the remaining sugar. Sift the flour with the salt. When the milk mixture has cooled, add to the flour with the yeast. Mix to a dough and knead thoroughly until smooth. Leave to rise until doubled in bulk in a greased bowl, covered with a cloth. Punch down, knead again until springy. Divide into 2 pieces, shape and place each piece in a 9 × 5 inch loaf pan. Leave to prove, and bake at 425° for 25 minutes. Check to see if the loaf is cooked by tapping the underside. If it sounds hollow, turn on to a wire rack to cool. If the loaf is still soft, return for a further 10 minutes, or until cooked.

Recipes for "American white bread" vary by the square mile, and much depends on the quantities of sugar and salt used. While European white breads are generally quite salty and made with water, Americans prefer a milk bread, made with butter and sugar – the amounts used vary according to taste. The above recipe cannot possibly be "standard" – it is just one more recipe for American bread.

English Cottage Loaf

4 cups flour
1 teaspoon salt
1 package dry yeast
1 cup water

Sieve the flour and salt, put into a large bowl. Dissolve the yeast in a little warm water with a $\frac{1}{2}$ teaspoon of sugar. When frothy, pour into the flour, mix with a wooden spoon, adding a $\frac{1}{2}$ pint of warm water. Mix to a dough and knead until smooth and springy. Set the dough

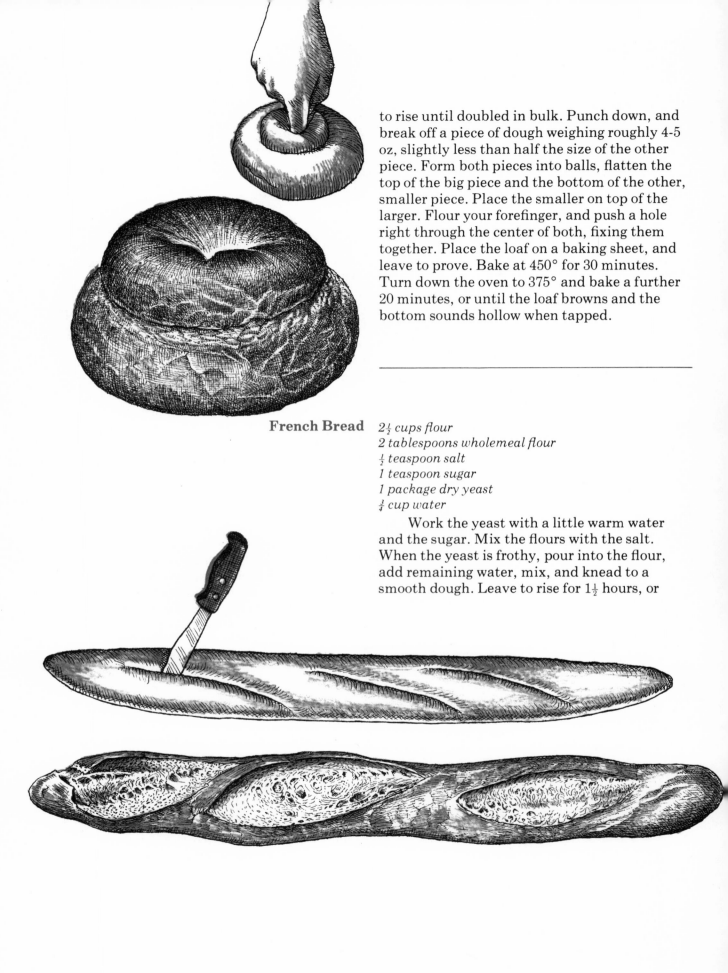

to rise until doubled in bulk. Punch down, and break off a piece of dough weighing roughly 4-5 oz, slightly less than half the size of the other piece. Form both pieces into balls, flatten the top of the big piece and the bottom of the other, smaller piece. Place the smaller on top of the larger. Flour your forefinger, and push a hole right through the center of both, fixing them together. Place the loaf on a baking sheet, and leave to prove. Bake at 450° for 30 minutes. Turn down the oven to 375° and bake a further 20 minutes, or until the loaf browns and the bottom sounds hollow when tapped.

French Bread

$2\frac{1}{2}$ cups flour
2 tablespoons wholemeal flour
$\frac{1}{2}$ teaspoon salt
1 teaspoon sugar
1 package dry yeast
$\frac{3}{4}$ cup water

Work the yeast with a little warm water and the sugar. Mix the flours with the salt. When the yeast is frothy, pour into the flour, add remaining water, mix, and knead to a smooth dough. Leave to rise for $1\frac{1}{2}$ hours, or until doubled in bulk. Punch down, knead thoroughly until smooth and satiny. With your floured hands, and on a floured work surface, shape the dough into two long loaves, about 2 by 15 inches. Leave to prove on a greased baking sheet. Set the oven at 475°. When the loaves have risen again, make long slits, about three in all, along the length of the loaf, holding a sharp knife or razor blade at an angle as you cut. Brush with water, and bake on the top shelf for about 25 minutes, or until golden brown. Every 5 minutes, slide the loaves half out of the oven, and quickly brush with slightly salted water.

Quick French Bread

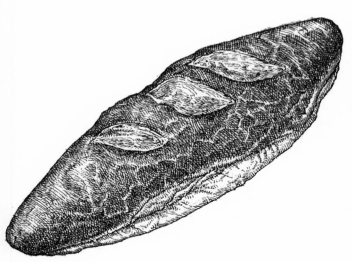

2½ cups flour
2 tablespoons wholemeal flour
½ teaspoon salt
1 teaspoon sugar
1½ packages dry yeast
¾ cup water

Mix the flours together in a mixing bowl and warm in a gentle oven for about 5 minutes. Meanwhile, warm the water to blood-heat, and add the yeast with the teaspoon of sugar. When frothy, pour into the flour, and mix to a stiff dough, adding either more flour or water as required. Knead thoroughly for 5 minutes, or until the dough feels smooth and springy. Shape the dough into two long loaves, about 2 by 15 inches, rolling them with the palms of your hands on a floured board or work surface. Put the loaves on a greased, lightly floured baking sheet (you can use either flour or cornmeal) and allow the bread to rise for about ¾ to 1 hour, in a warm place. Just before putting in the oven, make long, slightly diagonal cuts along the length of each loaf, brush with salted water, and bake on a top shelf at 450° for 25 minutes. If you wish, the loaves may be brushed with a glaze of egg yolk, mixed with two tablespoons of milk, to give a stronger color.

199

Simple Rye Bread

2½ cups white flour
2 cups rye flour
2 teaspoons salt
1 tablespoon caraway seeds
1 tablespoon sugar
½ cup corn syrup
1 package dry yeast
2 tablespoons butter
1½ cups warm water

Blend the two flours together with the salt and caraway seeds. Dissolve yeast in a little tepid water with a ½ teaspoon of the sugar. Warm the rest of the water, dissolve the sugar and add the butter. Pour all the liquids into the flour when the yeast is frothy. Add the syrup and mix to a dough, then knead until smooth. Place in a greased bowl, cover and leave to rise until doubled in bulk – about 2 hours. Punch down, knead again, then shape into a round hearth bread. Leave to prove, and bake at 375°–400° for 30 minutes. Test to see if bread is cooked, if not, return to the oven for a further 10 minutes.

Swedish Rye Bread

4 cups white flour
2 cups rye flour
1 teaspoon caraway seeds
3 tablespoons brown sugar
1 package dry yeast
2 tablespoons butter
1 cup water
1 cup milk

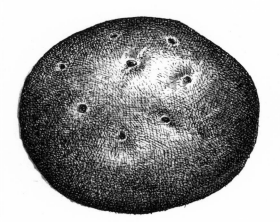

Mix the two flours with the salt and caraway seeds. Warm the milk, and dissolve the sugar (reserving a ½ teaspoon) in it and melt the butter. Put the yeast in a little warm water with a ½ teaspoon of sugar. Add to it the milk-sugar mixture, the melted butter, and the flour mixture; mix to a dough then add the water by degrees until a stiffish and sticky dough is obtained. Knead until smooth, put in a greased bowl, cover and allow to rise until doubled in bulk. Punch down, shape into loaves as desired. Prove and bake at 375° for 30 minutes, or until the loaves sound hollow when tapped.

European Black Rye Bread

In this recipe a sour starter is used to give the bread its characteristic flavor, the dark color may be obtained by adding commercial caramel or gravy browning. Neither affects the taste of the bread.

2 cups rye flour
2½ cups ryemeal
1 cup white flour
1 teaspoon salt
1 teaspoon sugar
1 package dry yeast
3 cups water
1 tablespoon caraway seeds
a slice of onion
3 teaspoons cornstarch

You will need to make your starter 2 or 3 days in advance of breadmaking, to give it time to ferment – much depends on the weather. Put 1 cup of ryemeal and 1½ cups of water in a bowl. Add a sprinkling from the package of dry yeast and the slice of onion, also the caraway seeds. Cover, and leave to ferment. When the starter begins to smell faintly alcoholic, and bubbles appear on the surface, prepare for breadmaking.

Mix the rye flour, the white flour and the remaining ryemeal with salt. Set the rest of the yeast working with a ¼ cup of the water, warmed to tepid, and a teaspoon of sugar. When frothy, pour into the flour. Remove the onion from the starter, add all the starter to the flour along with the remaining water. Mix to a stiff dough, adding more rye flour if required. Work in coloring as desired. No accurate quantities can be given, for it depends on the quality of the caramel, but a rough estimate of 1 tablespoon to the above quantities should suffice. Knead thoroughly and place in a greased bowl. Cover and leave to rise until doubled in bulk. Punch down and knead again until smooth. Shape the dough in the form of a roll, and leave to prove. Glaze the loaf with a cornstarch glaze, made with 3 teaspoons of cornstarch mixed to a paste with cold water, add sufficient boiling water to thicken, and brush over the loaf. Bake at 425° for 30 minutes, then reduce heat to 350° and bake for about 15 – 20 minutes, until the loaf sounds hollow when tapped underneath.

Granary Bread

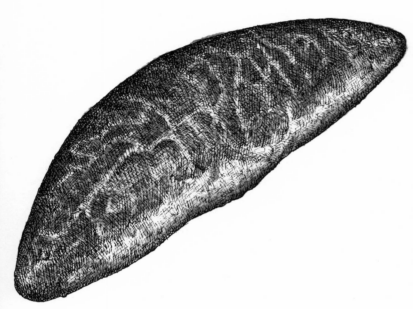

Granary flour is a mixed, malted grain flour, usually rye and wholemeal, and sold ready mixed in packs.

4 cups granary flour
2 teaspoons salt
1 teaspoon sugar
1 package dry yeast
1 tablespoon shortening
1 cup water

Mix the flour with the salt, and rub in the shortening. Set the yeast working with ½ cup of the water and the sugar. When frothy, add to the flour with the rest of the water. Mix to a firm dough. Leave to rise in a greased bowl, about 1 hour. Punch down, knead again until smooth, shape as a round hearth loaf, and prick surface in several places with a fork. Leave to prove, then bake in an oven at 400° for 30 minutes, or until the loaf sounds hollow when tapped underneath.

Milk Bread

4 cups flour
1 teaspoon salt
¼ teaspoon sugar
1 package dry yeast
1 cup milk
1 egg

Warm the milk until tepid, add the sugar and yeast and leave until the yeast is frothy. Sift the flour with the salt, add the milk and yeast mixture and mix to a softish dough, and knead until smooth and satiny. Put the dough in a greased bowl and leave to rise, covered with a cloth. Punch down, knead again until smooth, and place in a greased loaf pan, 9 × 5 inches. Or this loaf can be divided into three or four equal parts after punching down, and then plaited: roll the pieces into strips about 2 inches wide, join them at one end, and make a plait, securing them at both ends. The loaf may be brushed with a glaze of beaten egg yolk mixed with 2 tablespoons of milk, then sprinkled with poppy seeds. Leave to prove, then bake at 425° for about 40 minutes. The loaf is cooked when the underside sounds hollow when tapped.

German Vollkornbrot

Vollkornbrot simply means "whole grain bread" and recipes vary considerably from area to area. Some breads are darker than others, some are *sauerteig* or sourdough breads, some made with beer, or dusted with oatmeal. This recipe comes from a city famous for its beer – Munich.

1½ cups wholemeal flour
1½ cups coarse ryemeal
2 teaspoons salt
1 tablespoon brown sugar
1 package dry yeast
1 cup beer, preferably a dark, draught beer

Put the beer, the yeast and a teaspoon of the sugar in a bowl. Mix the flours with the salt and remaining sugar. Add yeast and beer when frothy, and mix to a stiff dough, adding more wholemeal flour or beer if required. Knead on a well-floured board (the dough will be fairly sticky) until smooth. Put the dough in a greased bowl and cover with a cloth. Leave to rise about 2 hours. Punch down, knead again until smooth, and shape the dough either as a roll, a round hearth loaf, or bake in a 9 × 5 inch loaf pan. Leave to prove in a warm place, and brush occasionally with warm water. Just before baking, sprinkle the surface with fine oatmeal, or coarsely crushed wheat grains. Bake at 425° for 10 minutes, then reduce heat to 375° and continue baking for 30 minutes, or until loaf sounds hollow when tapped underneath.

203

The Doris Grant Loaf

3¼ cups stoneground, wholewheat flour
1 teaspoon salt
2 teaspoons Barbados sugar, honey or black molasses
1 package dry yeast
1½ cups warm water

Mix the salt with the flour. Put in a bowl 3 tablespoons of the water, and add the yeast. Leave for a few minutes to allow yeast to soak, then add the sugar. When frothy, pour into the flour and add the rest of the water. Mix for a minute or so, until the dough feels smooth and elastic. Put the dough in a 9 × 5 inch loaf pan, and leave for about 20 minutes, or until the dough is within half an inch of the top of the tin. Bake at 400° for about 35 to 40 minutes.

Haidd: Welsh barley bread

4 cups barley flour
2 teaspoons salt
1 teaspoon sugar
1 package dry yeast
1 cup warm water

Set the yeast working with some of the warm water and the sugar. When frothy, add to the flour which has been sifted with the salt. Add the remaining water and mix to a dough with a wooden spoon, until all ingredients are thoroughly blended. Place the dough in a greased bowl, cover and leave to rise. Punch down, knead lightly, and place in a round layer cake pan, about 8 inches in diameter. *Haidd* is a round hearth loaf. Bake at 400° for 25 minutes, or until the loaf sounds hollow when the underside is tapped.

Vienna Bread

8 cups flour
1 tablespoon salt
1 tablespoon sugar
2 packages dry yeast
1 cup water
1 cup milk

Sift flour with the salt. Dissolve the yeast

in about $\frac{1}{4}$ cup of warm water with a $\frac{1}{2}$ teaspoon of the sugar. When frothy add the milk, water, sugar and flour, and mix. Turn out on to a floured board and knead until the dough is smooth. Use more flour if the dough is too slack. Put the dough into a greased bowl, and leave until doubled in bulk. Punch down, knead until smooth, and divide into 2 equal pieces. Shape as for French loaves, making diagonal slanting cuts across the top. Brush with egg and milk glaze and leave to prove. Bake in an oven set at 450° for 10 minutes, then turn down to 350° and bake until loaves sound hollow when tapped on the underside – about 30 to 40 minutes.

Buttermilk Bread

3 cups flour
1$\frac{1}{2}$ teaspoons salt
$\frac{1}{4}$ cup sugar
1 package dry yeast
pinch of baking soda
$\frac{1}{2}$ cup butter
$\frac{1}{4}$ cup warm water
1 cup buttermilk

Warm the buttermilk gently and stir in the sugar, the salt and the butter, which will melt. While this is cooling, set the yeast to work in the warm water and when it has dissolved, add it to the buttermilk mixture. Sift half the flour and the baking soda into the mixture and beat well. Gradually add the remaining flour until you have a firm dough. Knead it until it is smooth, place in a greased bowl, cover and leave to rise until doubled in bulk. Punch down and, on a floured board, shape it into a loaf. Put it in an 8 × 8 inch pan, brush the top with melted butter and leave to prove. Bake at 400° for 45 minutes, or until brown, and the loaf sounds hollow when tapped underneath.

Cracked Wheat Bread

2 cups flour
¾ cup cracked wheat
½ teaspoon salt
¼ cup brown sugar
½ tablespoon white sugar
1 package dry yeast
1 tablespoon softened butter
¾ cup boiling water
¼ cup warm water

Put the cracked wheat in a bowl and pour the boiling water over it. Add the brown sugar, the salt and the softened butter. Set the yeast working in the warm water and when frothy, add the white sugar. Pour this into the cracked wheat mixture. Now add the flour and mix to a firm dough. Knead it until it is quite smooth, then put it in a greased bowl, cover and leave to rise until doubled in bulk. Punch down and make it into a loaf shape. Put the dough in a greased 7 × 4 inch loaf pan, cover and leave to prove for 30 minutes. Bake at 350° for about 70 minutes, or until brown, and the loaf sounds hollow when tapped underneath.

Good-For-You Bread

2 cups flour
1 cup wheat germ
1 teaspoon salt
1 tablespoon brown sugar
½ tablespoon molasses
1 package dry yeast
¼ cup softened butter
¼ cup warm water
½ cup milk, gently heated then left to cool
1 egg

Set the yeast working with a teaspoon of the brown sugar in the warm water. Put the milk into a bowl and add the butter, the remaining brown sugar, the molasses, the salt and the beaten egg. Stir the yeast mixture into it, add half the flour and beat well. When the mixture is smooth, stir in the remaining flour and the cup of wheat germ. Knead the dough well on a floured board, then put it in a greased bowl, cover and leave to rise until doubled in bulk. Punch down and shape into a loaf. Put the loaf in a greased 7 × 4 inch loaf pan, cover and leave to prove until dough reaches the top of the pan. Bake at 400° for 40 minutes, or until loaves sound hollow when tapped underneath.

Pain de Mie, French Sandwich Bread

4 cups flour
2 teaspoons salt
1 teaspoon sugar
1 package dry yeast
¼ cup butter
1 cup water

Set the yeast working with a little water, about ¼ cup, warmed to tepid, and the sugar. Mix the salt with the flour, and rub in the butter with your fingertips. When the yeast is frothy, pour into the flour, and add the remaining water to make a stiff dough. Knead thoroughly on a floured board until smooth and springy, then leave to rise, covered, for 2 hours, or until doubled in bulk. Punch down, re-knead for about 10 minutes until smooth. Leave to rise again until doubled in bulk, punch down, knead, and press the dough into a loaf pan. *Pain de Mie* is a square-shaped loaf, and is commercially baked in a pan with a close-fitting lid. Choose a 1 – 1½ pound loaf pan, and bake the loaf with a greased baking sheet resting on top of the pan, weighted if possible. Bake at 375° for 20 minutes, turn the pan upside down and continue baking for a further 15 minutes. Remove the loaf, from its pan, and continue baking on the sheet until all sides are a golden brown, and the loaf sounds hollow when tapped.

Hungarian Fennel Bread

4 cups flour
2 teaspoons salt
4 teaspoons fennel seeds
1 teaspoon sugar
1 package dry yeast
2 tablespoons butter
1 cup water
1 egg yolk
milk

Set the yeast working in half of the water, warmed to tepid, with the teaspoon of sugar. When frothy, add to the flour sifted with the salt. Add half the fennel seeds, melt the butter and add it, and work to a stiff dough with the water, adding more water or flour as required. Knead until smooth and springy, put the dough in a greased bowl, cover and leave to rise. When doubled in bulk, after about 1 hour, punch down and knead again for a minute or two, then shape as one large or two small hearth loaves. Leave to prove. Mix the egg yolk with sufficient milk to make a wash, or glaze. Glaze the loaf and sprinkle the remaining fennel seeds over the top. Bake at 375° for 30 minutes or until the loaf sounds hollow when tapped.

Anadama Bread

4½ cups flour
¾ cup yellow cornmeal
1 tablespoon salt
½ teaspoon sugar
¼ cup molasses
1 package dry yeast
2 tablespoons butter
1¼ cups water

Dissolve the yeast until frothy in the tepid water with the sugar. Blend the cornmeal and the flour with the salt, the butter, previously softened, and the molasses. Add the yeast liquid and mix to a stiffish dough, then turn on to a floured board and knead until springy. Put the dough in a greased bowl, and leave to rise. Punch down, knead again, divide the dough into 2 equal pieces and bake either in loaf pans, layer cake pans, or shape into round loaves. Anadama bread was originally a hearth-type loaf, probably an ash or hoecake. Leave the loaves to prove, then bake at 400° for 45 minutes or until nicely browned. Tap loaves to test whether they sound hollow, an indication that they are cooked.

Good Corn Bread

¾ cup flour
1 cup cornmeal
½ teaspoon salt
¼ cup sugar
1 tablespoon baking powder
¼ cup vegetable oil
1 cup milk
1 egg

Sift together the flour, salt, cornmeal, sugar and baking powder into a bowl and add the egg, the milk and the oil. Beat very hard for a few minutes or until the mixture is free of lumps and very smooth. Pour into a greased 8 × 8 inch baking pan and bake at 425° for 20 – 25 minutes.

Southern Spoonbread

1 cup cornmeal
1¼ teaspoons salt
2 tablespoons softened butter
3 cups milk
4 egg yolks, well beaten
4 egg whites, beaten till stiff

Blend the milk, the cornmeal and the salt over a low heat until the mixture thickens – about 15 minutes. Stir in the butter, allow the mixture to cool and then stir in the egg yolks. Fold the whites into the mixture and pour it into a greased soufflé or baking dish. Bake at 400° for about 35 minutes or until puffed up and brown and firm on top.

209

Corn Dodgers or Corn Pone

4 cups cornmeal
1 teaspoon salt
1 tablespoon butter
1 cup water

Rub the butter into the cornmeal, add the salt and water to form a soft dough. Corn Pone was baked under ashes as a hoecake, or on a skillet. For corn dodgers, cut into thin rectangles, and place on a greased baking sheet. Bake at 400° for 20 minutes, or until golden brown.

Johnnycake or Journeycake

1 cup flour
1 cup cornmeal
1 teaspoon salt
1 teaspoon baking soda
2 tablespoons sugar
2 tablespoons butter
1 cup milk
2 eggs

Combine the flour, the cornmeal, the soda and the salt. Beat the eggs, melt the butter. Whip eggs, sugar and butter together and add to the dry ingredients. Add the milk to make a batter and pour into a greased, square baking pan, about 7 × 7 inches. Bake at 425° for 20 minutes, or until a fork inserted in the bread comes out clean.

Rye 'n' Injun

2½ cups ryemeal
3 cups Indian cornmeal
2 teaspoons salt
½ cup molasses
1 package dry yeast
1 cup rye starter (see recipe page 279)
boiling water
1½ cups tepid water

210

Scald the cornmeal with just enough boiling water to make it wet. Mix the ryemeal with the salt, then with the cornmeal. Add the starter, the yeast and the molasses, and sufficient tepid water to make a stiffish dough. Mix thoroughly with a wooden spoon, cover, and leave to ferment. Stir again after 2 hours, then shape into a round loaf, and bake on a baking sheet at 350° for 1 hour, or until the loaf sounds hollow when the underside is tapped.

Mormon Rye Bread

3 cups flour
1 cup rye flour
1 teaspoon salt
½ cup honey
1 teaspoon sugar
½ cup brown sugar
1 package dry yeast
½ cup vegetable oil
2 tablespoons softened butter
1 cup water
1 tablespoon milk
1 egg

Warm half the water gently and set the yeast working in it; stir in the teaspoon of sugar. Meanwhile sift the flours, the brown sugar and the salt in a bowl, make a well in the center, and pour in the yeast mixture, the remaining water, the honey and the vegetable oil. Stir until the mixture is a stiffish dough. Knead the dough on a lightly floured surface for 5 minutes adding more flour as required to make it firm and smooth. Knead for a further 5 minutes. Put the dough in a greased bowl. Cover, and leave to rise until doubled in bulk. Punch the dough down and, on a lightly floured board, shape it into a loaf. Put it in a greased 9 × 5 inch loaf pan and leave to prove. Blend the milk with the egg and brush the top of the loaf with the mixture. Bake at 375° for 40 minutes, or until loaf sounds hollow when underside is tapped.

Scandinavian Rye Bread

1½ cups flour
1½ cups rye flour
1½ teaspoons salt
½ cup brown sugar
¼ cup molasses
1 package dry yeast
¼ teaspoon baking soda
¼ cup softened butter
½ cup warm water
½ cup buttermilk
½ tablespoon grated orange rind
½ teaspoon anise seed (or caraway seeds if preferred)

Heat the buttermilk, the molasses and the softened butter together until just warm. Meanwhile, put the rye flour, the brown sugar, the salt, orange rind, the anise seed, the baking soda and the dry yeast into a bowl; now add the buttermilk mixture and the warm water, so that the yeast is set to work. Stir, and leave for 10 minutes. Then mix in white flour to form a stiffish dough. Knead it on a floured board for 5 minutes until smooth, then place the dough in a greased bowl. Cover and leave to rise until doubled in bulk. Punch down and shape into a round loaf. Place on a greased baking sheet, cover and leave to prove, until doubled in size again. Bake at 350° for 45 minutes, when the crust will be a rich golden brown.

Pumpernickel

4 cups flour
2 cups coarse, dark ryemeal
3 teaspoons salt
½ cup molasses
2 tablespoons shortening
1½ cups water
(coloring)

Set the yeast working with a teaspoon or two of molasses in a ½ cup of water, warmed to tepid. Warm the rest of the water just enough to dissolve the rest of the molasses and the shortening in it. Thoroughly mix the flours and the salt. When the yeast is frothy, add it with the other liquid to the flours. To obtain really

212

dark pumpernickel, add a teaspoon of commercial coloring, such as caramel or gravy browning. Mix dough and knead on a floured board until smooth. Place in a greased bowl and cover with a cloth. Allow to rise for about 2 hours, or until doubled in bulk. Punch down, and re-knead until smooth. Put the dough in a greased 9 × 5 inch loaf pan, or shape as a round loaf, and leave to prove for about 45-50 minutes. Brush with water and bake at 425° for 15 minutes, then reduce the heat to 350° and bake a further 30 minutes.

Swedish Limpé

3 cups flour
2 cups rye flour
1 teaspoon salt
2 teaspoons caraway seeds
2 teaspoons fennel seeds
½ cup brown sugar
1 package dry yeast
1 tablespoon butter
1½ cups boiling water
1 teaspoon grated orange rind

Add the sugar, the butter, and the grated orange rind, with the caraway and fennel seeds, to the boiling water and continue to boil for 2 or 3 minutes. When the mixture has cooled to tepid, add the yeast and stir well. Add the 3 cups of white flour gradually to make a soft dough and place it in a greased bowl, cover and let rise till doubled in bulk. Punch down the dough and work in the salt and the rye flour to form a stiffish dough. Leave to rise until doubled in bulk again. Knead for a minute or two and then shape the dough into a loaf, place it in a 9 × 5 inch greased loaf pan and leave to prove for 50 minutes. Bake at 350° for 1 hour.

Tortillas *3 cups fine corn flour*
1 teaspoon salt
1½ cups water

Mix the salt with the flour in a bowl, and gradually add half the water, stirring constantly, then the rest of the water by degrees, until the dough becomes stiff enough to shape. Take small pieces of dough, about the size of a walnut, and roll each into a circle of about ⅛ inch thickness. So that they won't stick to the rolling pin, you may have to flour each tortilla as you roll it, or roll between waxed paper. The *tortillas* should be rounds of approximately 5 or 6 inches. To cook, heat a griddle or frying pan, and brown the *tortillas* gently, about 2 to 3 minutes on each side. They can be kept warm in the oven, wrapped in batches in damp paper towels and then in foil.

Naan *4 cups all-purpose white flour*
1 teaspoon salt
1 teaspoon sugar
1 package dry yeast
½ teaspoon baking soda
*2 tablespoons **ghee** or butter*
¼ cup milk
¼ cup of yogurt
2 eggs

Set the yeast to work with a little tepid milk and the teaspoon of sugar. Warm the remaining milk gently, and stir in the yogurt. Add the soda, the beaten eggs and the *ghee.* Sift the flour with the salt, add the yeast and the milk and yogurt mixture. Work to a dough, adding more milk if the mixture is too stiff. The result should be a smooth and springy dough. Leave to rise until doubled in bulk. Punch down, then divide into 6 pieces.

Roll out each piece into a ball, then flatten with your hands, or roll out to an oval 6 by 3 inches, and about ⅜ inch thick. Grease some kitchen foil, and place the dough pieces on it, and bake in an oven set at 450° for 7 minutes, until light brown and puffy. The traditional appearance of *naan* is a pear-shaped bread, unevenly puffed, and scorched in places. The bread should be eaten hot, so when you have taken them from the oven, transfer to the broiler for a minute or two, then serve. Some *naan* breads are flavored with sesame seeds, others with finely sliced raw onion, which can be worked into the dough before it is shaped.

Chupattis

*2 cups **atta** (wholewheat flour)*
1 teaspoon salt
*3 tablespoons **ghee** (Indian clarified butter, obtainable in tins, from Indian stores)*
1 cup water

Rub the *ghee* into the flour combined with the salt, until the mixture resembles fine crumbs. Warm the water, add to the flour and mix to a stiff dough. Knead until smooth, then leave covered to rest for an hour. Shape pieces of the dough into balls, about 1½ inches, flatten and then roll each one to about 6 inches in diameter. Heat a skillet or griddle, and cook each *chupatti* until blisters appear in the dough, and it begins to brown. If you overcook them, they become like cardboard. They should be soft enough to fold easily.

Paratha

2 cups wholewheat flour
1 teaspoon salt
*2–3 tablespoons butter or **ghee***
1 cup milk and water, mixed

Sift the flour with the salt, add the liquid to make a softish dough, then knead thoroughly until smooth and supple. Leave for at least two hours; overnight in the refrigerator makes a

215

better dough. Roll out the dough to about the thickness of $\frac{1}{4}$ inch, spread with softened butter, fold in half, then in half again, roll out, spread with butter, and repeat the folding, until you have used all the butter. After the final rolling, cut into small circles of 5 or 6 inches in diameter, and cook on a lightly greased skillet or griddle until light brown; turn the *paratha,* and cook the other side. *Parathas* may be stuffed with a variety of vegetables: onion, minced meat, potato purée. Place the stuffing in the center, fold in half, then over again into a triangular shape, and fry in vegetable shortening.

Churek

6 cups flour
1 tablespoon salt
1 tablespoon sugar
$\frac{1}{4}$ lb butter
2$\frac{1}{2}$ cups water
2–3 tablespoons sesame seeds

Warm the water, add the butter and sugar. Sift the flour with the salt. Pour the butter/water mixture into the flour. Mix thoroughly to a soft dough, knead and then put the dough on a floured board. Divide into 10 pieces, form into balls, flatten with the hand, and then roll out into oval pancakes as thin as possible. Sprinkle each circle with sesame seeds and bake for 20 minutes at 400°, or until light brown.

Pita

4 cups white flour
2 teaspoons salt
$\frac{1}{4}$ teaspoon sugar
1 package dry yeast
1$\frac{1}{4}$ cups water

Set the yeast working with 3 tablespoons of the water, warmed to tepid, and the sugar.

When frothy, add the flour and salt. Mix to a stiff dough, then thoroughly knead until smooth and springy. Cover, and leave to rise.

Punch down, then knead again until smooth. Divide into 6 pieces and shape each piece into a ball. Roll each ball into a long oval of about ¼ inch thickness. Cover and leave to prove, then slide on to a greased baking sheet and bake at 475° for about 15 minutes until puffed and light brown. *Pita* is usually cut in half and filled with broiled kebab, chopped onion and quartered tomatoes.

Arabic Bread

8 cups flour
1 tablespoon salt
2 tablespoons sugar
1 package dry yeast
2½ cups water

Sift the flour with the salt and sugar, dissolve the yeast in tepid water with a ½ teaspoon of the sugar. Mix thoroughly to a firm dough, but not too stiff, adding either more flour or water as required. Knead well, and leave to rise in a covered bowl. When doubled in bulk, punch down, knead again, divide into about 10 pieces. Roll each into a ball then roll to a thickness of about a ½ inch, making sure the dough is smooth and uniform. Leave to prove for 15 minutes, then bake on a greased baking sheet at 450° until browned.

Portuguese Bread

5 cups flour
1 tablespoon salt
1 tablespoon sugar
1 package dry yeast
1 tablespoon butter
2 cups water

Sift the flour and the salt in a bowl. Dissolve the sugar and melt the butter in one cup of the water, which must be gently heated and stirred. Set the yeast working with a $\frac{1}{2}$ teaspoon of the sugar in the remaining water, warmed to tepid. When the butter and sugar mixture is cool, ideally at blood heat, pour into the flour with the yeast. Mix to a dough, then knead until smooth, adding more flour if required. Put the dough in a greased bowl, cover, and leave to rise until doubled in bulk. Punch down, and divide into 2 pieces. Shape into round loaves, and leave to prove. Cut a cross on each loaf, about $\frac{1}{8}$ inch deep, and bake at 425° for 15 minutes, then at 350° for a further 30 minutes, or until the loaves sound hollow when tapped on the underside.

Sourdough French Bread

4 cups flour
2 teaspoons salt
1 teaspoon sugar
1 package dry yeast
1 cup warm water
1 cup starter (use yogurt starter on page 279)

Put into a large mixing bowl the warm water, the sugar, the yeast, the starter and 2 cups of the flour. Cover, and leave to ferment for about 2 hours, stirring occasionally. Now add the remaining flour, more if necessary, to make a stiff dough. Knead on a floured board until smooth and springy. Put the dough in a greased bowl and leave to rise, covered, for about 2 hours. Punch down, knead again until smooth, and divide into 2 pieces. Shape each piece as an oval, then slightly taper the ends. Leave to prove, place on a greased baking sheet, and make slanting, diagonal cuts along the length of each loaf. Brush with water and bake at 450° for 10 minutes, then turn the heat down to 400°, brush with water again, and continue baking for a further 15 minutes, or until the loaves are brown, and sound hollow when tapped underneath.

Italian Bread

3½ cups flour
¼ tablespoon salt
1 tablespoon honey
1 package dry yeast
1 tablespoon softened butter
1 cup water

Set the yeast working in a ¼ cup of water, warmed to tepid. Add 1 teaspoon of the honey, and when the yeast is frothy, add it with the salt, the softened butter, the rest of the honey and the water to half the flour. Beat thoroughly and add the remaining flour. On a floured board, knead the dough until smooth, adding more flour if required to prevent sticking. Put the dough into a greased bowl, cover and leave to rise until doubled in bulk. Punch down and roll the dough out to form a circle 9 or 10 inches in diameter. Taking hold of one edge of the dough, roll it up into a tight roll, tucking the ends neatly under. Leave to prove until doubled in bulk on a baking sheet sprinkled with cornmeal. Bake at 375° for 30 minutes.

Caraway Seed Bread

4 cups flour
1 teaspoon salt
1 tablespoon caraway seeds
2 teaspoons sugar
1 package dry yeast
¼ lb butter
¼ cup warm water
½ cup milk
1 egg

Set the yeast working with the warm water and the sugar. Warm the milk to tepid, add it to the yeast, gradually add the flour, the well-beaten egg, the salt and the caraway seeds. Knead, working in the butter piece by piece. When it is a smooth dough, cover in a greased bowl and leave to rise until doubled in bulk. Punch down, re-knead until smooth, and shape as a round hearth loaf. Leave to prove about 30 minutes, then bake at 375° for 50 minutes, or until the loaf sounds hollow when tapped underneath.

Scots Barley Bannocks

4 cups barley flour
1 cup all-purpose flour
1 teaspoon salt
3 teaspoons baking soda
2 teaspoons cream of tartar
1½ cups buttermilk

Mix the flours with the salt and cream of tartar. Stir the baking soda into the buttermilk and add to the flour mixture. Make into a pliable dough, and roll out to ½ inch thickness. Cut into 8 inch discs, and bake on a hot griddle, turning the bannocks so that they brown lightly on both sides.

Scots Oatcakes, Bannocks or Farls

1 cup rolled oats
1 teaspoon salt
1 teaspoon baking soda
3 teaspoons melted shortening
¼ cup hot water

Mix the oatmeal, baking soda and the salt. Add the melted fat, and sufficient hot water to make a stiff dough. Knead until smooth, and roll out on a floured board as thinly as possible; use plenty of dry oatmeal to prevent sticking. Dust with dry meal, and cut into 5 inch discs, (bannocks) which if further cut into quarters become farls. Bake on a hot griddle until dry and crisp. Oatcakes burn easily, so watch them carefully.

Irish Corn Bread

In Ireland this is known as *Yalla Male* (yellow meal) bread, and uses cornmeal, also called "Indian Meal." In Scotland, a similar bread was made, called *Aran Isenach,* a bannock of cornmeal, white flour and butter.

3 cups all-purpose flour
1 cup fine cornmeal
1 teaspoon salt
1 teaspoon sugar

2 teaspoons baking soda
1½ cups buttermilk

Thoroughly mix the flours with the salt, soda, and the sugar. Add the buttermilk by degrees to make a soft dough, and knead lightly for a minute. Flour a baking sheet or griddle. Shape into a round hearth loaf, and cut a cross ½ an inch deep so that the cuts reach the edge of the loaf. Bake at 400° for 40 minutes, or until the loaf sounds hollow when tapped underneath.

Salt Rising Bread

5 cups all-purpose flour
¼ cup cornmeal
1 teaspoon salt
2 tablespoons sugar
2 tablespoons melted butter
1 cup water
1 cup milk

Scald the milk and add the cornmeal, half of the sugar, and the salt. This is, in fact, a starter and should be left, covered by a cloth, in a warm place to ferment, which depends on the presence of yeast in the air, and also the climate. When the starter begins to bubble (which may take 2 or 3 days), stir in the remaining sugar, the water and 2 cups of the flour. Mix, and leave to continue fermentation (at least 10 hours), until you have a light sponge, well aerated with bubbles. Add the rest of the flour to make a smooth dough, and knead for about 5 minutes. Shape or place in loaf pans, brush with melted butter, cover and leave to rise until doubled in bulk. Bake at 375° for 15 minutes, then reduce the heat to 350° and bake a further 30 minutes.

Irish Oatmeal Bread

2½ cups all-purpose flour
2 cups oatmeal
2 teaspoons salt
2 teaspoons cream of tartar

221

2 teaspoons baking soda
3 tablespoons butter
1½ cups milk

Soak oats overnight in the milk. Sift together the flour, salt, soda and cream of tartar. Rub in the butter until it resembles fine crumbs. Add the oatmeal and milk and mix to a soft dough. Bake in a greased loaf or layer cake pan at 375° for about 1 hour, or until light brown.

Irish Potato Bread

¼ cup white flour
1 cup (½ lb) mashed potato
1 teaspoon salt
2 tablespoons butter

Add the salt and the butter to the mashed potato, then incorporate the flour to make a pliable dough, adding more flour if needed. Roll out to ½ inch thick. Cut into triangles or discs, and bake in an oven at 450° or on a griddle until brown, turning over during cooking to ensure that they are brown on both sides.

Oatmeal Yeast Bread

5 cups flour
1½ cups rolled oats
¼ teaspoon sugar
1 teaspoon salt
1 package dry yeast
¼ cup butter
2 cups milk

Warm the milk, add the butter and the oats, leave to stand for about 1 hour. Set the yeast to work with a little warm water and a ½ teaspoon of sugar. Sift the flour with the salt, add the yeast when frothy, also the oats in milk. Mix to a soft dough, place in a greased bowl, cover and leave to rise. Punch down, knead again until smooth. Make into a round hearth loaf, mark with a cross and bake at 400° for about 35 minutes, or until loaf sounds hollow when the underside is tapped.

Irish Soda Bread

4 cups all-purpose flour
1 teaspoon salt
1 teaspoon baking soda
1–1½ cups buttermilk

Sift flour, soda and salt together, then add the buttermilk until the dough is firm. If it crumbles, add more buttermilk as required. Shape the dough into a round loaf about 8 inches in diameter and 1½–2 inches thick. Cut a cross in the dough about ¾ inch deep. Bake on a griddle, or in the oven at 400° until light brown. This bread is usually eaten warm.

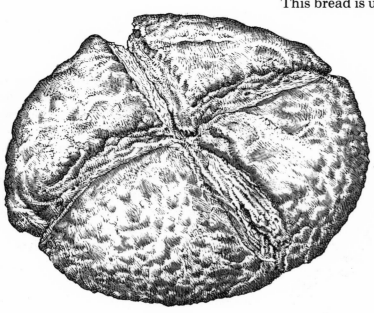

Fruit, Festive and Tea Breads

Swedish Tea Ring

5 cups flour
2 teaspoons salt
½ cup sugar
1 package dry yeast
¼ lb of butter
¼ cup water
1 cup milk
2 eggs

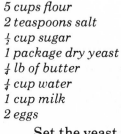

Set the yeast working in the water, warmed to tepid, with a teaspoon of the sugar. Scald the milk, add to it the butter and remaining sugar. Sift the flour with the salt, add the yeast, then the milk mixture cooled to tepid; beat and add the eggs. Mix to a soft dough, adding more flour if required. Knead until smooth. Put in a greased bowl and cover with a cloth. Leave to rise until doubled in bulk. Punch down and knead again until smooth. Roll out to a rectangle 12 × 5 inches, and a ½ inch thick.

Filling:

1 cup raisins or currants
2 teaspoons cinnamon
2 heaped tablespoons blanched and chopped almonds
2-3 tablespoons melted butter
Confectioners' sugar frosting

Brush dough with melted butter, scatter the fruit, chopped nuts and cinnamon over the surface. Roll fairly tightly so that you have a 12 inch length. Form a circle, joined at both ends by brushing ends with water to make them adhere. Leave to prove until well-risen, about 30 minutes. With a sharp knife or scissors, make deep cuts almost through the ring at intervals of 1 inch, twisting each segment at an angle. Bake at 375° for 25 minutes. When cool, cover the top with confectioners' sugar frosting, made in the proportions of 2 parts sugar to 1 part cold water.

Bohemian Braid
Sweet dough (as for Swedish Tea Ring, above)
2 tablespoons softened butter
½ cup blanched, chopped almonds
Confectioners' sugar frosting.

Let the dough rise for the first time until doubled in bulk, then divide into 9 pieces. Roll each piece into a long roll and braid 4 of the rolls together loosely. Now braid another 3 of the rolls and place this braid on top of the first braid. Twist the last 2 rolls loosely and place them on top of the 2 braids. Now tuck all the ends in neatly. Cover and leave to rise until doubled in bulk. Bake at 350° for 45-50 minutes. Brush with the confectioners' sugar frosting (2 parts confectioners' sugar to 1 part water) and sprinkle with the chopped almonds.

Streusel
2 cups flour
1 teaspoon salt
3 tablespoons sugar
1 package dry yeast
½ cup softened butter
⅔ cup milk
2 eggs
rind of 1 lemon

Set the yeast to work in the milk warmed to tepid, with a teaspoon of the sugar. When frothy, add to the flour with the well beaten eggs, the grated lemon rind and the butter. Knead to a smooth dough, place in a greased bowl, cover, and leave to rise for about 2 hours. Punch down, knead again, then roll out to a ½ inch thickness. Separate the dough into 2 pieces and place in greased pans 8 × 11 inches. Leave to prove for an hour. Cover with *streusel* topping:
¼ cup flour
1 tablespoon cinnamon
¾ cup sugar
3 tablespoons butter
⅓ cup raisins
⅓ cup blanched almonds

Rub the butter into the flour, mix with cinnamon, raisins and sugar. Brush top of dough with melted butter, sprinkle on the crumbled topping, and the chopped almonds. Bake at 400° for 25-30 minutes.

Stollen

Sweet dough (as for Swedish Tea Ring on page 224)
4 tablespoons softened butter
¼ cup raisins
¼ cup blanched, chopped almonds
confectioners' sugar

Let the dough rise for the first time until doubled in bulk. Add the raisins and almonds and knead them in, then shape the dough into a ball. Cover, leave to rise for 15 minutes. Roll out the dough to an oval. Brush half the oval with the melted butter and fold the other half over it, pressing down and sealing the edges. Leave on a greased baking sheet until doubled in bulk. Bake at 350° for 30 minutes. Dust with the confectioners' sugar and sprinkle with the chopped almonds.

Dresdner Stollen

6 cups all-purpose flour
¼ teaspoon salt
½ teaspoon almond extract
¾ cup sugar
2 packages dry yeast
¼ lb softened butter
¼ cup water
1 cup milk
2 eggs
½ cup raisins
½ cup currants
½ cup candied peel
¼ cup candied angelica
½ cup maraschino cherries
½ cup blanched, chopped almonds
grated peel of 1 lemon
grated peel of 1 orange
2 oz. rum or brandy
2 oz. kirsch
¼ cup confectioners' sugar

Soak the raisins, currants, candied peel and angelica in the rum or brandy. Cut maraschino cherries in half and soak in the kirsch; leave for about 2 hours. Set the yeast to work with the water warmed to tepid and a teaspoon of the sugar. When the yeast is frothy, pour it into a bowl containing 5 cups of the flour, half the butter and the beaten eggs. Warm the milk with the sugar and salt, till dissolved. Drain the fruit and the cherries, reserving the brandy or rum and the kirsch. When the milk mixture is cool, add it to the flour and yeast mixture along with the reserved liquids from the fruit and the almond extract. Mix to a dough and knead thoroughly, incorporating the rest of the flour if required. Cover and leave to rise until doubled in bulk. Punch down, and work the fruit and the lemon and orange peel into the dough. Roll or press the dough into a rectangle about $\frac{1}{2}$ inch thick. Brush with the remaining butter and sprinkle with sugar. Fold lengthwise to the center, bring the remaining piece across, press down gently, seal the seam and taper the ends of the loaf. Leave to prove for about an hour. Brush with melted butter, place on a greased baking sheet and bake at 375° for 40 minutes until golden brown. When cool, dust with confectioners' sugar.

Jewish Challah

7 cups flour
2 teaspoons salt
2 tablespoons sugar
2 packages dry yeast
6 tablespoons shortening
1½ cups milk and water, mixed half and half
¼ cup warm water
3 eggs
poppy seeds

Set the yeast working in the $\frac{1}{2}$ cup of warm water with the sugar. Scald the milk and add the shortening, allowing it to melt. Sift the flour with the salt. When the milk and shortening has cooled, add the beaten eggs, reserving one yolk. Add the flour by degrees to the egg and milk, also the yeast. Mix to a

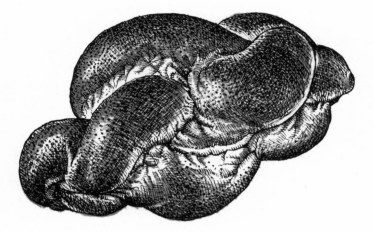

stiffish dough, and knead thoroughly on a floured board. Put the dough in a greased bowl, cover, and leave until doubled in bulk. Punch down, and knead again until smooth. The quantities of this recipe will make one very large, or three medium-sized loaves. To make one loaf, divide dough into three, roll each piece into a rope, tapered at either end. Secure the three ropes by pinching them together at one end, and tucking the join underneath. Now braid the ropes together, and secure ends as before. Beat the remaining yolk with a little milk, and brush the challah with it, then sprinkle with poppy seeds. Leave to prove until well-risen – about ¾ hour, and bake at 375° for 45 minutes, or until loaf sounds hollow when tapped underneath.

Panettone

3 cups flour
½ teaspoon salt
2 teaspoons vanilla extract
¼ cup sugar
3 packages dry yeast
¼ lb softened butter
½ cup water
6 egg yolks
¼ cup raisins
¼ cup sultanas
¼ cup candied peel
grated rind of a fresh lemon
melted butter

Set the yeast working with a teaspoon of the sugar in half the water, warmed to tepid. When the yeast is frothy, add to the flour, also the egg yolks, vanilla extract, salt, remaining sugar, grated lemon rind. Thoroughly mix with a wooden spoon and work in the softened butter. If the dough is too stiff, add a little more water. Turn dough onto a floured board and knead to a smooth and satiny texture. Put in a greased bowl, cover and leave to rise for an hour, or until doubled in bulk. Punch down dough, knead again, working in the fruit and candied peel. The panettone should be baked in a round cake pan, ring mold, or a paper collar 6 inches deep and about 8 inches in diameter. Place the dough in the pan and leave to prove for about 40 minutes. Brush panettone with melted butter, and bake at 400° for 15 minutes. Turn down the heat to 350°, brush again with melted butter, bake for a further 35-40 minutes, until a rich golden brown. The more times you brush with melted butter during baking, the crisper the panettone will become.

Poppy Seed Braid

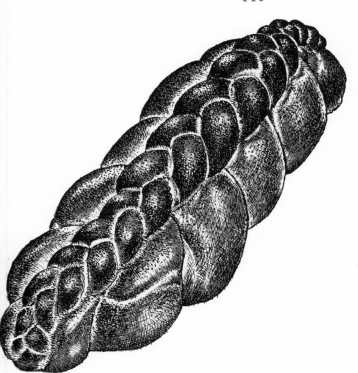

1 lb sweet dough (as in the recipe for Swedish Tea Ring on page 224)
½ cup poppy seeds
½ cup chopped, pitted prunes
2 teaspoons grated lemon rind
confectioners' sugar
nuts for decoration

Make a sweet dough as for the recipe for Swedish Tea Ring, adding to the jixture the poppy seeds, the prunes and the grated lemon rind. Work these into the dough, knead thoroughly, and leave to rise. Punch down and knead again. Now divide the dough into 5, rolling each piece until it is about 18 inches long. On a greased baking sheet, braid 3 of the pieces, sealing the ends firmly. Twist the other two pieces along the top of the braid, tucking under the ends neatly. Cover and allow to rise until doubled in bulk. Bake at 350° for 45 minutes and when cool, decorate with confectioner's sugar and nuts.

Russian Kulich (Easter Bread)

6 cups flour
1 teaspoon salt
1 teaspoon vanilla
¾ cup sugar
1 package dry yeast
½ cup butter
¾ cup milk
5 eggs
grated lemon peel

229

Confectioners' frosting:
¼ cup confectioners' sugar
2–3 tablespoons cold water

Warm half the milk until tepid. Add the yeast and a teaspoon of the sugar. Gently heat the rest of the milk, add to it the remaining sugar, and the butter. Add vanilla extract. Pour yeast mixture and milk mixture into flour. Add grated lemon peel. Add beaten egg yolks. Mix thoroughly with a wooden spoon, fold in the stiffly-whipped egg whites. Cover and leave to rise until doubled in bulk. Punch down, knead lightly for a minute, then put dough in a round deep pan, or use a paper collar 8 or 9 inches deep. *Kulich* should be a tall, tubular cake-bread. Bake at 350° for 1 hour. When cool, pour a fairly liquid confectioner's frosting over the top, so that it dribbles down the sides like candle wax.

Kugelhopf

2 cups all-purpose flour
½ teaspoon salt
1 teaspoon vanilla extract
½ cup sugar
1 package dry yeast
½ lb softened butter
¼ cup water
6 egg yolks
4 egg whites
½ cup raisins
confectioners' sugar

Set the yeast working in the tepid water with a teaspoon of the sugar. Cream together the butter and the remaining sugar and beat in the egg yolks by degrees. Add the vanilla, salt, raisins, and yeast, and gradually work in the flour. Beat the egg whites until stiff, fold into the dough until well incorporated. Put into a greased and floured bowl, kugelhopf mold or savarin mold. Cover and leave to rise for 2 hours. Bake at 375° for about 30–40 minutes, until golden brown. When cool, invert mold and dust Kugelhopf with confectioners' sugar.

Portuguese Sweet Bread

3 cups flour
1 teaspoon salt
1 cup sugar
1 package dry yeast
1 tablespoon softened butter
¼ cup unsalted butter
½ cup water
½ cup milk
2 eggs

Warm the water gently and set the yeast working in it with a teaspoon of the sugar. Put the remaining sugar, most of the flour, and the salt into a bowl. Add the yeast mixture and the milk, warmed to tepid. Stir and add the eggs, leaving a little of the egg remaining. Beat well, adding the unsalted butter and the remaining flour until you have a firm dough. On a floured board, knead the dough for 10–15 minutes until it is smooth. Put it in a lightly greased bowl, turning it around once to grease the entire surface. Cover and leave to rise until doubled in bulk. Punch the dough down and leave to prove for 30 minutes. Shape the dough into a flattened, round loaf and place it on a greased baking sheet. Brush the top of the loaf with the remaining beaten egg and bake at 350° for 1 hour, or until loaf sounds hollow when tapped underneath.

Scots Selkirk Bannock

4 cups flour
1 teaspoon salt
¾ cup sugar
1 package dry yeast
¼ lb butter
4 tablespoons lard
1 cup water
2 cups raisins

Sift the flour with the salt. Set the yeast working with a teaspoon of the sugar and a ¼ cup of the water; when frothy, add to the flour with remaining water and make a stiff, bread dough. When well-mixed, knead until smooth and springy. Now work in the butter and the

231

lard by degrees, also the rest of the sugar and the raisins. It will become a sticky dough, so use flour as you knead. When these last ingredients have been thoroughly worked in, place the dough in a greased bowl, and leave until doubled in bulk, about $1\frac{1}{2}$ hours. Punch down, re-knead for a few minutes, shape as a round hearth loaf, and leave 30 minutes to prove. Bake on a baking sheet or in a buttered layer-cake tin at 400° for 1 hour, or until golden brown on top. Test to see if the bannock is cooked by tapping the underside. If it sounds hollow, the bannock is done.

Irish Barm Brack, Bairgen or Boreen-brack

4 cups all-purpose flour
1 teaspoon salt
1 teaspoon mixed spice
1 teaspoon cinnamon
3 tablespoons sugar
1 package dry yeast
3 tablespoons butter
$1\frac{1}{4}$ cups milk
2 eggs
1 cup raisins
$\frac{1}{4}$ cup candied peel

Sift the flour with the salt, sugar and spices, reserving a teaspoon of sugar. Add the yeast to a $\frac{1}{4}$ cup of milk and the teaspoon of sugar, and leave until frothy. Rub the butter into the flour. Beat the eggs, warm the remaining milk to tepid, and mix eggs, milk and yeast. Pour this into the flour, add the fruit, and mix to a stiffish dough, then knead until smooth. Proceed as for Selkirk Bannock.

Welsh Bara Brith

4 cups all-purpose flour
1 teaspoon salt
2 teaspoons caraway seeds
1 cup brown sugar
3 tablespoons molasses

2 teaspoons baking soda
3 teaspoons cream of tartar
¼ lb butter
1 cup buttermilk
(or plain milk)
1 egg
1½ cups raisins
juice of 1 lemon

Rub the fat into the flour, add the sugar, beaten egg, molasses, salt, raisins and caraway seeds. If you are using buttermilk, omit the cream of tartar. Add the baking soda to the buttermilk, or to the plain milk add baking soda plus cream of tartar, and add to the flour mixture with the lemon juice. Stir all the ingredients thoroughly to a stiffish dough. Grease a 9 × 5 inch loaf pan, and bake at 400° for 20 minutes, then lower heat to 350° and bake for about 1½ hours more.

Yorkshire Spiced Loaf

2½ cups all-purpose flour
1 teaspoon salt
1 teaspoon nutmeg
1 teaspoon cinnamon
1 teaspoon ginger
2 cups brown sugar
1 package dry yeast
¼ lb butter
2 tablespoons lard or margarine
¾ cup milk
1 egg
2 cups currants or raisins

Rub the shortenings into the flour, add the spices, the currants or raisins, and the salt. Set the yeast working with a teaspoon of the sugar and a ¼ cup of tepid milk. Beat the egg and add to the remaining milk. Pour this and the yeast into the flour, and mix to a stiffish dough, adding more flour or milk as required. Put in a greased bowl and leave to rise for 1 hour. Now punch down, and knead in the remaining sugar until well incorporated. Put into a greased 9 × 5 inch loaf pan, and leave to prove for about 30 minutes. Bake at 350° for 2 hours.

233

Yorkshire Gingerbread

2 cups all-purpose flour
1 teaspoon salt
2 teaspoons ginger
½ cup sugar
4 tablespoons molasses
2 teaspoons baking soda
4 tablespoons butter
½ cup milk and water, mixed

In a pan, gently melt butter, sugar and molasses with milk and water. Do not allow to boil. When mixture has cooled a little, stir in flour, salt, spices and soda. Mix thoroughly, pour batter into a greased 8 inch square gingerbread tin. Bake in a 350° oven for about 1½ hours, or until a folk inserted in the bread comes out clean.

Honey Bread

1½ cups flour
1¼ cups wholewheat flour
1 teaspoon salt
½ cup honey
1 package dry yeast
1 tablespoon softened butter
1 cup warm water
1 cup milk

Heat the milk and the butter gently. Put the wholewheat flour, the honey, the salt, and the yeast into a bowl and then add the warm milk with the butter, and the warm water to set the yeast to work. Beat well for several minutes once the yeast has dissolved. Stir in the white flour gradually, to form a stiffish dough and knead on a floured board until smooth. Put the dough in a greased bowl, turning once to grease the entire surface of the dough. Cover and leave to rise until doubled in bulk. Punch down and shape the dough into a loaf. Put it in a greased 9 × 5 inch loaf pan, cover and leave to prove. Bake at 350° for 50 minutes, then cool before glazing with the following:

Honey Glaze

½ cup confectioners' sugar
¼ cup finely chopped pecans
½ tablespoon honey
1½ tablespoons milk

234

Blend these ingredients together and when the consistency of hot candle wax, pour it over the nearly cool loaf so that some of the glaze dribbles down the sides.

Dutch Honey Bread

2 cups all-purpose flour
¼ teaspoon salt
½ teaspoon cloves
½ teaspoon cinnamon
½ teaspoon ginger
1 cup brown sugar
¾ cup honey
1 teaspoon baking soda
½ cup softened butter
¾ cup buttermilk
3 eggs
¼ cup almonds
¼ cup raisins

Stir the baking soda into the honey and then stir in the buttermilk. Cream the brown sugar and the butter together and beat in the eggs. Sift the flour, the salt, the ginger, the cinnamon and the cloves and stir this dry mixture into the egg mixture; mix to a batter with the buttermilk liquid. Dust the almonds and raisins with a little flour and fold them into the batter. Pour the batter into a greased 9 × 5 inch loaf pan and leave it to stand for 1 hour. Bake at 350° for 50 minutes, or until a loaf inserted in the centre comes out clean.

Boston Brown Bread

1 cup wholemeal flour
1 cup rye flour
1 cup cornmeal
2 teaspoons salt
¾ cup molasses
¾ tablespoon baking soda
2 cups buttermilk
1 cup raisins

Mix the flours and cornmeal with the salt, the soda and the raisins. Add the molasses and buttermilk, mix to a battery and pour into greased molds – 1 pound cans of any type that

235

will produce a cylindrical loaf. Cover tightly with waxed paper or foil. Place cans in a "water jacket," a cassesole containing boiling water $\frac{3}{4}$ way up the sides of the cans. Cover with a lid and steam on top of the cooker for at least 2 hours, adding more water if required. Unmold, and dry the bread in the oven at 359° for a few minutes.

Molasses and Oatmeal Bread

4 cups wholemeal flour
1 cup medium oatmeal (not rolled oats)
1 teaspoon salt
1 teaspoon sugar
1 package dry yeast
$\frac{1}{2}$ cup molasses
$2\frac{1}{2}$–3 cups warm water

Combine the oatmeal, 2 cups of the water, molasses and salt, and set aside for 10 minutes. Set the yeast working with the remaining warm water, and the sugar. When frothy, add to the oatmeal, and add the flour. Mix thoroughly. Place in a greased bowl, cover with a cloth and allow to rise for $1\frac{1}{2}$ hours. Knead on a floured board for about 10 minutes, using more flour as required. Divide the dough for 2 small loaves, or for one 8 × 4 or 9 × 5 inch loaf pan. Allow to prove for a further hour. Bake at 425° for 15–20 minutes, then reduce the heat to 400° and bake for 50 minutes to 1 hour. The bread will be cooked when well browned, and the bottom sounds hollow when tapped.

Lardy Cake

1 lb of dough as for Chelsea Buns (p 264)
$\frac{3}{4}$ cup lard
$\frac{1}{2}$ cup currants
$\frac{1}{2}$ cup sugar

Put the dough on to a floured surface, and roll out to an oblong 12 × 5 inches. Spread $\frac{3}{4}$ of the dough's surface with about a third of the lard. Scatter over the lard a third of the currants and a third of the sugar. Fold the unlarded portion toward the center, fold the rest on top, so that you have three layers. Press down lightly, then turn the open end toward you. Roll out, spread with lard, currants and sugar, repeating the process until you have used all remaining. The aim is to have layers of fruit/lard/sugar within the dough. Try and avoid rolling too thinly, otherwise the currants will break through the surface, also try and leave the edges unlarded each time, so that you can seal them to prevent the lard escaping during baking. Shape the dough into a round cake with your hands, turning the edges underneath, and making sure they are well sealed. Put the cake in a baking tin, and bake at 425° for 20 minutes, or until risen and brown. Leave for a few minutes to cool, then brush with a sugar syrup glaze, made with equal proportions of sugar and water, boiled for 3–4 minutes.

Malted Fruit Bread

2 cups flour
1 teaspoon salt
2 tablespoons molasses
2 tablespoons malt extract
1 package dry yeast
1 tablespoon lard
½ cup water
½ cup raisins

Sift the flour with the salt, rub in the fat. Set yeast working, with half the water warmed to tepid and 1 teaspoon of molasses. Put the remaining molasses and malt in the rest of the water, heat gently until dissolved. When yeast is frothy, add to the flour, along with the other liquids; mix to a stiffish dough. Knead for a few minutes until smooth, put in a greased bowl, covered, to rise until doubled in bulk. Meanwhile, soak raisins in warm water. Punch down dough, drain the raisins and knead into the dough. Put dough in a 7 × 3 inch loaf pan. Leave to prove for about 20 minutes and bake at 400° for 15 minutes. Reduce heat to 350° and bake for a further 40 minutes or until loaf sounds hollow when tapped underneath.

237

Raisin Bread

3 cups flour
½ teaspoon salt
¼ cup brown sugar
½ teaspoon cinnamon
1 package dry yeast
¼ cup softened butter
2 eggs
¼ cup water
½ cup milk
1 cup raisins

Warm the milk to tepid. Set the yeast working in half of this milk, with a teaspoon of the brown sugar. Beat the eggs and add to them the water, the remaining milk, the softened butter and the sugar. When the yeast is frothy, mix it with the other liquid, and stir in 2 cups flour to make a batter. Cover, and leave for 1 hour, or until doubled in bulk. Now, stirring, add by degrees the rest of the flour, the salt, cinnamon and the raisins. Knead thoroughly on a floured board, put the dough in a greased 8 × 4 inch loaf pan, and leave to prove. When the dough has risen to just within the top of the tin, bake in an oven set at 400° for 15 minutes, then lower to 375° and bake a further 30 minutes, or until the loaf is well-risen and brown. Test to see if it is cooked by tapping the bottom of the loaf. If it sounds hollow, the loaf is done.

Date Bread

2 cups all-purpose flour
1 teaspoon salt
1 teaspoon baking soda
¾ cup soft brown sugar
2 oz butter
½ cup water
1 egg
½ cup pitted dates

Put the butter and sugar in the water, and heat gently until the butter melts and the sugar is dissolved. When cool, pour on to the egg, well-beaten. Sift the flour with the salt and soda, add the liquid, then the dates, roughly chopped. Stir to a smooth batter, and pour into a greased 8 × 4 inch loaf pan. Bake at 350° for about 45 minutes. Test by inserting a fork into the center of the loaf; if it comes out clean, the loaf is done.

Apple Bread

2 cups flour
1 teaspoon salt
1 cup unsweetened apple sauce,
slightly warmed
¼ cup sugar
1 package yeast
1 tablespoon softened butter
1 tablespoon tepid water
1 egg white, beaten
poppy seeds

Set the yeast working in the water and then add the apple sauce. Stir, and add the butter, the salt and the sugar. Still stirring, add enough of the flour until there is a light dough. Leave to rise until doubled in bulk. Punch down and on a floured board, knead for another minute or two. Shape the dough into a long loaf, put it on a greased baking sheet, and with a sharp knife, make 2 or 3 slashes across the top. Cover and leave to rise until doubled in bulk. Bake at 400° for 10 minutes, then reduce the oven to 350° and bake for a further 50 minutes. Just before the loaf is ready, brush the top of it with the beaten egg white and sprinkle the poppy seeds on top before returning it to the oven for 5 minutes.

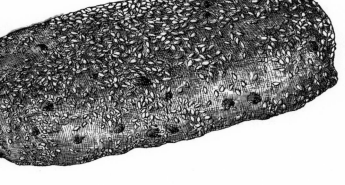

Apricot Bread

2 cups flour
1 cup bran
½ teaspoon salt
½ cup sugar
4 teaspoons baking powder
½ teaspoon baking soda
2 tablespoons butter
1 cup orange juice
2 eggs
1 cup cooked, drained, and chopped apricots
½ cup blanched, chopped almonds
1 teaspoon grated orange rind

239

Cream the sugar and the butter in a bowl. Add the eggs, the orange juice, and stir in the bran, the chopped almonds, the apricots and the orange rind. Sift the flour, the salt, the baking powder, the baking soda and stir into the egg and orange juice mixture. Pour into a 9 × 5 inch greased loaf pan and leave for 30 minutes. Bake at 350° for 1 hour.

Orange Bread

4 cups flour
1 teaspoon salt
1 teaspoon vanilla extract
½ cup sugar
1 package dry yeast
½ cup softened butter
2 tablespoons warm water
2 eggs
1 cup orange juice
3 tablespoons grated orange rind

Set the yeast to work in the warm water and when dissolved, add the mixture to the orange juice, the eggs, the butter, the salt, the sugar, the grated rind and ½ the flour. Mix well and add the remaining flour to make a stiffish dough, using more if required. Add the vanilla extract and knead the dough for a minute or two, until smooth. Place the dough in a greased bowl, turning once to lightly grease entire surface, cover and leave to rise until doubled in bulk. Put it in a 9 × 5 inch greased loaf pan, and leave to prove. Bake at 350° for 45 minutes.

Date, Pecan and Orange Bread

2½ cups all-purpose flour
1 teaspoon salt
1 cup sugar
2 teaspoons baking powder
4 tablespoons softened butter
1 cup orange juice
1 egg
3 teaspoons grated orange peel
½ cup chopped pecans
½ cup pitted, chopped dates

Sift the flour, the baking powder, and the

salt into a bowl. Cream the butter and the sugar well and add the egg, still beating. Beat into it a little of the flour mixture at a time, using some of the orange juice to moisten it, until all the juice and all the flour is used up and blended. Dust the chopped pecans, the dates and the orange rind with a little extra flour and stir into the mixture. Pour the batter into a greased 9 × 5 inch loaf pan. Bake at 350° for 1 hour, or until a fork inserted in the loaf comes out clean.

Pecan Bread

3 cups all-purpose flour
1 teaspoon salt
1 cup sugar
2 teaspoons baking soda
$\frac{3}{4}$ cup milk
2 eggs
1 cup finely-chopped pecans

Thoroughly beat the eggs in a bowl and stir in the milk. Sift the flour, the salt, the sugar and the baking soda and add the chopped nuts. Stir the egg and milk mixture into the flour mixture, mix well, and pour into a greased 9 × 5 inch loaf pan. Bake at 350° for 1 hour, or until the bread is risen and brown.

Mixed Nut Bread

2 cups flour
$\frac{1}{2}$ teaspoon salt
$\frac{1}{2}$ teaspoon vanilla extract
$\frac{1}{3}$ cup sugar
3 teaspoons baking powder
$\frac{1}{4}$ cup lard
1 cup milk
2 eggs
1 cup chopped nuts

Put the sugar, the eggs and the lard into a bowl and beat thoroughly. Sift the flour, the baking powder and the salt and stir them into the egg mixture, adding the milk and the vanilla extract. Stir in the nuts and put the batter into a 9 × 5 inch loaf pan. Bake at 350° for 1 hour. The bread is cooked when a fork inserted in the center comes out clean.

Walnut Bread

3 cups all-purpose flour
1 teaspoon salt
½ cup sugar
4 teaspoons baking soda
½ cup softened butter
1 cup milk
2 eggs
1 cup finely chopped walnuts

Beat the eggs with the milk and the butter. Sift the flour, the salt, the baking soda and the sugar in a bowl. Add the egg mixture to the flour mixture and stir well. Add the chopped walnuts and pour into a greased 9 × 5 inch loaf pan. Bake at 350° for 1 hour. The bread is cooked when a fork inserted in the center comes out clean.

Savory Breads

Avocado Bread

2 cups all-purpose flour
¼ teaspoon salt
½ cup sugar
½ teaspoon baking soda
½ teaspoon baking powder
¾ cup buttermilk
1 egg
¾ cup finely chopped pecans
1 ripe avocado, mashed

Beat the egg lightly, then add the mashed avocado, the buttermilk and the chopped nuts. In another bowl, sift the flour, the salt, the baking powder and the baking soda. Add the avocado mixture to the flour mixture, and very lightly stir the ingredients together, but do not beat. Pour the mixture into a greased 8 × 4 inch loaf pan. Bake at 350° for 1 hour. The loaf is better if kept 24 hours before slicing, when it will prove to be a delicate green inside.

Carrot Bread

1½ cups all-purpose flour
¼ teaspoon salt
1 cup sugar
1 teaspoon baking powder
1 teaspoon baking soda
¾ cup vegetable oil
2 eggs
1½ cups raw carrot, grated
1 teaspoon cinnamon

Beat the eggs and add the sugar. Add the vegetable oil, ¼ cup at a time, still beating well. When all the oil has been added, beat for a further minute or two. Now stir into the mixture the flour, the baking powder, the baking soda, the salt, the cinnamon, and the carrots. Pour the mixture into a greased 8 × 4 inch loaf pan, and leave for 30 minutes. Bake at 350° for 1 hour. The loaf is done when a fork, inserted in the center, comes out clean.

Pumpkin Bread

5 cups all-purpose flour
1 teaspoon salt
1 teaspoon cinnamon
½ teaspoon nutmeg
2 cups brown sugar
2 tablespoons baking powder
½ cup softened butter
2 cups canned pumpkin
3 eggs, beaten
2 teaspoons grated orange rind

Sift together the flour, the salt, cinnamon, nutmeg, the orange rind and the baking powder. Blend the sugar, the softened butter, the beaten eggs and the canned pumpkin. Combine the flour mixture and egg mixture, blending thoroughly. Pour into a greased 9 × 5 inch loaf pan, and leave for 30 minutes. Bake at 350° for 1 hour.

Tomato Bread

2½ cups flour
2 teaspoons salt
¾ cup sugar
3 teaspoons baking powder
¼ cup shortening
1½ cups milk
2 eggs
1 cup canned tomatoes, drained

Sift together the flour, salt, baking powder and sugar. Melt shortening, and add with the well-beaten eggs, the tomatoes mashed to a pulp, then as much milk as makes a stiff batter. Pour into a greased 1 pound loaf or baking pan. Bake at 375° for 50 minutes, or until a fork inserted in the bread comes out clean.

Potato Bread

2 cups flour
1½ teaspoons salt
1 teaspoon sugar
1 package dry yeast
2 tablespoon softened butter
¼ cup warm water
¼ cup milk
½ cup boiled and mashed potatoes

Sift half the flour and the sugar into the milk and water and add the yeast to set it working. Meanwhile, mix the potatoes with the softened butter and the salt and add it to the yeast mixture, with some of the remaining flour to make a stiffish dough. On a lightly floured board, knead the dough for about 10 minutes until smooth, then leave it in a greased bowl, covered, until doubled in bulk. Punch down and on a floured board shape it into a ball, then flatten it a little. Leave to prove again, for about 50 minutes, then bake at 400° for 20–30 minutes or until a deep golden brown on top.

Onion Bread

3 cups flour
1 teaspoon salt
1¼ tablespoons sugar
1 package dry yeast
1 tablespoon melted butter
1¼ cups water
1 tablespoon water
1 egg white
1 cup finely chopped raw onion,
or reconstituted dried onion.

Simmer the onion in 1½ cups of water until soft. When cool, strain, but keep the water. Set the yeast working with a teaspoon of sugar in ½ cup of this onion water. When frothy, add to the flour, sifted with the salt, the remaining sugar, and the butter. Add sufficient of the remaining onion water to form a stiffish dough, and knead until smooth. Put in a greased bowl, cover, and leave for an hour, or until doubled in bulk. Punch down, re-knead until smooth. Form into one long loaf, or a round hearth loaf, and allow to prove for a further hour. Beat the egg white with a tablespoon of cold water until suitable for brushing on the top of the loaf. Make 3 or 4 diagonal cuts with a sharp knife and bake at 375° for 40 minutes, or until the loaf sounds hollow when tapped underneath.

Non, Central Asia

3 cups flour
1 teaspoon salt
5 tablespoons butter
½ cup water
1 cup finely chopped onions

Cook the onions gently in a little butter and allow to cool. Soften the remaining butter and to it add the water, gently heated, the onions and the salt. Beat in the flour gradually to make a firm dough. Divide into 15 pieces, and shape each piece into a ball the size of a walnut. Roll out each ball on a floured board so that is is about 6 inches in diameter. Heat an ungreased pan and cook the *Non,* one at a time, for 3 minutes on each side, placing them upright on a rack lined with a paper towel to dry out.

Herb Bread

4 cups flour
1 teaspoon salt
½ teaspoon nutmeg
2 teaspoons fine sage
2 teaspoons caraway seeds
2 tablespoons sugar
1 package dry yeast
2 tablespoons melted butter
1 cup milk
1 egg

Gently heat the milk to dissolve the sugar and salt. When cooled to tepid, add the yeast. Sift the flour with the herbs and spices. Beat the egg, add to the flour with the yeast mixture. Add the melted butter and knead to a smooth dough, using more flour as required. Cover, and leave to rise until doubled in bulk. Punch down, re-knead for a minute or so, until smooth, and place in a loaf pan, about 7 × 4 inches. Leave to prove, and bake at 400° for 15 minutes, then reduce the heat to 375° and bake a further 30 minutes, or until the loaf sounds hollow when tapped underneath.

Dill Bread

2 cups flour
1 teaspoon salt
2 teaspoons dill seed
2 tablespoons sugar
1 package dry yeast
¼ teaspoon baking soda
4 tablespoons softened butter
½ cup water
1 tablespoon milk
2 eggs
1 cup cottage cheese
2 tablespoons chopped onions

Heat the water gently, and set the yeast working in it, with a little of the sugar. Stir well. Cook the onions gently in a little of the butter until soft. Sift the flour, the remaining sugar, the baking soda and the salt in a bowl and into a well in the center, put the cooked onions. Add the yeast mixture, the cup of cottage cheese, 1 egg and the dill seed and stir until you have a smooth dough. On a lightly floured board, knead the dough, adding a little more flour if required. Put it in a greased bowl, turning it around once to lightly grease the entire surface, cover and leave to rise until doubled in bulk. Punch the dough down and shape it into a loaf. Put it in a greased 8 × 4 inch loaf pan and leave to prove. Mix the second egg with the milk and brush the top of the loaf with the mixture, then bake at 375° for 40 minutes.

Cheese Bread

4 cups flour
1 teaspoon salt
1¼ tablespoons sugar
1 package dry yeast
1 cup water
1 egg
2 cups finely grated cheddar cheese

Warm water to tepid, add half of the sugar and the yeast. When the yeast is frothy, add it to the flour with the remaining sugar, the salt, the cheese and the well-beaten egg. Mix to a stiff dough, then knead thoroughly until smooth. Leave to rise in a greased bowl, covered, until doubled in bulk. Punch down, knead again

247

until smooth, divide into 2 pieces and shape for loaves, pressing the dough into 2 loaf pans, 7 × 4 inches. Leave to prove, then bake at 400° for 15 minutes, then reduce the heat to 375° and bake a further 30 minutes, or until the loaves sound hollow when tapped underneath.

Rice Bread

4 cups flour
3 cups cooked rice
1 teaspoon salt
2 tablespoons sugar
1 package dry yeast
3 tablespoons butter
1 cup milk

Scald the milk and add the butter, sugar and the salt. When cooled to tepid, add the yeast. When the yeast is frothy, mix in the cooked rice and flour. Knead thoroughly on a well-floured board, as the dough will be sticky. Because of the rice, this will not be as smooth textured as most bread doughs. Put in a greased bowl, cover, and leave to prove until doubled in bulk, about 1 hour. Punch down, re-knead and put into 2 loaf pans, 7 × 4 inches. Allow to prove, and bake at 375° for about 30 minutes, or until loaves sound hollow when tapped underneath.

Ancient Breads

Cappodocia

1 cup white flour
1½ cups wholemeal or graham flour
1 teaspoon honey
1 package dry yeast
1 tablespoon olive oil
1 cup milk

Work the yeast with the honey and a few tablespoons of the milk, warmed to tepid. When frothy add to the mixed flours with the oil, and knead to a springy dough. Put the dough in a greased bowl, cover and leave to rise until doubled in bulk. Punch down, knead again for a few minutes, shape as a domed hearth bread, leave to prove, then mark with a cross. Bake at 400° for 25 minutes, or until well risen and light brown. If the bottom of the loaf is firm, and sounds hollow when tapped, the loaf is done.

Melitutes

1½ cups white flour
¾ cup wholemeal flour
½ teaspoon salt
2 tablespoons honey
1 package dry yeast
1 cup milk

Work the yeast with a little warmed milk and a teaspoon of the honey. When frothy add to the mixed flours with the salt, the rest of the milk and honey. Knead to a springy dough, then leave to rise until doubled in bulk. Punch down, knead again, form into a hearth loaf, and bake as for *Cappodocia.*

Artologanos

1½ cups wholemeal flour
1 cup barley flour
1 teaspoon freshly ground black pepper

1 teaspoon honey
1 package dry yeast
1 tablespoon olive oil
¾ cup milk

Set the yeast working with a little tepid milk and the honey. When frothy, add to the mixed flours with the salt, oil and pepper. Work to a dough with the milk, knead until smooth and springy, cover and leave to rise until doubled in bulk. Punch down, re-knead and form into a hearth loaf, bake at 400° until well risen and brown, about 30 minutes.

Pain d'epices (French Spice Bread), fourteenth century

4 cups flour
1 teaspoon salt
1 teaspoon mixed spice
1 teaspoon ginger
1 teaspoon nutmeg
½ cup brown sugar or honey
1 package dry yeast
1 teaspoon baking soda
¼ lb butter
1 cup milk

Sift the flour and add the spices and salt, rub in the fat until the mixture resembles fine crumbs. Work the yeast with a little tepid milk and a teaspoon of sugar or honey. When frothy, add to the flour with the beaten egg, the soda and the remaining honey or sugar. Mix to a stiffish dough with the milk, and either beat well or knead. Because the mixture is sticky, you will require plenty of flour on the work-surface as you knead. Put the dough in a greased bowl, cover and leave to rise until double in bulk. Punch down, knead again for a few minutes. Put the dough in a greased bowl, cover and leave to rise until doubled in bulk. Punch down, knead again for a few minutes. Put the the dough in a loaf pan, or round layer cake pan, leave to prove. Brush the surface with milk. Bake at 400° for 15 minutes, cover the top with foil, reduce the heat to 350° and bake a further 20 minutes.

York Mayne Bread, fifteenth century

3 cups flour
2 teaspoons crushed coriander seeds
2 teaspoons caraway seeds
1 cup sugar or honey
1 package dry yeast
½ cup mixed milk and water
3 teaspoons rose water
3 egg yolks
2 egg whites

Mix the flour, spices and sugar. Add the egg yolks to the rose water and beat together. Beat the whites of the eggs until stiff. Set the yeast to work with a little tepid milk and a teaspoon of honey or sugar. Pour the yeast, when frothy, into the flour; add the egg yolk and rose water mixture and the egg whites; mix to a stiff dough, knead thoroughly and leave to rise until doubled in bulk. As with the spice bread, the mixture will be very sticky, so use plenty of flour while kneading. Punch down, prove and bake as for the French Spice Bread.

Trencher Bread, medieval

12 cups wholemeal flour
4 cups barley flour
1 tablespoon salt
1 teaspoon sugar
1 package dry yeast
6 cups water

Set the yeast working with a little warm water and the sugar. Mix the flours and sift with the salt. Pour the yeast, when frothy, into the flour and work to a stiff dough. Knead, then leave to ferment for half an hour. Knead again, then shape into discs 10 inches in diameter. Leave to prove for one hour, then bake for 45 minutes at 400°. When the *trenchers* have baked for half this time, turn over to give an even finish. The *trenchers* are then stored, wrapped in a cloth, for 4 days, and trimmed square with a sharp knife, before being used as plates to hold food.

251

Small Breads and Buns

Croissants

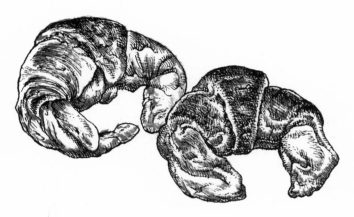

2½ cups flour
1 teaspoon salt
1 teaspoon sugar
1 package dry yeast
1½ tablespoons lard
¼ lb softened butter
¼ cup water
1 cup milk
1 egg

Set the yeast working in the water warmed to tepid with the sugar. Scald the milk, add the lard. Allow to cool until tepid. Sift the salt with the flour, add the yeast, and the lard mixture; mix to a stiffish dough, adding more flour if needed. Leave to rise, covered, until doubled in bulk. Punch down, lightly knead, place in the refrigerator to chill for 30 minutes. Roll out the dough on a floured board to a rectangle about ¼ inch thick. Cream the butter and spread a thin layer over the dough. Fold in both ends to meet in the center and then fold again like a book. Roll out again to a rectangle, spread with butter, repeat this process twice. Place in the refrigerator for another 15 minutes, then roll to a thickness of about ⅛ inch. Now cut the dough into squares, then into triangles. Roll each triangle, starting from the widest edge toward the apex. Shape into crescents, leave to rest for about 30 minutes. Brush with the yolk of an egg, mixed with a little milk. Bake on a greased baking sheet at 450° for 5 minutes, then at 375° for a further 8 minutes or until golden brown.

Nairn Butteries

4 cups flour
1 teaspoon salt
2 teaspoons sugar
1 package dry yeast
¾ cup softened butter
¾ cup lard
1 cup water

252

Set the yeast working with the sugar and half of the water warmed to tepid. Sift the flour with the salt. When the yeast is frothy, add it to the flour. Mix to a stiffish dough, adding remaining water as required. Knead until smooth, leave to rise, covered, for about an hour. Punch down, place in the refrigerator for 20 minutes. Roll out dough to a rectangle, 6 × 18 inches. Thoroughly cream the lard and the butter, spread a third of this mixture on the dough, keeping it clear of the edges. Fold both ends toward the center, then fold over again. Roll out, and repeat the process until the fat mixture has been used up. Don't worry if the butter breaks through the surface, just dust with a little flour. Stamp out into discs with a 3 or 4 inch pastry cutter. Fold the edges of each underneath to form a small bun shape, making sure they are well sealed. Place on a greased baking sheet. Allow to prove for about 20–30 minutes. Bake at 400° until golden brown – about 25 minutes. Makes about 18 butteries.

Baps

4 cups flour
1 teaspoon salt
1 teaspoon sugar
1 package dry yeast
¼ cup lard
1 cup milk and water (half and half)

Set the yeast working with the sugar and half the liquid warmed to tepid. Sift flour and salt, rub in the lard. When the yeast is frothy, add it to the flour with the remaining liquid. Mix to a soft dough, cover and leave to rise for 1 hour. Punch down, knead lightly, divide into small pieces to make ovals 2 × 3 inches. Leave to prove for about 20 minutes, brush with water, dust with flour and bake at 425° for about 15–20 minutes. Makes about a dozen baps.

Brioche

2 cups flour
¼ teaspoon salt
1 tablespoon sugar
1 package dry yeast
¾ cup softened butter
3 eggs

Sift flour and salt into a bowl. Dissolve yeast with a little warmed milk and a ½ teaspoon of the sugar. When frothy, add to the flour, also add the well-beaten eggs. Mix to a dough with a wooden spoon and work in the butter by degrees, beating well into the dough. Use a fork to lift the dough, which will be very soft and sticky, beating air into it. Cover, and leave to rise for 2 hours. Punch down, cover and leave overnight on the lowest shelf of the refrigerator; brioches should be prepared well in advance, for they need long periods of rising. Shape the dough as required, or put small portions into muffin or patty pans. Leave to prove for 30 minutes, bake at 450° for 20 minutes until well risen and golden brown.

Bagels

4 cups flour
1 teaspoon salt
1½ tablespoons sugar
1 package dry yeast
¼ cup butter
1 tablespoon water
1 cup milk
1 egg

Warm the milk to tepid, add butter, sugar and salt. Add yeast. Separate the egg, beat the white to a stiff froth. Add the milk mixture and egg white to the flour. Knead to a smooth dough, put in a greased bowl, cover and leave to rise until doubled in bulk. Punch down, knead again for a minute or two. Take pieces of dough of sufficient size to roll out (about the width of a finger and twice the length). Shape into rings, making sure the ends are well joined. Leave to prove about 20 minutes. Cook the bagels in a pan of water near boiling for 5–6 minutes after they have risen to the surface. Transfer them gently to a greased baking sheet; leave them to cool, meanwhile beating up the egg yolk with a tablespoon of water. Brush the bagels with the egg mixture and bake at 375° for 30 minutes or until golden brown. Makes about 20 bagels.

Spanish Churros

2 cups flour
1 teaspoon salt
2 cups water
Fat for deep-frying

In a saucepan boil the water and salt, add all the flour at once, and stir briskly until the dough leaves the sides of the pan, then remove from heat. This dough is similar to that used for making *choux* paste. When cool, roll into pieces of a thickness slightly larger than a pencil, and about 6 inches long. Ideally, the *churros* paste should be passed through a special press fitted with a star-shaped cutter, giving them their characteristic ribbed shape. Fry in hot fat for about five minutes, or until golden brown. *Churros* are usually eaten at breakfast time, plain and unsweetened.

Grissini

4 cups flour
2 teaspoons salt
1 tablespoon sugar
1 package dry yeast
2 tablespoons butter
½ cup water
½ cup milk

Warm water to tepid, add a teaspoonful of the sugar, and the yeast. In a bowl, combine flour, salt and remaining sugar. Warm the milk, add the butter; heat till butter melts. Cool to lukewarm, add to the flour along with the yeast. Knead to a smooth dough, put in a greased bowl and leave till doubled in bulk. Punch down, knead again until smooth. Take pieces of dough and roll them to the thickness of a pencil, about 9–12 inches long. Place on a greased baking sheet, leave to prove, about 20 minutes. Just

255

before placing in the oven, brush them with cold water, bake at 425° until *grissini* are golden brown. Makes about 15 *grissini*.

Pretzels

4 cups flour
1 teaspoon salt
1 tablespoon sea salt
1 tablespoon sugar
1 package dry yeast
1 cup water
1 egg

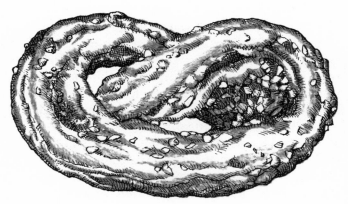

Set the yeast working in half of the water warmed to tepid, with a teaspoonful of the sugar. Sift the flour with the salt and remaining sugar. When the yeast is frothy, add it to the flour and knead to a smooth dough. Take pieces of dough and roll to the thickness of a pencil, each about 6 inches long. Fashion into the shape of a traditional pretzel, brush with the beaten egg and sprinkle with the sea salt. Place pretzels on a greased baking sheet and bake at 425° until brown. Makes between 20 and 25 pretzels.

The Hamburger Bun

4 cups flour
1 teaspoon salt
2 tablespoons sugar
4 ounces butter
1 package dry yeast
1 cup milk

Set the yeast working in half the milk, warm to tepid, and a teaspoon of the sugar. Sift the flour with the salt, melt the butter, and add to the flour with the remaining sugar. When the yeast is frothy, add to the flour with remaining milk, and mix together; then knead to a smooth dough. Put in a greased bowl, cover, and leave to rise until doubled in bulk, about 1 hour. Punch down, and knead again until smooth and springy. Break off small pieces of the dough to form balls, each about 3 inches across. Place on a greased baking sheet, flatten

256

each one slightly, to the shape of a hamburger bun, and leave to prove for about 20 minutes. Brush with a glaze of cold milk, and bake at 425° until the buns are well-risen and brown, about 20 minutes. If liked, the buns can be sprinkled with sesame seeds, a modern refinement to the bun.

Soda Scones

4 cups flour
1 teaspoon salt
1 teaspoon baking soda
4 tablespoons butter
1 cup buttermilk or
1 cup fresh milk with the
addition of 2 teaspoons
cream of tartar

In Scotland, cooks make scones with either self-rising flour, or soft cake flour, some even use self-rising plus the extra teaspoon of baking soda and cream of tartar. Sift the flour with the baking soda and the salt, rub in the butter until you have the texture of fine crumbs. Add the buttermilk or milk with cream of tartar. Quickly knead with the tips of the fingers to a stiff dough. Flour a board and press the dough or roll it to $\frac{1}{2}$–$\frac{3}{4}$ inch thickness. Cut circles with 2–2$\frac{1}{2}$ inch pastry cutter or the rim of a glass tumbler. Bake in a hot oven, about 450° for 7 to 10 minutes, until well-risen and lightly brown. The Scots eat these with butter for tea. The English, hedonistic souls that they are, serve them with butter, thick cream and strawberry jam.

Paker House Rolls

7 cups flour
1 teaspoon salt
2 tablespoons sugar
1 package dry yeast
2 tablespoons butter
$\frac{1}{4}$ cup water
2 cups milk
1 egg

Set the yeast working in the water warmed

257

to tepid with a teaspoon of the sugar. Warm the milk with the remaining sugar, the salt and the butter. When the yeast is frothy, mix with 3 cups of flour, and the rest of the liquid. Beat well with a wooden spoon, cover and leave for 30 minutes. Then add remaining flour and the well-beaten egg. Knead thoroughly and allow to rise until doubled in bulk. Punch down and knead until smooth. The dough is now ready to be fashioned in the traditional shapes. Makes about 25 rolls.

Parker House Rolls: To make the classic rolls, cut the dough into 3 inch rounds. With a knife, make a crease in each round, slightly off center. Brush with melted butter. Fold the smaller section onto the larger one and nip edges together. Place on a greased baking sheet, cover, leave to rise again till doubled in bulk. Bake at 425° for 15 minutes.

Clover Leaf Rolls: Shape the dough into small balls, about an inch in diameter, brush them with melted butter and place them 3 at a time side by side, in greased muffin cups. Cover and leave to rise until doubled in bulk. Bake at 425° for 15 minutes.

Crescent Rolls: Roll out dough until it is circular and about $\frac{1}{4}$ inch thick. Cut the dough into triangles, the wide end of each being about 3 inches long. Starting with the wide end of each piece of dough, roll it toward the apex, and shape into a crescent, turning the ends in neatly. Place on a greased baking sheet, cover and leave to rise until doubled in bulk, then bake at 425° for 15 minutes.

Fan Tans: Roll out the dough into a rectangle about $\frac{1}{4}$ inch thick. Brush with melted butter and cut it into 1 × 8 inch strips. Pile 6 strips on top of each other and cut into six 1 × 1 inch pieces; place each bundle cut side up in a greased muffin cup. Cover and leave to rise until doubled in bulk. Bake at 425° for 15 minutes.

Bow Knots: Roll out the dough into a long shape about $\frac{1}{4}$ inch thick. Brush with melted butter and fold half the dough over the other half, to double the thickness. Cut into strips about $\frac{1}{2}$ inch thick and 5–6 inches long, and, greasing your hands first, roll these pieces into cylinders and tie into loose knots, without, if possible, stretching the dough too much. Place on a greased baking sheet, cover and leave to rise until doubled in bulk, then bake at 425° for 15 minutes.

Pieces of Eight Rolls: Roll dough out to a long oblong about $\frac{1}{4}$ inch thick. Brush with melted butter and fold half the dough over the other half, to double the thickness. Cut into strips $\frac{1}{2}$ inch thick and 5–6 inches long, then shape these into figure-eights. Place on a greased baking sheet, cover, leave to rise until doubled in bulk, and bake at 425° for 15 minutes.

Snails: Roll dough out to a long oblong shape about $\frac{1}{4}$ inch thick. Brush with melted butter and fold half the dough over the other half, to double the thickness. Cut into strips $\frac{1}{2}$ inch thick and 5–6 inches long. Hold the end of each strip down on a greased baking sheet and wind the other end round and round to form a snail shape, tucking the end firmly into the center. Cover and leave to rise until doubled in bulk and then bake at 425° for 15 minutes.

Pan Rolls: Take pieces of dough and shape them into balls the size of large walnuts (about $1\frac{1}{2}$ inches in diameter). Place them in the bottom of a round or square but deep-sided greased pan to make one layer only, the sides of each ball just touching. Brush with melted butter, cover and leave to rise until doubled in bulk. Bake at 425° for 15 minutes. When baked, the rolls will pull apart easily.

Four Leaf Clover Rolls: With your hands well greased, take pieces of dough and roll each into a ball about 2 inches in diameter. Put each ball into a well greased muffin cup and with a very sharp knife, cut each ball into halves, then quarters, each time nearly cutting through to the bottom, but not quite. Brush with melted butter, cover and leave to rise until doubled in bulk, then bake at 425° for 15 minutes.

Butterfly Rolls: Roll the dough into a rectangle about $\frac{1}{4}$ inch thick, and 5–6 inches wide. Brush with melted butter and roll up. Cut the roll into

259

2 inch wide slices. Place each piece on a greased baking sheet with an inch or two between each one. With the back, not the blade, of the knife, make a firm indent in the middle of each piece (to mark the body of the butterfly). Cover, leave to rise until doubled in bulk, then bake at 425° for 15 minutes.

Long Rolls: Roll out the dough until it is $\frac{1}{2}$ inch thick, then divide it into strips 5–6 inches long and $\frac{1}{2}$ inch thick. With well greased hands, roll each piece into a cylinder, brush it with butter, place on a greased baking sheet and leave to rise, covered, until doubled in bulk. Bake at 425° for 15 minutes.

Triple Decker Rolls: Roll out the dough to an oblong shape about $\frac{1}{4}$ inch thick. Brush with melted butter and fold in both ends of the dough to meet in the center and then fold again like a book. Cut into strips 1–2 inches wide, nipping the ends in firmly to seal. Place well apart on a greased baking sheet, cover and leave to rise until doubled in bulk. Bake at 425° for 15 minutes.

Kaiser Semmeln

5 cups flour
2 teaspoons salt
1 teaspoon sugar
2 teaspoons malt extract
1 package dry yeast
1 tablespoon melted shortening
1 cup milk
Poppy seeds

Set the yeast working in half of the milk, warmed to tepid, with a teaspoon of sugar. Sift the salt with the flour, and add the melted shortening with the malt extract. When the yeast is frothy, add to the flour mixture and mix to a stiff dough with the remaining milk. Knead thoroughly, then put in a greased bowl, cover, and leave to rise until doubled in bulk. Punch down, knead again for a few minutes, then break off small pieces of dough to shape as rolls. Kaiser rolls used to have a portrait of the reigning Hapsburg monarch stamped in them.

Now, any fancy shape will suffice. Sprinkle with poppy seeds, and bake at 450° for 20 minutes, or until crisp and golden brown.

English Muffins

2½ cups flour
1 teaspoon salt
2 tablespoons sugar
1 package dry yeast
3 tablespoons butter
¾ cup water
1 egg

Set the yeat working with a ½ teaspoon of the sugar and half the water. When frothy, add to the flour. Warm the remaining water and dissolve the sugar in it and and the butter. Add the water mixture and the beaten egg to the flour and yeast; mix to a stiffish dough and knead for about 5 minutes. Put in a greased bowl, cover and leave till doubled in bulk. Punch down, knead again for a minute or two, then roll out dough on a floured board to a ¼ inch thickness. With a pastry cutter, cut into 3-inch rounds. Cover with a cloth, leave to prove for 50 minutes. Sprinkle with wholemeal flour or cornmeal, heat griddle, but not too hot, cook each muffin for 3 minutes on each side, check that they are not scorching, and then for a further 5–7 minutes each side. English muffins should never be cut with a knife, but pulled apart and buttered. Makes about 20 muffins.

English Crumpets

Crumpets are as institutional as wet Sundays in England. The word is of unknown origin, it might have derived from the Old English *cruma,* a small fragment of bread. "Crumpet" is also an English slang word for "girl," the reasons for which might not be wise to pursue.

4 cups flour
1 teaspoon salt

1 package dry yeast
1½ cups milk

Sift the flour with the salt. Warm a little of the milk to tepid and add yeast. When frothy, add to the flour with the rest of the milk to make a smooth batter, the consistency of heavy cream. Cover, and leave to rise for about 50 minutes. To make crumpets you will require a skillet or griddle, and some crumpet rings, flan rings, or a shallow can with the bottom removed. Either way, the rings ought to be about 3½ inches diameter and an 1–1½ inches deep. Grease the rings and the griddle with lard. Pour the batter into each ring set on the hot griddle, and fill to a depth of a ½ inch. Be sure that the griddle is not too hot, otherwise the crumpets may burn. When brown on the underside, turn them and cook the top surface for about 2–3 minutes. They should be only lightly brown. To serve, allow the cumpets to cool, then toast them on both sides under the broiler, until crisp and golden. They require mountains of butter and ladles of jelly, and are served with tea, in the time-honored fashion. Makes about 15 to 20 crumpets.

Corn Muffins

2 cups flour
1 cup cornmeal
1 teaspoon salt
¼ cup sugar
1 package dry yeast
¼ cup butter
¼ cup warm water
1 cup milk
2 eggs, beaten

Gently heat the milk and dissolve the sugar and salt. Add the corn meal and the butter. While the milk mixture is cooling, set the yeast working in the warm water. Add the beaten eggs and the yeast mixture to the other ingredients. Knead on a floured board to a soft dough, adding more flour if required. Leave, covered, until doubled in bulk. Punch down, and knead lightly for a minute or two. Now roll out the

262

dough and divide it into pieces which will roll into balls the size of a walnut. Bake in greased muffin pans at 425° for about 20 minutes. Makes 20–25 muffins.

Jelly Doughnuts

2 cups flour
1 teaspoon salt
2 teaspoons sugar
1 package dry yeast
1 tablespoon softened butter
¼ cup warm milk
some raspberry jelly
fat for frying

Sift the flour, while setting the yeast to work in half the warm milk with 1 teaspoon of sugar. Add the salt and softened butter to the remaining milk and allow to cool. Add both the yeast mixture and the butter liquid to the flour and remaining sugar, stir and knead to a firm dough. Leave in a greased bowl to rise until doubled in bulk. Knead again for a minute or two, then divide the dough into 15 pieces, forming each piece into a ball. Flatten out each ball slightly, place some raspberry jelly in the middle and fold the edges over. Allow to prove for half an hour, then fry in hot fat at 375°. Drain and cool.

Glaze for Doughnuts

2 cups sugar
2 cups water
1 teaspoon vanilla extract, or grated lemon rind
cinnamon or any similar spice

Bring the sugar and the water to the boil, and boil for 5 minutes. Cool well and stir in the flavoring of your choice. When the doughnuts have cooked in the hot fat, dip them in the syrup, and leave to cool.

Baba au Rhum

2 cups flour
½ teaspoon salt
¼ cup sugar
1 package dry yeast
½ cup butter
½ cup milk
3 eggs, beaten
1 tablespoon grated orange rind

Warm the milk to tepid and with a teaspoon of sugar and set the yeast working. When frothy stir in ½ cup of the flour and 1 tablespoon of the sugar, and beat well. Cover and leave to rise until doubled in bulk. Cream the butter, stir in the remaining sugar and beat for 2 or 3 minutes until smooth. Then add the salt, the orange rind, the eggs and beat well. When smooth, stir in the remaining flour. Combine with the yeast mixture and beat thoroughly for 20 minutes. Pour into a greased mold, cover and leave to rise until doubled in bulk. Bake at 350° for 50 minutes. Place a plate on top of the mold, and invert it quickly, when the baba should slide out neatly. Serve with Apricot Sauce:

Apricot Sauce

¾ cup sugar
1½ cups apricot juice
2 teaspoons lemon juice
½ cup rum

Put sugar and apricot juice in a pan and bring to the boil. Let the sauce boil for 5 minutes. Cool slighly, and stir in 2 teaspoons lemon juice and the rum. Pour this sauce over the baba.

Chelsea Buns

4 cups flour
1 teaspoon salt
1 teaspoon sugar
1 package dry yeast
4 tablespoons butter
2 tablespoons water
¾ cup milk
2 eggs

Sift flour with salt into a bowl. Dissolve the

264

yeast with the sugar in the tepid water, leave until frothy. Beat the eggs and add to the milk, also warmed to tepid. Now add the liquids to the flour, mix to a dough and work in the butter, previously softened. Make a soft dough, and knead until smooth. Leave it to rise in a greased, covered bowl. Punch down, knead until smooth again, and roll out on a floured board or table top, to an oblong 12 by 6 inches.

1 tablespoon sugar
Egg and milk glaze
¼ lb of butter
1 cup mixed currants and white raisins
Sugar

Soften the butter and spread over the rolled out dough. Scatter the fruit, washed and dried, over the butter, also sprinkle on the sugar. Roll up as for a jelly roll, fairly tightly. Cut into 1 inch lengths, and place the pieces in a square 7 or 8 inch baking tin. Glaze with beaten egg and milk and bake in a hot oven at 450° until well risen and brown – about 20 minutes. When the buns have cooled slightly, dust lightly with caster sugar.

Bath Buns

2½ cups flour
½ teaspoon salt
4 tablespoons sugar
1 package dry yeast
4 tablespoons butter
¾ cup milk
1 egg
1 cup sultanas
2 tablespoons candied peel
egg and milk glaze
sugar syrup glaze
1 tablespoon coarse white
sugar or coffee sugar

Sift the flour with a ½ teaspoon salt. Dissolve the yeast in a little tepid milk with a ½ teaspoon of the sugar. Heat the rest of the milk with the butter and rest of the sugar (not the coarse sugar) until the butter melts. Allow to

265

cool slightly before adding to the flour along with the yeast. Beat the egg and add to the flour mixture, mix to a soft dough with a wooden spoon. Leave for 2 hours to rise, punch down and work in the dried fruit. Leave to rise again for 30 minutes. Punch down again, and knead for a few minutes.

The dough will be very sticky, so use plenty of flour on the work surface. Break off pieces of dough, and make balls measuring about 3 inches in diameter, and try to prevent the dried fruit breaking through the surface. Place the buns on a greased baking sheet, and brush each one with an egg and milk glaze. Bake in the oven at 375° for 20 minutes on middle shelf, or until nicely browned. Before they cool, brush with sugar syrup glaze and sprinkle tops with coarse sugar or white coffee sugar.

Cornish Saffron Buns

Tradition maintains that saffron was introduced to the west of England, to Devon and Cornwall, by the Phoenician traders who came to mine the rich deposits of tin. The Phoenicians were said to be remarkably partial to saffron, both as a dye and a flavoring for food.

4 cups flour
1 teaspoon salt
½ teaspoon saffron powder or saffron threads
1 tablespoon caraway seeds
¾ cup sugar
1 package dry yeast
2 tablespoons butter
1 cup water
2 eggs
¼ cup candied citron peel

Bring a ½ cup of the water to the boil, then steep saffron powder or threads for 10 minutes. Warm remaining water to tepid, add 1 teaspoon of the sugar and add the yeast. Mix the flour with the rest of the sugar and the salt. Add the caraway seeds, melt the butter and add to the flour. Add the yeast, then the saffron water, beat the eggs and add to the mixture. Stir thoroughly, then knead on a well-floured board – the dough will be very sticky, so use plenty of flour. Knead until smooth, place in a greased, covered bowl, and allow to rise until doubled in bulk. Punch down, re-knead, and shape into small buns on a greased baking sheet, each about 2–2½ inches in diameter. On each bun place a few small pieces of the candied citron peel for decoration, then allow to prove for 40 minutes. Bake at 425° for 10 minutes, then lower heat to 350° and bake a further 10 minutes, or until buns are lightly brown, and sound hollow when tapped underneath. The buns can be brushed with a little light sugar syrup if desired.

Hot Cross Buns

4 cups flour
1 teaspoon salt
1 teaspoon mixed spice
3 tablespoons sugar
1 package dry yeast
¼ lb. butter
1 cup milk
2 eggs
1 cup currants
thin sugar syrup

Sift flour with salt, spice and all but 1 teaspoon of the sugar of tepid milk, and the remaining teaspoon of the sugar. When yeast is frothy, pour into the flour. Beat the eggs, add these with the remaining milk to the flour, mix to a dough. Turn on to a floured board. Work in the currants and knead dough until smooth and elastic. Then place in a greased bowl. Leave to rise until doubled in bulk. Punch down, knead again for a minute. Now, for each bun, take a small piece of dough to form a ball about 1½ inches in diameter. Arrange them about 2 inches apart on a baking sheet and allow to prove for about 20 minutes. The crosses may be made by cutting with a sharp knife about ¼ inch deep on the top of each bun, or with a light flour and water paste just thick enough to pipe. Bake the buns at 450° for about 15 minutes or until golden brown. The tops of the buns may be brushed with a thin sugar syrup. Boil for 3 minutes ¼ cup of granulated sugar with ¼ cup water. Glaze the buns while the syrup is still warm. Makes about a dozen buns.

Sally Lunns

3 cups of flour
pinch of salt
2 tablespoon sugar
1 package dried yeast
4 tablespoons butter
¼ cup of milk
1 egg

Sift flour with salt. Dissolve the yeast with a ½ teaspoon of the sugar in a little tepid milk. Leave yeast to work for about ten minutes. Warm the rest of the milk with the butter and sugar until the butter melts and the sugar dissolves. Allow to cool until tepid. Add well-beaten egg, and mix in with the flour to a soft dough, using a little extra milk if required. The dough will be fairly soft and sticky. Beat or knead on a floured surface until smooth, and leave to rise until doubled in bulk. Punch down, divide the dough into two equal pieces. Put each piece in separate Sally Lunn, Charlotte pans, or any round cans of about 5 inches diameter. Leave for 20 minutes to prove, glaze with egg and milk, or plain milk. Bake for 25 minutes at 425° or until brown on top. Sally Lunns should be either split in two while hot, and spread with butter, or sliced into three, toasted, spread with butter and reassembled.

Hamantaschen

2 cups flour
½ teaspoon salt
2 tablespoons sugar
1 package dry yeast
½ cup milk
2 eggs

Gently warm the milk to tepid, add the butter, the yeast and a teaspoon of the sugar.

Sift the flour and salt, add yeast mixture and make a soft dough. Knead until smooth, place in a greased bowl, cover, and leave to rise until doubled in bulk. Punch down, work in remaining sugar with the beaten egg. This will produce a sticky dough, so knead on a well-floured board. Leave to rest for 10 minutes, then roll out to a ¼ inch thickness. Cut into 4 inch discs with a cutter, and place a tablespoon of filling in the center of each. Fold three edges toward the center, making a triangle, like the tricorn hat worn by Haman, the villain of the Jewish Purim festival. Leave to prove, then brush each with beaten egg yolk mixed with a little milk. Bake at 375° for 20 minutes, or until golden brown.

Filling:

1 cup poppy seeds
½ cup water
¼ cup honey
¼ cup sugar
1 egg
Pinch of salt

Combine poppy seeds with honey, sugar and salt. Cook gently in a small pan, adding sufficient water to make a thick paste. When cool, add the well-beaten egg.

Scots Cookies

The Americans have their "cookies," and the English their "biscuits." The Scots have cookies too, which are more like buns or like muffins, served with jelly and cream.

4 cups flour
1 teaspoon salt
¼ cup sugar
1 package dry yeast
5 tablespoons butter
1 cup milk
2 eggs
Sugar/milk glaze

Set the yeast working with a ¼ cup of the

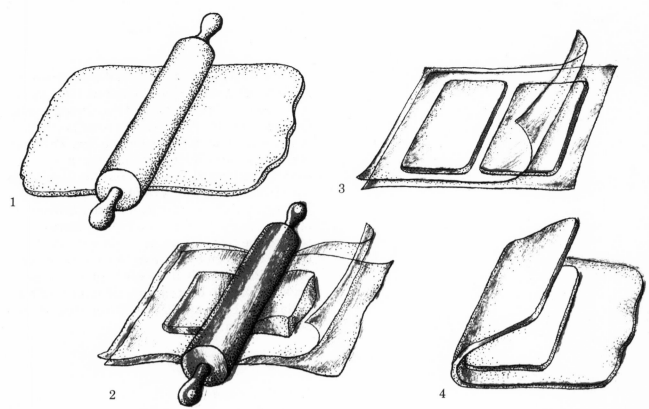

1

2

3

4

milk, warmed to tepid, and a teaspoon of the sugar. Gently warm the remaining milk, add the butter and stir until it melts. When luke-warm, add this and the yeast mixture to the flour. Then add the well-beaten eggs. Mix to a soft dough. Put in a greased bowl, cover, and leave to rise – about 1 hour. Punch down, work in the remaining sugar, and knead until smooth and silky, using flour to counteract the stickiness of the dough. Divide the dough into $2\frac{1}{2}$–3 inch pieces, shape into balls, then press lightly with the hand. Place them on a greased baking sheet, and leave to prove. Bake at 400° for about 20–25 minutes, or until golden brown. Make a glaze with a tablespoon of sugar boiled for a minute in a little hot milk, or a glaze of sugar and water.

Shortbread

1¼ cups flour
6 tablespoons rice flour
¾ cup fine sugar
¾ cup unsalted butter

Cream the butter and work in the sugar.

Sift the two flours, add to the butter cream, and mix to a paste. Press into a 5 × 5 inch pan, and bake at 350° until a pale fawn color, about 10–15 minutes. Remove from the oven, and cut into fingers while still warm.

Danish Pastries Basic Dough

6 cups flour
1 teaspoon salt
¼ cup sugar
1 teaspoon vanilla sugar
2 packages dry yeast
1 tablespoon butter
¼ cup water
½ cup milk
2 eggs
1 lb unsalted butter

Set the yeast working with the water warmed to tepid and a teaspoon of the sugar. When frothy, add to 4 cups of the flour; then add the milk, the tablespoon of butter, the well-beaten eggs, salt, remaining sugar and the vanilla sugar. Mix with a wooden spoon, gradually adding more flour until you have a

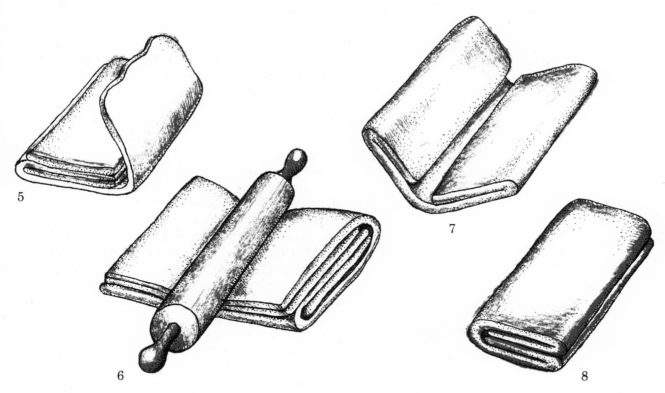

5

6

7

8

softish dough. Knead thoroughly on a floured board for about 5 minutes, or until the dough is smooth and satiny. Dust with flour and put in the refrigerator for at least 30 minutes. The next step is to work the unsalted butter into the flour as for flaky pastry. The butter must be cold, but not hard, and must be rolled flat between sheets of waxed paper. Take the dough from the refrigerator, and roll out to a rectangle about $\frac{1}{8}$ inch thick.

Roll out the butter to a rectangle slightly smaller than that of the dough. If the butter becomes too soft to roll, return it to the refrigerator for a few minutes. Cut the rectangle of butter in half. Place one half on the center of the dough, fold one flap over it, place the other half of the butter on top, then fold the remaining flap of dough over the butter. Thus you have a parcel of layers of dough and butter. Carefully roll this out into a rectangle twice as long as wide, about 9 × 18 inches. Fold both ends toward the center, then fold again. Chill again until firm, then repeat this last folding process twice more, chilling when necessary. The aim is to achieve a flaky dough containing

layers of butter. Try not to roll out the dough too vigorously, or too thinly as this might cause the butter to break through the surface – if it does, dust the break with flour. Chill the dough before using, preferably overnight. Makes about 24 pastries.

Fillings
Each to fill one dozen pastries.

Almond Filling

$\frac{1}{2}$ cup almonds, finely ground
$\frac{1}{2}$ cup fine sugar
1 egg

Mix the almonds and sugar, beat the egg, and add sufficient egg to bind to a thick paste.

Apple Filling

2–3 large cooking apples
3–4 tablespoons fine sugar
rind and juice of a lemon
2 tablespoons butter

Stew apples until soft, with the sugar, the lemon juice and the grated rind. When cool, work in the butter.

Frangipane Filling

1 teaspoon flour
6 tablespoons almond paste
1 tablespoon rum
2 teaspoons finely chopped almonds
3 tablespoons butter

Cream the butter, add the almond paste and the rum, beat for a moment before adding the flour. Mix to a paste.

Vanilla Cream

2 tablespoons all-purpose flour
2 tablespoons cornstarch
2 tablespoons sugar
$\frac{1}{2}$ cup milk
1 egg yolk
vanilla extract

Blend the flour and cornstarch with the egg yolk, the vanilla extract and a little cold milk. Scald the remaining milk, pour into the mixture, stir and return to the heat. Allow it to come to the boil, stirring constantly, then leave to cool.

Envelopes

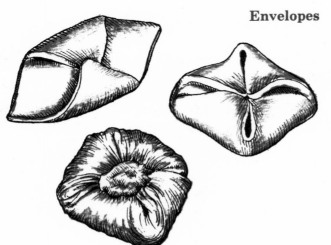

The amount of dough used in the following recipes depends on the number of pastries you require. As a rough guide, the dough made according to the recipe on page 270 makes about 24 pastries.

pastry dough
red currant jelly
vanilla cream

Roll out the dough to about $\frac{1}{8}$ inch thickness, and cut into 4 inch squares. Fold the corners to meet the centre, pressing down the points. Place a good tablespoon of cream in the center, and dot with a teaspoon of the jelly.

Place envelopes on a greased baking sheet, then allow them to prove. Bake at 375° for about 20 minutes.

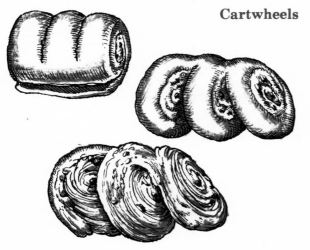

Cartwheels

pastry dough
raisins
flaked or chopped almonds
almond filling
beaten egg for glaze

Roll out dough to about $\frac{1}{8}$ inch thickness. Spread thinly with almond filling, then sprinkle raisins over the surface. Roll as for jelly roll, cut the roll into $\frac{1}{2}$ inch slices. Place them on a greased baking sheet, brush with beaten egg. Leave to prove, then sprinkle each cartwheel with flaked almonds. Bake at 375° for about 20 minutes.

Cock's Combs

pastry dough
frangipane filling
egg white
sugar

Roll out dough to about $\frac{1}{8}$ inch thickness. Spread one half of the dough with a layer of frangipane filling, fold other half over it. Cut into strips approximately $2\frac{1}{2}$ inches wide by 4 inches long.

Make 3 equidistant cuts $\frac{3}{4}$ of the way along the length of each strip, so that you have 4 small rectangles joined along the bottom. Bend strip into a crescent, forming the cock's comb. Brush with a mixture of egg white diluted with a little water, and sprinkle the cock's combs with sugar. Allow to prove, and bake at 375° for 20 minutes.

273

Crescents
pastry dough
almond or frangipane filling
egg white

Roll dough to rectangle $\frac{1}{8}$ inch thick, then cut into 4 inch squares. Cut each square into two triangles, spread a little almond or frangipane filling on each triangle, roll the widest edge toward the apex, and bend into crescents. Brush with egg white and water and glaze, allow to prove, and bake at 350° for 20 minutes.

Apricot Slips
pastry dough
vanilla cream
canned apricot halves

Roll out dough to $\frac{1}{8}$ inch thickness. Cut into 5 inch squares, spread a little vanilla cream over each square, and two apricot halves. Fold corners toward the center. Leave to prove, then bake at 375° for 20 minutes.

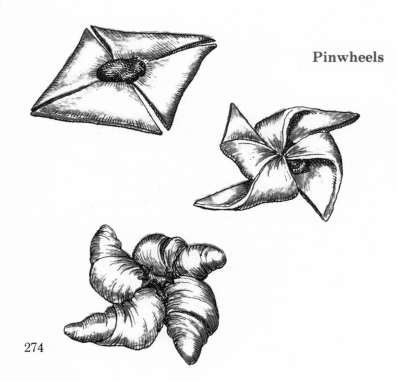

Pinwheels
pastry dough
egg white
almond, frangipane, apple or vanilla cream filling

Roll out dough to $\frac{1}{8}$ inch thickness, cut into 4 inch squares. Cut from each corner to about $\frac{1}{2}$ inch from the center. Put a little filling in the center, then fold alternate points to the center. Brush with egg white mixed with a little water. Leave to prove, and bake at 375° for 25 minutes.

Graham Muffins   *3 cups graham flour*
1 cup cracked wheat
1 teaspoon salt
2 tablespoons sugar
1 package dry yeast
1 tablespoon softened butter
1 cup warm water
3 cups milk

Set the yeast to work with the warm water. In a bowl sift the graham flour and the wheat and add the sugar, the salt and the softened butter, mixing well. Add the yeast mixture and the milk and beat well. Cover, leave to rise and pour into muffin pans. Bake at 425° for 20 minutes.

Leberknodel (Liver Dumplings)   *2 slices stale white bread*
1 cup dry bread crumbs
½ teaspoon salt
¼ teaspoon fresh ground black pepper
1 tablespoon unsalted butter
½ cup milk
2 egg whites
¼ cup chopped onions
½ lb chicken livers
2 teaspoons chopped parsley

Chop the bread, having first soaked it in the milk, and squeezed it dry. Chop the chicken livers into the bread. Cook the onions in the butter gently for 5 minutes and add them to the bread mixture. Stir in the egg whites, the salt, the pepper and the parsley. Add ½ the bread crumbs, stir well and form the mixture into small balls the size of a walnut adding more bread crumbs as required. Bring to the boil the soup in which the dumplings are to be cooked, allow it to cool a little and put the dumplings in. Bring the soup to the boil again to bring the dumplings to the surface. Cook gently for a further minute or two, and serve in the soup. Makes 30 dumplings.

275

Dishes with Bread

Brown Betty

4 cups bread crumbs
pinch of cinnamon
½ teaspoon nutmeg
½ cup sugar
¼ cup brown sugar
¼ cup butter
½ cup water
¼ cup orange juice
6 apples, peeled, cored and sliced

Cook the apples in the water and orange juice, adding a little more water if required. When the apple slices are cooked but still quite firm, add the sugar, the nutmeg and the cinnamon. Mix the brown sugar with the bread crumbs. Put a layer of the apples in the bottom of a baking dish, then a layer of the crumbs and brown sugar; repeat until ingredients are used up, but ending with a layer of bread crumbs. Dot the top all over with butter and bake at 375° for 20 minutes, or until the top is crusty and brown.

Poor Knights of Windsor (French Toast)

Also called *pain perdu,* "lost bread," in medieval times known as *perknollys,* and now known as "French toast." As everything points to this delicacy as having French origins, the English in their perversity called it "Poor Knights of Windsor" at a time when the *entente* was less than *cordiale.* There is no standard recipe for this famous dish, it calls for slices of bread, traditionally stale, dipped in beaten egg and milk and then fried. Successive cultures added their own refinements: cinnamon and fine sugar dusted on the slices after frying; brandy and orange-flower water mixed with the egg, rum and grated lemon rind or, as with "Poor Knights," jam or jelly on each slice – at one time quite a luxury. There was never any real poverty at Windsor ...

276

Summer Pudding

3 lb ripe raspberries, blackberries,
blueberries or red currants (if the
fruit is nor ripe, cook it gently
with sugar, until soft and sweet)
1½ cups sugar
12 slices white bread
1 cup heavy cream

Wash the fruit (if ripe and uncooked) and put on paper towels to drain. Put it in a large bowl and sprinkle with the 1¼ cups sugar, moving it about with a spoon until the sugar dissolves in the juice. Taste for sweetness, adding more sugar if required. With a sharp knife cut a circle in one of the slices of bread, to fit the bottom of a 2-quart earthenware pudding basin or charlotte mold. Then trim 7 slices of the bread into wedge shapes 4 inches across the top and 3 inches at the bottom and stand them round the inside of the bowl, narrow end down, each wedge overlapping the next by about ¼ inch. Now that the bottom and the sides of the bowl are lined with bread, ladle the fruit mixture in and cover the top of it with the remaining slices of bread, trimmed. Cover the top of the pudding with a heavy flat plat plate and a heavy pan or weight on top of that. Refrigerate for at least 12 hours until the bread is saturated and marbled with the fruit syrup. Remove the weight and the plate, ease a knife-blade around the pudding in case it sticks, and invert the whole thing quickly on to a fresh plate. The pudding should slide out neatly, intact. Serve with the cream, whipped.

Bread-and-Butter Pudding

12 slices white bread
pinch of cinnamon
pinch of nutmeg
¼ cup sugar
8 tablespoons softened butter
1 cup heavy cream
3 cups milk
5 eggs
½ cup currants
½ cup raisins

277

Trim the crusts from the bread and brush each slice on both sides with softened butter. Put 4 of the slices on the bottom of a greased 7 × 10 inch baking pan, fitting them snugly against each other. Mix the raisins, the currants and the cinnamon in a bowl and sprinkle $\frac{1}{3}$ of the mixture over these 4 slices. Repeat the process until dish is filled, then place the last 4 slices on top omitting the topping, which would burn during baking. Beat the eggs well and then beat in the milk, the cream, the sugar and the nutmeg and pour this carefully over the pudding; the bread will take about 20 minutes to absorb the liquid. Cover with a lightly greased piece of foil and bake at 350° for 30 minutes, then, removing the foil, for a further 30 minutes until golden brown on top.

Bread Sauce

3 cups white breadcrumbs from a fresh loaf
$\frac{1}{2}$ teaspoon salt
$\frac{1}{2}$ teaspoon white pepper
1 small bay leaf
1 small onion studded with 2 or 3 cloves
5 tablespoons butter
2 cups milk

Boil the milk with the onion, bay leaf, salt, 4 tablespoons of the butter, and the pepper, stirrring to melt the butter. Allow the onion to steep in the liquid for 30 minutes, then discard it. Re-boil milk, then add the breadcrumbs, mashing to as smooth a consistency as possible, and stir until sauce thickens. Add remaining butter, stir and check for seasoning. Bread sauce is served in Britain as an accompaniment to roast poultry.

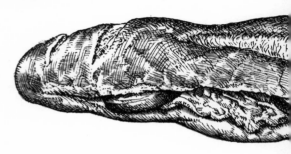

Starters

Hops Starter

3 cups flour
¼ cup hops
2 cups mashed potato
½ cup sugar
8 cups water

    Boil the water, add the hops, let them steep for an hour while the water gently simmers. Strain the water into an earthenware bowl, add the sugar, the flour and the mashed potato. Cover and leave for 2 days to ferment.

Honey and Rye Starter

2 cups rye flour
2 tablespoons honey
3 cups water
a sprinkling of dry yeast

    Warm the water just enough to dissolve the honey, when cool, add the flour and the yeast. Cover and leave to ferment.

Yogurt Starter

2 cups flour
1 cup milk
1 cup yogurt

    Combine the three ingredients, leave in an earthenware bowl, covered, to ferment for about three days.

The Hero Sandwich

GLOSSARY

Aerate: to charge with carbon dioxide, or with air, or to beat with a high-speed mixer.

Alum: double phosphate of aluminum and potassium, an old technique for bleaching flour.

Barm: a leavening agent obtained from malted liquor, usually a by-product of brewing, used before the introduction of commercial yeast.

Batch: a quantity of loaves, usually refers to the number baked in an oven at one time.

Bolt: a method of sieving flour, the old method was to pass the flour through cloths of varying textures, thus a silk bolting cloth would produce a finer flour than would a cotton cloth.

Bran: the husk of the grain, separated from the endosperm.

Docking: scoring or puncturing the surface of dough to permit expansion of gases, called "oven spring," while baking.

Dough: basic mixture of flour and a liquid, kneaded.

Endosperm: the white starchy part of the wheat grain.

Enrich: to add vitamins or improvers to flour, also to add ingredients such as sugar, eggs, milk, to dough.

Extraction rate: the milling rate of flour, and the amount retained after milling. Wholemeal flour, or wholewheat flour is 100 percent extraction. White flour is 70 percent extraction.

Farl: wedge shape of scones, buns and some hearth breads, a term of Gaelic origin.

Ferment: leavening of dough with yeast, sourdough or barm.

Fourse: wedge-shape of some English breads. Term is of Anglo-Saxon origin.

Glaze: to coat or make shiny the surface of breads with a wash of egg, water or milk, or a syrup.

Gluten: the protein substance which gives bread flour its characteristic texture, part of the wheat grain.

Griddle: metal disc, usually of iron, for baking bread over heat. Also called **girdle** and **bakestone.**

Knead: to work the dough to a required degree of smoothness, or elasticity, and to strengthen the gluten.

Knock-back: same as to **punch down,** removing air or gases from the dough after the preliminary rising.

Leaven: to ferment the dough, or a substance used for the purpose.

Malt: a substance, maltose, obtained from the roasting of germinating grain, usually barley.

Peel: term used for a baker's long-handled shovel, the means of handling loaves when in the oven.

Plait: a fancy bread where ropes of dough are plaited together.

Prove: second period of rising after punching down.

Proofer: a chamber used in a bakery, where dough is proved in a humid, steamy atmosphere.

Quern: stone hand-mill for grinding corn.

Rise: the expansion of dough during fermentation.

Roller milling: the process in which grain is torn apart by being passed through a series of ribbed rollers, the modern flour mill.

Scale: weighing off pieces of dough for molding and baking.

Sourdough: a dough fermented by wild yeast, or a portion of fermenting dough used to leaven a fresh dough.

Sponge: usually a fermenting batter, and a technique of dough-making in which flour and other ingredients are worked into the batter.

Starter: a batter fermented by wild yeast, used to "start" the fermentation in sourdough bread.

Strong or hard flour: from a hard wheat, possessing a high quantity of gluten. The flour used to make most bread.

Unleavened: when no yeast or raising agent is used. A flat bread.

Weak or **soft flour:** the flour from weak wheat with a low percentage of gluten.

Wheat: the principle grain of bread flour.

Wheatmeal: flour of about 85 percent extraction.

Wholemeal: flour of 100 percent extraction, containing all the wheat grain or berry, also called **wholewheat,** and **Graham** flour.

Yeast: the unicellular, living organism that ferments, leavens or aerates bread, produced commercially as compressed yeast or dry yeast. Also called "German yeast," probably because it comes from Holland. . . .

BIBLIOGRAPHY

Allinson, T. R.: *The Advantages of Wholemeal Bread*, London, 1889.

Amendola and Lundberg: *Understanding Baking*, Chicago, 1970.

Amos, A. J.: *Bread of Ancient Egypt*, London, 1974.

Ashton, John: *The History of Bread*, London, 1904.

Baker, Margaret: *Folklore and Customs of Rural England*, Devonshire, 1974.

Bakers Digest: vol. 47, no. 5, Pontiac, Illinois, 1973.

Baking, American Institute of: *Egyptian Bread*, Chicago, 1973.

Beaven, E. S.: *Barley*, London, 1947.

Berger, Joseph: *Maize Production and the Manuring of Maize*, Geneva, 1962.

Brown, Frank C.: *North Carolina Folklore*, North Carolina, 1964.

Buller, A. H. Reginald: *Essays on Wheat*, New York, 1919.

Burnett, John: *Plenty and Want*, London, 1966.

Cameron, Allan G.: *Food – Facts and Fallacies*, London, 1971.

Cobbett, William: *Cobbett's Rural Rides*, London, 1830.

Cobbett, William: *Cottage Economy*, London, 1823.

Cobbett, William: *A Treatise on Cobbett's Corn*, London, 1831.

Cole, Sonia: *The Neolithic Revolution*, London, 1970.

Day, Harvey: *About Bread*, London, 1966.

Dodlinger, Peter Tracy: *The Book of Wheat*, New York, 1922.

Drummund, J. C. and Anne Wilbraham: *The Englishman's Food*, London, 1957.

Dundonald, The Earl of: *Letters on Making Bread from Potatoes*, Scotland, 1791.

Edgar, William C.: *The Story of a Grain Of Wheat*, London.

Evans, George Ewart: *Pattern Under the Plough*, London, 1966.

Flour Milling and Baking Research Association: "Trencher Bread", *F.M.B.R.A. Bulletin*, no. 3, Chorleywood, 1973.

Fuller, John G.: *The Day of St Anthony's Fire*, New York, 1968.

Graves Robert: *The Greek Myths*, London, 1955.

Guy, Christian: *An Illustrated History of French Cuisine*, New York, 1962.

Harris, I.: *The Calcium Bread Scandal*, London, 1942.

Hartley, Dorothy: *Food in England*, London, 1951.

Hole, Christina: *English Folklore*, London, 1940.

Hone, William: *The Year Book*, London, 1832.

Hunter, Herbert: *Oats*, London, 1924.

Hyams, Edward: *Plants in the Service of Man*, London, 1971.

Irish Bakery World: "Bread in the Course of History", *I.B.W.* vol. 2, no. 1, Dublin, 1973.

Jackson, H.: *An Essay on Bread*, London, 1758.

Jacob, H. E.: *Six Thousand Years of Bread*, New York, 1944.

King, Charles: *The Story Behind a Loaf of Bread*, London, 1966.

Kuhlmann, Charles Byron: *The Development of the Flour Milling Industry in the United States*, Chicago, 1929.

Labarge, Margaret Wade: *A Baronial Household of the 13th Century*, London, 1965.

Laverty, Maura: *Flour Economy*, Dublin, 1941.

Lee, Laurie: *Cider with Rosie*, London, 1959.

Lloyd, Rev. W. F.: *Prices of Corn in Oxford in the 14th Century*, Oxford, 1830.

Manning, James: *The Nature of Bread*, London, 1757.

Masters, John: *The Nightrunners of Bengal*, London, 1951.

McNeill, Marian F.: *The Scots Kitchen*, London, 1963.

Mitchell, J.: *A Treatise on the Falsification of Food*, London, 1848.

Moritz, L. A.: *Grain Mills and Flour in Classical Antiquity*, Oxford, 1958.

Nesbitt, Leonard D.: *The Story of Wheat*, Alberta, 1949.

Opie, Peter and Iona: *Dictionary of Nursery Rhymes*, Oxford, 1951.

Penkethman, John: *"Artachthos"*, *The Assize of Bread*, London, 1638.

Physician: *Poison Detected*, London, 1757.

Powell, John, *The Assize of Bread*, London, 1600.

Prebble, John: *The Highland Clearances*, London, 1963.

Pyke, Magnus: *Townsman's Food*, London, 1963.

Renfrew, Jane M.: *Palaeothnobotany*, London, 1973.

Richardson, B. W.: *The Healthy Manufacture of Bread*, London, 1884.

Santillana, G. De, and H. von Dechand: *Hamlet's Mill*, London, 1970.

Searle, Alice Morse: *Customs and Fashions in Old New England*, London, 1893.

Sheppard and Newton: *The Story of Bread*, London, 1957.

Soyer, Alexis: *The Pentropheon*, London, 1853.

Stirling, A. M. W.: *Coke of Norfolk*, London, 1900.

Storck and Teague: *Flour for Man's Bread*, Minnesota, 1952.

Stutz, Howard C.: "The Origin of Cultivated Rye", *American Journal of Botany*, vol. 59, no. 1, 1972.

Syder, Harry: *Papers on Bread*, New York, 1930.

Tannahill, Ray: *The Fine Art of Food*, London, 1968.

Travis, W. G.: *The "Assize" System of selling Bread*, London 1968.

Usher, Abbott Payson: *The History of the Grain Trade in France*, Cambridge, Mass., 1913.

Wagner, Leopold: *Manners, Customs and Observances*, London, 1875.

White, John: *A Treatise on the Art of Baking*, Edinburgh, 1828.

Wymer, Norman: *Village Life*, London, 1951.

Yudkin, John: *This Slimming Business*, London, 1958.

INDEX OF RECIPES

INDEX

286